D1566612

# Rebuilding
# Arab Defense

# Rebuilding
# Arab Defense

## US Security Cooperation
### in the
## Middle East

Bilal Y. Saab

LYNNE
RIENNER
PUBLISHERS

BOULDER
LONDON

*The views expressed in this book are those of the author only and do not reflect in any way the official policy or position of the US Department of Defense or the US government.*

Published in the United States of America in 2022 by
Lynne Rienner Publishers, Inc.
1800 30th Street, Suite 314, Boulder, Colorado 80301
www.rienner.com

and in the United Kingdom by
Lynne Rienner Publishers, Inc.
Gray's Inn House, 127 Clerkenwell Road, London EC1 5DB
www.eurospanbookstore.com/rienner

**Library of Congress Cataloging-in-Publication Data**
Names: Saab, Bilal Y., 1980– author.
Title: Rebuilding Arab defense : US security cooperation in the Middle East
    / Bilal Y. Saab.
Other titles: US security cooperation in the Middle East
Description: Boulder, Colorado : Lynne Rienner Publishers, Inc., [2022] |
    Includes bibliographical references and index. | Summary: "Explores the
    current state of US security cooperation in the Middle East, considering
    why the military capabilities of US allies in the region are still
    lacking and suggesting avenues for effective change"— Provided by
    publisher.
Identifiers: LCCN 2021053960 (print) | LCCN 2021053961 (ebook) | ISBN
    9781955055390 (hardback) | ISBN 9781955055444 (ebook)
Subjects: LCSH: Middle East—Defenses. | Middle East—Armed
    Forces—Forecasting. | National security—Middle East. | United
    States—Military relations—Middle East. | Middle East—Military
    relations—United States. | Middle East—Military policy—21st century.
    | United States—Military policy—21st century.
Classification: LCC UA832 .S23 2022 (print) | LCC UA832 (ebook) | DDC
    355/.033056—dc23/eng/20211110
LC record available at https://lccn.loc.gov/2021053960
LC ebook record available at https://lccn.loc.gov/2021053961

**British Cataloguing in Publication Data**
A Cataloguing in Publication record for this book
is available from the British Library.

Printed and bound in the United States of America

5  4  3  2  1

*For Mom,*
*who would have been proud*

# Contents

# Preface

FOR THE BETTER PART OF MY RESEARCH AND ANALYTIC career, I have examined with great interest and care various aspects of US-Arab defense and security cooperation, often enjoying a front-row seat in Washington and in the region. I've had the opportunity to observe joint US-Arab military training exercises in the field, to lecture in professional military education workshops and seminars run by US agencies, to brief the US defense and intelligence communities on military affairs in the Middle East, and to participate in consultations between US and Arab defense officials. From 2018 to 2019, I had the privilege of overseeing all US security cooperation programs in the broader Middle East as part of my responsibilities as a senior adviser in the Pentagon's Office of the Under Secretary of Defense for Policy.

Although I knew that Washington and its Arab partners had a fairly large security cooperation portfolio, what I did not know until after I assumed my government duties was *how much* they do together and *how much money* they spend to try to upgrade their military relations. The volume is staggering and imposing—but regrettably the output is not. Indeed, much has been invested by both sides ostensibly to develop Arab military capability, yet little of it has produced meaningful results.

Curiosity about this vastly disappointing outcome, which has increasingly important implications for US plans and strategic interests in the region and across the globe, led me to write this book. This issue matters to the United States in part because Americans have grown tired of the Middle East, and they can be forgiven for this weariness because

Washington's legacy in that part of the world, at least since its ill-fated intervention in Iraq in 2003, is not one of which to be proud. Whether it is due to idealism, ignorance, incompetence, or a combination thereof, US involvement in the Middle East over the past two decades has caused no small harm to the US national interest. It also has not done a good job of improving the lives of the very people the United States claims to want to support: the ordinary citizens of the region.

Precisely because of this overall dire US experience in the region, and because more Americans have reached Middle East fatigue, the goal of assisting Arab partners in their quest to reform their defense sectors and build credible military power is incredibly important. If we cannot help those partners become more competent and responsible warriors, and if we cannot encourage them to commit to all-inclusive defense reform, we are probably going to be deploying US troops and extinguishing fires in the Middle East for a longer period of time.

We cannot do that anymore. Our new global priorities require us to turn our attention to China—our biggest foreign policy challenge likely for many years to come. Yet we will not successfully be able to make that strategic shift if we keep our current level of military investment in the Middle East. At the same time, we cannot just leave or shrink our presence precipitously because we will make things a lot worse not only for us but also for regional and international security. Vacuums are almost always filled by adversaries.

Every time we tried to disengage, most glaringly under President Barack Obama, things flared up in the region, forcing us to return. There is a way out of the Middle East morass, however, and I believe it is through stronger and more sustainable defense and security relations with our key Arab friends. Only when they are willing and able to step up can we draw down. How the United States can try to achieve this difficult equilibrium is the subject of this book.

# Acknowledgments

SEVERAL PEOPLE MADE INVALUABLE CONTRIBUTIONS TO this book. They did that by generously sharing insights, sitting for long interviews in person and on-screen, and providing feedback on multiple drafts. I owe them and would like to thank them one by one.

But first, let me express my sincerest gratitude to those who, prior to me penning a single word, offered me an opportunity to pursue this project and to be where I am today. I am forever indebted to Janine Hill and Victoria Harlan of the Council on Foreign Relations (CFR) for granting me a fellowship that propelled my career like no other. The CFR International Affairs Fellowship indeed was a turning point in my professional life. This unique vehicle allowed me to serve in the US government in 2018–2019 and gain the practical experience I needed to write this book.

I am also extremely grateful to former Middle East Institute (MEI) president Wendy Chamberlin and her successor, Paul Salem, for approving my sabbatical that year and preserving my position at MEI despite the void my departure created. I'll always be appreciative of their kindness and support and, importantly, their recognition of the value of producing (I hope good) scholarship in an age of sound bites and Twitter analyses.

I also want to extend my sincere thanks to Greg Pollock and Michael Fortin in the Office of the Deputy Assistant Secretary of Defense for Security Cooperation. They brought me on board and entrusted me with the responsibility of overseeing all of the Pentagon's security cooperation programs and activities in the Central Command (CENTCOM) Area of Responsibility, to which more than a quarter of a billion dollars are allocated every fiscal year. Talk about taking a flier on someone with decent familiarity with the Middle East but zero government experience and no clue how to run an interagency meeting. In the end, I hope I made them proud. Michael, in particular, I'd like to thank because he was an ideal boss—a straight shooter and an educator. He was funny as hell, too, which made things in the often dry environment of the Pentagon more bearable. His ideas, more than anyone else's but my own, permeate this book.

Patrick Goodman's touch is all over the book as well. Pat, a retired US Air Force lieutenant colonel nicknamed "Grenade," took special interest in my work and did everything he could to support it. I guess he did that because he understood how important the subject was to the United States, having himself devoted his post-military career to helping partner nations around the world enhance their defense management processes. Pat was incredibly liberal with his time and quite patient with me. The "Pat Goodman principles of sustainment," as I call them, will guide my analyses for many years to come.

Aaron Taliaferro is also someone who has a passion for security cooperation and a wealth of experience in the field. My security cooperation colleagues and I would listen carefully every time Aaron would come and brief us in the Pentagon. I am very grateful to him for making himself available for several interviews—even once when he was sick due to food poisoning.

At MEI, I was the lucky recipient of research assistance from a stout group of interns. Amanda Taheri, Marie-Line Younes, Caitlyn Perkins, Charlotte Armistead, Allison Wolfe, and Elizabeth Boyer performed admirably, collecting news and scholarly articles, writing summaries, doing literature reviews, transcribing interviews, checking references, and helping with formatting. Victoria Jacobs was the best librarian I could have asked for. She's caring and dedicated. Like a paleontologist, she helped me dig up some impossible archival sources.

CENTCOM was very good to me while I was writing the book, despite the unfair criticisms I sometimes unloaded on its J5 leadership during my time in government. Brig. Gen. Duke Pirak, who led the command's security cooperation portfolio at the time and fully understood the importance of using a holistic approach to the discipline, has been an ally and a trusted friend. Duke, who goes by "Juice," opened doors for me and facilitated a number of interviews with his colleagues, including Maj. Sam Jason Boyd, who was in charge of the United Arab

Emirates (UAE) file; Lt. Col. Timothy Kogge, who was responsible for Saudi Arabia; and Maj. Kai Lee Labac, who handled Lebanon. Sam, Tim, and Kai were precise and perceptive. Phil Maxwell, CENTCOM's chief of plans, policy, and programs, was another invaluable interlocutor during my government service, and his friendship, calming influence, and ideas helped me shape some of the content of this book.

In the United States, I benefited from multiple interviews with Philip Archer, David DesRoches, Gerald Feierstein, Jeanne Giraldo, Heidi Grant, Tina Kaidanow, Peter Levine, Michael Patrick Mulroy, Michael Nagata, Allison Noor, Joseph Rank, Tommy Ross, Mark Tillman, Joseph Votel, Chuck Wald, and John Zavage. The depth of their knowledge was surpassed only by their generosity. Each made a contribution to various sections of the book.

In the region, I leveraged the wisdom and experience of dozens of US and Arab officials, officers, noncommissioned officers, and enlisted soldiers who lent me a good bit of their very busy time to help me better understand the ins and outs of US-Arab defense and security cooperation. I wish I could properly credit them all, but I cannot because most insisted on remaining nameless due to the sensitivity of the conversations. I'll respect their wishes, of course, and hope they recognize how incredibly thankful I am for their advice.

Maj. Gen. Wendul G. Hagler, our senior defense official/defense attaché (SDO/DATT) in the US embassy in Riyadh; Col. Brad Gandy, our chief of US Military Training Mission (USMTM) to Saudi Arabia; and Col. John White, our head of the Office of the Program Manager–Saudi Arabian National Guard Modernization Program (OPM-SANG), all provided priceless insights on US-Saudi security cooperation. Khalid bin Hussein Bayari of the Saudi Ministry of Defense and his team, including his skilled and hard-working adviser Brig. Gen. Ahmed bin Hasan Asiri, poured their hearts out and expertly educated me on all the inner workings of the Saudi defense transformation plan. Lebanese Armed Forces (LAF) Commander Gen. Joseph Aoun and his diligent office director Brig. Gen. Wassim Halabi provided much data on the US military assistance program in Lebanon. Retired LAF rear admiral Joseph Sarkis was a vital source of information on the LAF's operations in key battles since 2000. Col. Robert Meine, our SDO/DATT in the US embassy just outside of Beirut, was of immense help to me in making sense of our assistance priorities with the LAF. Col. David Kobs, our SDO/DATT in Amman, provided me with an honest and succinct overview of Military Assistance Program–Jordan, our primary means to help train and develop the capabilities of the Jordanian Armed Forces.

Maj. Gen. Michael Hindmarsh, who retired from the Australian Armed Forces in 2009 and has since commanded the UAE Presidential Guard, gave me a fantastic tutorial on Emirati military operations in Yemen and defense reform efforts in Abu Dhabi.

Without the input of anonymous reviewers, this book would be weaker and duller. Kenneth Pollack gave me excellent and extremely generous feedback on multiple drafts, for which I am deeply appreciative. Pollack's endorsement, given his impeccable work on military affairs in the Middle East, means the world to me. Bruce Riedel, a former Brookings colleague, vetted my Saudi case study. That he did not vehemently object to the analysis gave me great confidence because few in the United States know Saudi Arabia better than Bruce. I owe both Riedel and Pollack for all the support and encouragement they have provided me over the years.

Marie-Claire Antoine, senior acquisitions editor and my main point of contact at Lynne Rienner Publishers, was warm, calm, and meticulous. She provided invaluable advice on various aspects of the book, exercised remarkable patience, and ably guided the publication process from start to finish during very abnormal and challenging times. The senior project editor, Allie Schellong, skillfully managed the production process.

I also very much appreciate the help of staffers, and specifically Paul Jacobsmeyer, in the Pentagon's Defense Office of Prepublication and Security Review, who ensured that the book contains no classified material. At one point, Paul had dozens of manuscripts on his desk to review. "The global pandemic," he quipped, "inspired many to write!"

Last but certainly not least, this book would not have been possible without the ideal environment I am blessed to have in our home in Vienna, Virginia. My loving wife, Alison, and my two little girls, Lilian and Elena, were more than supportive when I had to work during too many weekends and holidays. "Daddy, did you talk about the world and speak on the phone again today?" Lilian would ask me every night before reading her a bedtime story. I could never come up with a more interesting or clever answer than "yes, I did, sweetie." My hope is that one day she, her baby sister, and her mommy find this book worth a read.

# 1

## The US-Arab
## Security Partnership

TERRORISTS. INSURGENTS. PIRATES. MILITIAS. CRIMINAL NET-
works. Mad dictators. Radical regimes. There is no shortage of odious
actors constantly vying for influence, causing bloodshed, and sowing
disorder in the Middle East.

Even for the United States, a power with vested interests and considerable military force in the region and beyond, that can be a lot to handle.
And in fact, it has been. Washington would have been able to pursue a
more sustainable policy in the Middle East and manage many of these
problems with a bit more ease had it enjoyed stronger defense ties with its
Arab friends. Yet, the reality is that no effective US-Arab defense bonds
exist, like they do in the North Atlantic Treaty Organization (NATO), for
example, and it is the relative military weakness of most of the Arab partners that has exacerbated all of the above-mentioned challenges, preventing the United States from drawing down in the Middle East to desired
levels and pursuing its new, Asia-centric foreign policy priorities.

Why do America's efforts to help its Arab partners build military
capability have such an unimpressive record, what can be done to
improve this record, and why does it all really matter? These are the
main questions I seek to answer in this book.

### An Enterprise in Disarray
Ever since the Pentagon issued its 2006 Quadrennial Defense Review
(QDR), there has been a flurry of US strategic documents emphasizing

1

the goal of helping to build the capabilities of foreign partners to promote collective action and burden sharing.[1] Yet despite the increasing policy prominence of this objective, in the Middle East the fruits of this US effort have been underwhelming and at times downright embarrassing.

Just on Iraq alone, since the 2003 US invasion Washington has spent north of $32 billion in military aid, and we know what happened during that period: Iraqi security forces melted away in 2014 as Islamic State fighters swept across Iraq.[2] Since then, the Iraqi government has done much better in fending off terrorists, but it has had a very hard time containing Iran-backed militant groups who have sabotaged politics in Baghdad and repeatedly targeted US personnel and interests using Katyusha rockets and explosive-laden and precision-guided drones.[3]

The picture in Afghanistan, where the United States sought for two decades to create strong local security forces that can protect the country from terrorists, is a lot bleaker. From 2002 to 2021, Washington spent more than $83 billion in US security assistance to Afghanistan only to see the Afghan army disintegrate in a matter of eleven days after US troops withdrew from the country in August 2021 and the Taliban swiftly established control.[4] There are several reasons why the Afghan military fell, some having nothing to do with the Afghans and everything to do with US policy. But the outcome was hardly surprising. According to confidential documents obtained by the *Washington Post*, over all those years most parts of the Afghan military were "incompetent, unmotivated, poorly trained, corrupt and riddled with deserters and infiltrators."[5]

Though Iraq and Afghanistan are the latest and perhaps most troubling examples of unsatisfactory US military assistance programs in the broader Middle East, they are not the only ones. Consider Egypt, a major regional partner of the United States. The country is one of the largest recipients of US aid in the world, with $1.3 billion per year in military assistance.[6] Yet the Egyptians struggle in battling Islamic militants in Sinai and in securing their border with Libya. Although Egyptian soldiers are some of the bravest and most experienced in the region, they are poorly trained for counterinsurgency operations, and their Soviet-based doctrine is largely designed to fight the conventional battles of the past, not the hybrid threats of the future.

Then there is Saudi Arabia and its highly ineffective military campaign against Houthi rebels in Yemen since 2015, which until very recently was enabled by American bombs.[7] Many of Riyadh's air strikes, partly due to the Saudi pilots' unskillfulness despite years of US training and advice, have killed thousands of innocent Yemeni civilians, including children on school buses and elderly men in funerals, while also worsening a humanitarian catastrophe.[8]

The overwhelming unproductiveness of US military assistance programs in the Arab world has clearly manifested itself in various wars and US military interventions in the region. For example, during the Iran-Iraq War in 1980–1988, the Gulf Arabs were nowhere near capable on their own of deterring and responding to Iranian aggression and intimidation at sea, and as a result they had to rely almost exclusively on the United States for protection.

In 1990–1991, the majority of the Arab states provided Washington with diplomatic cover to defend Saudi Arabia from Iraqi leader Saddam Hussein and dislodge Iraqi forces from Kuwait. But in Operation Desert Storm, the United States did all the planning and the bulk of the fighting because it had no confidence in the abilities of its Arab partners. Whenever those partners took part in US-led military operations, they performed rather poorly even though they possessed a boatload of lethal and sophisticated American weapons.

One would think that roughly two and a half decades after Desert Storm, the Arabs would be stronger militarily, and Washington would enjoy greater success with its US military assistance programs in the region. However, Operation Inherent Resolve (OIR), the 2014 US-enabled campaign to combat the Islamic State and destroy its caliphate mainly in Iraq and Syria, would clearly show otherwise.

Once it became clear to Washington that the Arab partners were in no position to stop this expanding terrorist army from wreaking havoc across the region and elsewhere, it had no choice but to step in forcefully and once again come to the rescue. Arab members of OIR did pack a punch from the air using their US-purchased fighter jets, but other than the Iraqis and a handful of Syrian rebels, they shockingly contributed almost nothing to the ground war, an outcome that much delayed military victory and raised the costs of war.

How did it all go so wrong? What can Washington do differently to achieve greater returns on its defense and security cooperation investments in the Middle East? What roles do the Arab partners themselves have to play in this process? And why does the issue of Arab military capability matter now more than ever for the United States and the region? I intend to address these increasingly important policy issues in these pages with candor, pragmatism, and humility.

## Building Arab Military Capability
## Was Not a US Priority

To begin to understand why most US military assistance programs in the Arab world have gone awry, one has to address the basic issue of willingness on the part of Arabs and Americans. Let's start with the American side. Until recent years, the Arab partners' possession of military capabilities that could be used to contribute to collective security interests was not a serious concern of Washington. Even more so, it was not an explicit goal or preference for three main reasons.

First, the Middle East was critical in US foreign policy for the better part of the twentieth century. Few regions were more indispensable to America's economic well-being and geostrategic position in the world than the Middle East. At the time, US interests centered on maintaining the free flow of cheap oil to the US (and international) economy, preventing any hostile power from dominating the region, and ensuring Israel's survival.

Because the stakes were so high and the margin for error was so small, Washington saw the need to adopt a more hands-on security approach to the region to protect its core interests there, eschewing any direct and substantial military help from less capable friendly powers, both Arab and non-Arab. Washington's priority vis-à-vis its Arab partners was not necessarily to strengthen their military capabilities, but rather to acquire access to their territories to permanently or temporarily station US troops and materiel and to get their permission to use their ports and airspace.

Arab money was another major motivation for the United States, and it was more valuable than Arab military capability. Washington needed its Arab partners' financial resources to wage war when necessary, like it did in Desert Storm, and to support various elements of the US defense posture across the region during peacetime. Kuwait, Saudi Arabia, and the United Arab Emirates (UAE) took on most of the costs of US military operations in Desert Storm, for example, all totaling $84 billion in direct payments to the United States, Britain, and France.[9] In addition, the Saudis and the Kuwaitis covered the expenses—roughly $51 billion—of logistical support for the hundreds of thousands of American and allied troops in Saudi Arabia.[10] The Arab partners also bankrolled various US clandestine activities in the region that served collective security interests, such as the Central Intelligence Agency's (CIA's) Operation Cyclone in the 1980s—meant to kick the Soviet army out of Afghanistan—and more recently Operation Timber Sycamore in Syria in 2013—intended to combat al-Qaeda and the Islamic State.

But the US interest in and use of Arab financial resources extended beyond the military realm. A major reason why Washington sold arms to the Arabs in such large quantities was, and to a large extent still is, because this pumped millions and then billions of petrodollars back into the US economy.

Second, the United States did not need much military help from its Arab friends because all its regional adversaries had vastly inferior military capabilities and thus did not pose significant security problems. Once the United States expanded its footprint in the Middle East following the issuance of the Carter Doctrine in 1980 and created a full-fledged regional combatant command three years later (the Rapid Deployment Task Force became US Central Command, or CENTCOM), it quickly attained regional military superiority. With it, Washington was able to contain and in some places even roll back Soviet regional influence, check both Saddam and the Iranian mullahs for most of the 1980s and 1990s, and liberate Kuwait from Iraqi occupation, all largely by itself. The US military also relied on minimal Arab military support to secure the critical waters of the oil-rich Persian Gulf.

Third, the United States was highly committed to preserving the Qualitative Military Edge (QME) of Israel. This is a US tradition that was written into law in 2008 but dates back to the Lyndon Johnson administration and has been honored by every US president since.[11] It means that Israel is to possess strategic and tactical advantages, enabled by the United States, that can help it deter its numerically superior foes and win in any conventional military confrontation.

In many respects, QME placed tangible constraints on any US attempt to seriously upgrade the military arsenals of its Arab partners. The idea was that as long as the Arab states were weaker militarily, they could not defeat Israel or threaten its existence.

## Bolstering Self-Defense Was Not an Arab Priority Either

During that same period, the Arab partners, with the exception of Egypt and to some extent Jordan and Morocco, did not consider the development of indigenous conventional military capabilities as a pressing priority either. To defend themselves against external threats, they focused most of their efforts on incentivizing the United States to play the role of protector. And US policymakers much obliged because the US national interest commanded it.

If the United States needed access, basing, and overflight rights, that's what the Arab partners readily provided. They also purchased American arms, frequently and in big amounts, not necessarily to improve their own military abilities but to preserve their political equities in Washington and the special political relationship with successive US presidents. For the most part, the Gulf Arab partners had no intention of using the arms they bought from the United States. In many cases, Washington sold equipment to them with explicit agreements that the US military could use it if it needed to defend them, which was another incentive for the Americans.

The wealthier Gulf Arab states happily bought their security by financing a good bit of America's deterrence and war-fighting architecture in the region. Some—like Kuwait, the UAE, Saudi Arabia, and Qatar—continue to do so to this day. For example, Doha covered all the costs of construction of Al Udeid Air Base—CENTCOM's forward headquarters in the region and the home of the Combined Air Operations Center (CAOC)—spending $8 billion since 2003 and committing another $1.8 billion since 2018 to expand the facility.[12] Riyadh helped finance the US return to Saudi Arabia in 2019 after a sixteen-year absence,[13] and Abu Dhabi paid for the building of permanent structures at Al Dhafra Air Base, where the United States has anywhere from 3,500 to 5,000 American military personnel and periodically deployed F-22 Raptors.[14]

It's hard to fault the Arab partners for not prioritizing self-defense capabilities in the pre-9/11 era. The United States had not only a relatively large and powerful military presence on their soil but also the *willingness* to protect them at any time from outside aggression. Moreover, the external threats to the Arab partners' safety weren't unmanageable or acute, especially after Tehran was severely battered following the Iran-Iraq War, the Soviet Union disintegrated, and Saddam's army was crushed by the United States in the sands of the Kuwaiti and Saudi desert. Internally, although terrorism was always a problem, it was more or less contained and until the early to mid-2000s, with the exception of the 1979 seizure of the Grand Mosque in Saudi Arabia by armed Islamic radicals, did not pose an existential threat to Arab governments.

## A Growing US and Arab Concern

Today, much of this Arab and American picture has changed. New priorities, challenges, and opportunities have emerged both in Washington and in the region, raising the strategic significance of Arab self-defense. Whereas US-Arab security cooperation was more or less a fiction throughout the twentieth century, in today's strategic environment both sides view it with a bit more seriousness and urgency.

First, there's a bipartisan consensus in Washington that the Middle East matters less to the United States in relation to other priority regions. The region still impacts long-standing US interests, including the safety of the US homeland, the stability of world energy markets, and the security of Israel. However, an outsized US military presence in the region may no longer be needed to defend those interests. There is now a greater US propensity to involve Arab partners in regional security designs, and concomitantly, there is a lot more room for their military contributions than in previous decades.

As Washington seeks to deprioritize the Middle East and shift its attention to Asia, it desperately needs its Arab partners to be able to stand on their own feet and share the burden of regional security. The US thinking, sharpened in recent years, is that with stronger Arab partners, the United States can afford to reduce its military engagements in the region and allocate more resources to the Indo-Pacific and Europe.

Regional access, basing, and overflight continue to matter a great deal to the US military, but these tools can no longer be relied upon almost exclusively to provide security for the region. US political and military leaders increasingly recognize that Arab military capability could be an additional and untapped contributor that ought to be effectively integrated into America's present and future approach to regional security.

Second, threats to US interests in the region have grown significantly in part due to the emergence of new security vacuums caused by the collapse of governance in various parts of the Arab world following the 2011 Arab Spring. In addition, to improve their capabilities and more effectively pursue their strategic agendas, America's regional adversaries have acquired more advanced, lethal, and dual-use technologies.

Transnational terrorist entities such as al-Qaeda and more recently the Islamic State have spread quickly and struck in all four corners of the globe, most shockingly on US soil on September 11, 2001. Though their military and fundraising capabilities have been degraded lately thanks to various US-led counterterrorism missions across the region, including OIR, these resilient actors were able not too long ago to shake the foundations of the Arab state system, particularly in Iraq and Syria, and they could do so again if the political and economic conditions that led to their rise in the first place continue to go unaddressed. Militant proxies with allegiances to Iran also have proliferated and now operate with more potent arms and greater political influence in places like Lebanon, Syria, Iraq, Bahrain, and Yemen. They have either weakened or destroyed state structures, threatened their neighbors' borders, and served as hotbeds of violence and extremism.

Iran itself has expanded its military capabilities and is believed to have technically gotten closer to producing an atomic bomb.[15] It has improved the range and accuracy of its missiles, while also procuring unmanned aerial systems that today pose serious problems for the US military and Arab partners.[16] It has intensified its efforts to provide advanced arms and technical know-how to its allies in the region.[17] And its elite military forces, the Islamic Revolutionary Guard Corps (IRGC), have gained expertise in cyber warfare and used it in offensive operations against Saudi Arabia, Bahrain, and others.[18]

The problem of piracy in the Red Sea, Arabian Sea, and Indian Ocean, once manageable, now has grown, threatening some of the world's most vital oil supply routes. Bolder and better armed and organized pirates operating in those areas have been able to conduct hijacking, kidnapping, and extortion operations against merchant ships using high-speed boats, night-vision equipment, waterborne improvised explosive devices, and sophisticated technologies including radar and Global Positioning System (GPS).[19] These actors have exploited conditions of state failure and the absence of local law enforcement, especially in places like Somalia and Yemen.

Yet, the maritime threat is not limited to piracy. Iran is a menace too, and a much bigger one, frequently endangering commercial shipping in the Strait of Hormuz and the Persian Gulf. The country has enhanced its ability to hit military ships with longer-range and more precise antiship missiles and to plant more lethal sea mines to deter and deny US access to key Arab ports.[20]

Then there is Russia, who never had as firm and strategic a military presence in the region as it does currently. Thanks to its rescuing of Syrian dictator Bashar al-Assad from a growing insurgency that almost toppled his regime in 2011, Moscow now has a long-term footprint in Syria—a "permanent group of forces" at the port of Tartus and an air base in Khmeimim[21]—and in the natural gas–rich Mediterranean near NATO's southern flank. The conflict in Syria has allowed Iran and Hezbollah, who also sent troops to Assad's aid, to set up shop near the Israeli-occupied Golan Heights. Iran's fast-developing military infrastructure in Syria is a major concern for the Israelis, who often have resorted to force to manage that threat.

Third, QME, while still a sensitive issue in US Middle East policy, is not as rigid a political and legal requirement as it once was because of new regional dynamics and much-improved Arab-Israeli relations. Ever since Egypt and Jordan signed peace agreements with the Jewish state in 1978 and 1994, respectively—thus minimizing if not eliminating the chances of another major Arab-Israeli war—Washington has been more than willing to bend the QME rules to some extent and equip its Arab partners with more powerful arms.

This trend has accelerated recently with Washington agreeing to sell dozens of F-35 American fifth-generation aircraft to the UAE in a side deal to a historic normalization accord between Israel and the UAE in August 2020 (shortly after, Bahrain joined the so-called Abraham Accords and normalized its relationship with Israel).[22] That Israel didn't oppose the sale, as it often used to do (for example, the Israelis rejected, though ultimately failed to stop, the sale of sophisticated surveillance planes to Saudi Arabia by Ronald Reagan's administration in the early 1980s),[23] underscores how Arab-Israeli ties have changed considerably for the better.[24]

Today, Israel has key interests in common with several Sunni Arab states as both sides seek to deter and counter the same foes, be it Iran and its proxy network or jihadists belonging to al-Qaeda and the Islamic State. And with Washington's decision in January 2021 to move the military responsibility for Israel from US European Command (EUCOM) to CENTCOM, the opportunities for greater security cooperation between Israel and the Arab states abound.[25]

On the Arab side, the interest in developing stronger self-defense capabilities has gone through a remarkable evolution too. Decreasing Arab trust in US policy has been a major factor. This process may have started with the 2003 Iraq War, which several Arab capitals, including Riyadh, thought was thoroughly misguided and a major distraction from the bigger and more pressing challenge of the hostile regime in Tehran.

How Washington responded to the 2011 Arab Spring didn't help in bridging the gap either. The Saudis and the Emiratis accused the Barack Obama administration of failing to save the regime of their ally, Egyptian president Hosni Mubarak, from a popular uprising (whether or not Washington could have done that, even if it wanted to, is a separate matter). Riyadh also was furious and perturbed over the perceived lack of US support for the Bahrainis, whose monarchy in February through March 2011 was under siege by protesters, some of whom were linked to the Iranian regime.

Exacerbating the mistrust in US-Arab ties was the infamous "red line" fiasco in Syria in the summer of 2012 when President Obama suggested resorting to military force if Assad used toxic agents against those who wished to depose him.[26] A year later, the Syrian leader did precisely that, killing more than 1,400 people with sarin gas.[27] However, Obama did not follow through with his threat, shocking many Arab and world leaders.

Yet, the one episode that most strikingly underscored the level of Arab concern over America's dependability as a protector is the fall 2019 attack by Iran against Saudi Arabia's oil infrastructure, to which President

Donald Trump did not respond. (Months later he went on to kill Iran's top military commander, Qassem Soleimani, but the operation arguably had nothing to do with the Iranian strike in Khurais and Abqaiq.)[28] This experience sent shivers down the spines of Gulf Arab monarchs who began to genuinely question America's security commitment.

Adding to those increasing Arab anxieties about American security reassurance is the reality that the domestic and foreign threats to the Arab partners' safety, as discussed previously, have proliferated. The growing problems of Sunni jihadism and Iran's intensified political violence in the region have compelled the Arab partners to get more serious about augmenting their self-defense capabilities and reducing their dependence on what they increasingly see, not unjustifiably, as an unpredictable and disinterested Washington.

## Areas of Improvement

Where Washington needs Arab military help the most is, quite logically, in the one area where it has struggled the most: combating violent extremism. Improved Arab capabilities in law enforcement, intelligence sharing, counterterrorism financing, terrorism prevention, and deradicalization would go a long way toward effectively and collectively tackling this resilient phenomenon.

Border security in the region is another area desperately in need of better US-Arab cooperation. Porous and dangerous frontiers—a key source of instability across the region—require much more reliable Arab skills in reconnaissance, surveillance, rapid reaction, and counterinsurgency. Washington has no desire to deploy more American soldiers to the region to prevent smuggling and halt cross-border infiltrations and attacks against Arab partner interests. The Arab states have to be able to secure their own borders and protect their own populations from rebels, militants, and criminal networks.

To counter the growing missile threat of Iran, the United States needs its Arab partners to be able to leverage their advanced, US-made missile defense assets and, with US help, commit to the critical mission of regional air and missile defense integration.[29] This is an old, shared priority but one that has yet to be met. Without it, Iran will continue to have an offensive aerial advantage, which it remarkably demonstrated in its successful 2019 strike against Saudi Arabia's oil facilities.

Yet, it's not enough to wholly rely on defense to deal effectively with Iran's more powerful and accurate missiles. Deterrence has to be a big part of the equation too. And to create a stronger joint deterrent against Tehran, the United States needs its Arab partners to more ably augment their offensive capabilities. Some of these partners, including the UAE, have more dependable air power capabilities than others.

At sea, the United States cannot further reallocate resources from the Middle East to the Indo-Pacific if it cannot rely more on its Arab partners' maritime forces to help police the regional waters.[30] Those Arab capabilities are slowly improving thanks to many years of cooperation with the Bahrain-based US Fifth Fleet.[31] However, the Americans are still doing the heavy lifting, and the Arab partners are still far from being able to take on more significant security responsibilities in those maritime areas largely because all of them have failed to make serious investments in naval power.

In the cyber domain, stronger Arab defensive capabilities are irreplaceable because, unlike other areas, the United States is simply in no position to directly contribute to the safety and security of its Arab partners. Washington can help with training and technology transfers, but it is not able to deploy a "cyber army" in the Middle East tasked with defending them against Iranian cyberattacks.

The United States may have American advisers embedded in the governments of some of these Arab partners, or American cyber experts based in US embassies in the region serving as liaison officers, but it doesn't have a cyber force constantly monitoring and responding to threats against Arab oil installations, power plants, and other critical infrastructure. Only the Arabs can be responsible for such missions and functions.

## Defense Institution Building

Some US decisionmakers and military leaders are coming to grips with the reality that the old model of US-Arab defense and security cooperation—where, in short, the Americans pretended to teach and the Arabs pretended to learn—has expired. However, the question remains *how* the United States can transition to a new model—one that is responsive to its new global priorities and can strengthen Arab military power more effectively.

In my view, the chief lesson Washington can learn from its efforts thus far to assist its Arab partners in developing effective and sustainable military capability—which, for reasons laid out above, didn't really commence until after 9/11 and the 2003 Iraq War—is that transferring more arms and conducting more tactical and/or operational training, while politically, economically, and sometimes practically beneficial, on its own is not going to make those partners more capable over the long run. That is my main argument in the book.

Defense institution building (DIB), also known as institutional capacity building (ICB), is the most critical ingredient that is missing or insufficiently incorporated into America's approach to strengthening the military capabilities of partners in the Arab world. The effects of this major shortcoming in US military assistance programs are more clearly felt in the Arab world (and other developing regions) because the Arab partners, unlike most NATO and other treaty allies of the United States, lack a proper civilian defense infrastructure to begin with and thus are less able to effectively absorb US equipment, technology, and advice.

Contrary to Britain, for example, which only needed American weapons to survive Adolf Hitler's vicious aerial bombing of London, the Arab partners need a lot more than US "tools" to "finish the job," as Winston Churchill confidently told Franklin Roosevelt at the height of World War II.[32] They badly need stronger defense institutional capacity to better employ and sustain the sophisticated military hardware, knowledge, and technologies they receive from the United States.

What is defense institutional capacity? It is a country's ability to create and enforce defense rules and effectively perform the critical duties of policymaking, planning, budgeting, managing, employing, training, equipping, and sustaining. It involves structures, norms, procedures, and most importantly people. It helps provide coherence and organization to the mission of national defense. Institutional capacity serves as the foundation of military capability development, which is the process to create the ability to deter and defend against threats and achieve a specified operational and/or tactical objective during wartime.[33] To attain a joint capability, the US military relies on the famous DOTMLPF-P formula, which stands for doctrine, organization, training, materiel, leadership and education, personnel, facilities, and policy.[34] Each of these terms constitutes a critical element of defense institutional capacity.

Think of a business that is well positioned to create a product because it has a large financial endowment, relatively easy access to top raw materials, and the best engineers and designers in the world. Yet, if that firm does not have a coherent plan and effective mechanisms for quality control, accounting, human resource management, distribution, logistics, storage, and creative marketing and advertising, the odds are that it will not succeed in selling that product, generating profit, and sustaining its growth. This in a nutshell is the story of the armies of America's partners in the Arab world and other developing regions.

Before I go any further, let me clarify right up front what defense institutional capacity can offer and, equally important, what it cannot. Defense institutional capacity, no matter how robust, does *not* guarantee military effectiveness. Neither does military capability, for that matter. Centuries of human warfare have taught us that it's one thing for an army to possess tools and skills and show high levels of military readiness, but it's another altogether to leverage all these assets and enablers and proficiently execute on the battlefield.

How the Arab states fight and why they display military ineffectiveness more often than they should is not the focus of this book. There is a growing body of analytical work, to which Kenneth Pollack has made an unparalleled contribution, devoted just to that particular subject.[35] Instead, what I hope to do here is to try to modestly complement this scholarship with an examination of how the national defense establishments of the Arab states are postured *prior to* their armed forces entering the battlefield and firing a single shot.[36] The US military calls this Phase Zero, that is, "everything that can be done to prevent conflict from developing in the first place."[37] It consists of activities meant to favorably shape the environment through better training, readiness, and management of national defense.

Existing analyses on civil-military relations in the Middle East explore parts of this dimension, but many areas remain understudied.[38] For example, Nathan Toronto's investigation of the relationship between human capital and battlefield effectiveness, in which he analyzes the experiences of Egypt, Turkey, the UAE, and others, is a welcome attempt to address this gap in the literature.[39]

Some armies are able to show degrees of operational and tactical effectiveness despite suffering from significant weaknesses in defense institutional capacity. The UAE's military intervention in Yemen in 2015–2020, hardly supported by its nascent defense-reform experiment, is a perfect example of that.[40] Egypt in the 1973 Arab-Israeli War is another (although some aspects of Egyptian defense institutional capacity, including strategic planning and military professionalization, had much improved by the time Cairo launched its operation).[41] It is also not uncommon for a country to have a highly functioning defense institutional apparatus, able to effectively plan, budget, force generate, manage, and run day-to-day affairs, but either suffer military defeat or perform poorly during combat. The list of historical examples here is quite long, with France in both world wars being a glaring one.

That said, it is generally harder to overcome operational challenges on the battlefield, especially during long and drawn-out military contests, and to achieve *strategic* victory with a dysfunctional defense institutional infrastructure. Weak defense governance was one important reason, for example, why both the Iraqis and the Iranians in their conflict throughout most the 1980s could not sustain their war machines or devise more effective military strategies and as a result each lost more than half a million men.[42] It is also the same reason why the Saudis are still stuck in Yemen, seven years after they launched Operation Decisive Storm. Providing food and water supplies to soldiers; conducting search and rescue operations; issuing orders to and communicating with commanders in the field; moving men and materiel; fixing damaged equipment; rotating forces; acquiring, deploying, and integrating new weapons; and so on—all of these functions and many others require a measure of administrative capacity not only in the military but also in the larger civilian defense establishment (assuming one exists).

For the United States, Arab defense institutional capacity is vital because, at the very least, it allows the Arab partner to better utilize and *sustain* US military assistance. It bears repeating that better defense governance will not robotically enhance the Arab partners' fighting prowess. But it *does* put them in a better position to build military capability, a process itself that has an effect on their ability to conduct more effective operations. Better combat performance, partly resulting from meaningful institutional capacity investments over several years, is what the Lebanese military, for example, was able to show in its 2017 campaign against the Islamic State along the country's northern border.

## US Security Cooperation Reforms

In Washington, some progress has been made over the past few years, both legislatively and bureaucratically, to steer military assistance programs in the Arab world and elsewhere in the right direction. In December 2016, Congress formulated a set of security cooperation reforms that were published in the Fiscal Year (FY) 2017 National Defense Authorization Act (NDAA). These reforms, designed primarily by the late senator John McCain and his staff, were monumental and unprecedented. They officially recognized for the first time in the history of US defense policy the strategic importance of integrating institutional capacity building into US security cooperation activities with allies and partners by codifying a stand-alone authority for the Department of Defense to conduct it—Section 332 of Title 10 of the US Code of Law. Moreover, the new, consolidated train-and-equip authority, Title 10's Section 333 (previously 1206), now requires the Department of Defense to certify it is undertaking defense institution building programs to complement train-and-equip efforts with foreign partners.

The gist of Congress's security cooperation reforms is that the United States would no longer throw money and hardware at its less capable partners around the world and expect them all of a sudden to become more competent and responsible fighters on their own. Rather, the United States would seek to help them develop the institutional capacities that are necessary to strengthen and sustain their national defense establishments, and it would establish mechanisms to assess, monitor, and evaluate its own assistance efforts in ways it had shockingly never done before, at least not systematically and consistently. Some of the fruits of this security cooperation reform process in Washington have been apparent in the region, as this book's case studies will demonstrate.

## Lingering Challenges

Despite these positive changes in US security cooperation both on paper and on the ground in the Middle East, Washington's goal of helping its key Arab partners develop real military capability still has a very long way to go. The entire US security cooperation enterprise, of which defense institution building is now supposedly an integral part (at least by law), remains far too heavily biased in favor of US arms transfers and military exercises and insufficiently attentive to defense governance. The United States continues to provide copious amounts of lethal and sophisticated weapons to its Arab partners worth trillions of dollars with little regard to their capacity to use and maintain them.

There are multiple reasons for this, as I explain in Chapter 7, but it all starts with the acute lack of American leadership of security cooperation in the Department of Defense. There is no way defense institution building can become a firm and integrated part of the US security cooperation ecosystem, consistently preached and practiced, if there is no one at the top taking on the mantle of this crucial domain. And to this date, no one in the Pentagon has seriously assumed that responsibility.

The US military, which understandably has emphasized regional access and basing in security cooperation above all else, still dominates the planning and prioritization processes, partly because of the lack of effective civilian oversight in the Pentagon over security cooperation. Further, the Pentagon technically has no official strategy for security cooperation like it does for irregular warfare or cybersecurity, for example. As a result, there is some confusion and lack of clear guidance in the Department of Defense regarding how this increasingly important functional area, especially as it pertains to institutional capacity building, is practiced with partner nations.

How Arab rulers assess the risks and rewards of defense institution building ultimately will determine the likelihood of success and failure of this process and whether or not it even takes off. The good news is that more key Arab leaders, including Crown Prince Mohammed bin Zayed of the UAE (known as MBZ), Crown Prince Mohammed bin Salman of Saudi Arabia (known as MBS), and King Abdullah II of Jordan are eager to reform elements of their defense establishments and to some extent reconsider the strict hierarchical structures their predecessors had imposed for many decades. The bad news is that the executional struggles of holistic military capability development among *all* of Washington's Arab partners are wide and deep. This is so for the simple reason that the Arabs have not worried about how to properly build military capability for many decades. And because of that, all of their defense institutions are a mess and in need of overhaul.

Not unlike their economies and various parts of their social and governance systems, the Arab partners' militaries and ministries of defense require *structural* reforms. Both the remarkable longevity of the Arabs' neglect of military capability development and the very dire state of their defense establishments should very clearly point to the fact that the journey of Arab defense reform will be a very long and demanding one.

Looking at the various elements of defense institutional capacity as laid out here, perhaps the most obvious and common Arab deficiency is in the area of acquisition. Even if someday they kick the habit of buying prestige US weapons they don't need, most if not all Arab partners are unable to effectively address their security requirements because they have largely dysfunctional and sometimes even nonexistent defense procurement processes. Saudi Arabia, Bahrain, Qatar, Oman, and Egypt are obvious examples.

The existing civil-military imbalance in the Arab world suggests that national defense governance is dominated by military personnel. Arab soldiers are responsible for not only fighting but also strategizing, planning, equipping, analyzing, managing, force generating, and intelligence gathering. Arab defense continues to receive very little guidance and input from defense and national security professionals because very few of those exist and even fewer are competent and empowered.

It's doubtful that any Arab defense establishment has useful job descriptions and qualification documents to attract the right kind of talent and assign them to the right job. As I will show in this book's case studies, abilities in this space vary across the Arab world, but only very little. Personnel development in most cases is not based on specific and strict merit criteria, and performance assessments are not standardized. Arab officers tend to be promoted primarily because they are loyal to the leadership, come from an influential tribe, and/or are connected to power circles.

Military universities and staff colleges in the Arab world range from awful to mediocre, and very few teach anything useful in the field of military sciences. Indeed, the educational material in military universities and staff colleges in the Arab world is not a dependable source of knowledge on strategic, operational, and technical issues for officers, noncommissioned officers (NCOs), and regular soldiers.

Managing defense resources is not the Arab partners' strongest suit either. Decades of wasted US military assistance funds by the Egyptians, the Bahrainis, the Omanis, the Jordanians, the Moroccans, and others offer plenty of evidence to support this argument. Accounting in Arab defense ministries is optional. Costs for military capabilities as well as the employment of such capabilities are hardly ever collected and analyzed, which has always made planning and budgeting for the future virtually impossible.

In terms of logistics, not one Arab partner has effective automated systems, proper inventory control and distribution, and enough stockage levels. Some, like the Saudis and the Emiratis, seem to be more interested lately in doing maintenance, repair, and overhaul, but their logistics systems, strategies, and workforces still require a ton of development.

Why the Arab partners run their defense affairs the way they do is no mystery. Their societal cultures and their bureaucracies are two important factors. An in-depth analysis of the role of culture, in all its different dimensions, manifestations, and levels at which it operates, is outside the scope of this book.[43] I tip my hat to Pollack for taking on this vastly complicated issue with grace and precision. But suffice it to say here that Arabs, more so in government than in the private sector, tend to jealously guard information, memorize more than they engage in critical learning, shirk responsibilities, centralize decisionmaking, and insufficiently coordinate in group activities.[44] That's why the Arab bureaucracy, which at the end of the day is a reflection of societal and political culture, generally is hierarchical, inefficient, and inflexible.

Many of these cultural patterns are reinforced by the Arab rulers' priorities, which center on upholding political control and protecting economic privileges in the system. It's no wonder, then, that the Arab bureaucracy, without which defense institution building practically cannot be pursued, has historically underperformed.

That's not to say that the Arab bureaucracy is destined to frustrate all attempts at building Arab defense institutional capacity. Several examples of administrative success in the Arab world over many decades, including Egypt's Suez Canal and Aswan High Dam and Saudi Arabia's national oil company, Aramco, show that, if properly enabled and incentivized by political leadership, the Arab bureaucracy can be as competent and productive as any other in the world.

Arab governments and militaries have been unable to build stronger defense institutional capacity not because they do not know that there are different and better ways of doing things, but because that is how they have always done things, and they are comfortable doing them *their way*. In their eyes, they have not resisted "best" practices (as the United States sees it); they are resisting *American* practices. And they are not always wrong about that, because often what Americans claim are best practices are simply how *they* like to do things. Let's be honest, sometimes there is a good bit of illogic and inefficiency in the preferred approaches of Americans.

## The Plan of the Book

The book proceeds as follows: In the next chapter, I begin by briefly discussing what US military assistance in the Arab world primarily consisted of from the 1970s to the early to mid-2000s. This is what I call the "old model" of US military assistance, where the train-and-equip approach reigned supreme in US policy and process. Then I examine how in recent years US officials began to incorporate some elements of defense institution building into US military assistance in the region. I highlight the drastic changes in US security cooperation policy since 2017, both legally and administratively, and introduce the concept of defense institution building, providing some historical background and defining various elements of this process.

After that, I assess the challenges and opportunities of US military assistance programs in Saudi Arabia, Jordan, and Lebanon—three countries that lately have shown more interest in defense institution building than the rest of America's Arab partners. I also shed light on the UAE and its own attempts in more recent years to create military capability and pursue some measure of defense reform without the official involvement or help of Washington. I have selected these countries as case studies because they have been more eager to comprehensively reform their defense and military structures than the rest of America's Arab partners.

Saudi Arabia (Chapter 3) is the model of dysfunctional US military assistance in the Arab world, representing everything that has gone wrong in US-Arab defense and security cooperation. In that respect, Saudi Arabia provides this book's baseline. Many of the insights gained from US-Saudi military ties very much apply to all other cases of US military assistance in the region.

In addition, Saudi Arabia is one of the most important and long-standing Arab partners of the United States. Therefore, success and failure in US-Saudi defense and security relations carry greater policy and strategic significance for Washington than in most other US relationships in the region.

Jordan's example (Chapter 4) is important because the country has occupied a special place in US foreign policy toward the Middle East for several decades. The Hashemite Kingdom's role in the Israeli-Palestinian so-called peace process and the direct impact of its stability on Israeli security continue to matter a great deal to the United States.

Jordan in many respects is similar to Saudi Arabia in terms of US military assistance, but also very different because Amman is a pure *recipient* as opposed to a buyer of US security sector assistance. This distinction and several others demand scrutiny because they have real implications for how Washington administers, and how Amman utilizes, US military assistance.

Lebanon (Chapter 5) is an interesting case from both an analytical and policy perspective in large part because of how peculiar it is. Indeed, even outliers have merit. The country suffers from old, structural problems that typically would make any external attempt at helping to rebuild its armed forces virtually impossible. And yet, over the past decade or so, Washington has succeeded in transforming the Lebanese military from an irrelevant force into a respectable and competent national institution. Important US lessons can be gleaned from the Lebanese example.

Finally, there is tremendous value in looking at the UAE example (Chapter 6) for two main reasons. First, the UAE today is the closest and most militarily dependable partner of the United States in the Arab world. How US military assistance may have contributed to the UAE's elevated status certainly is worth investigating.

Second, the UAE has been able to achieve a higher level of military effectiveness than that of all other Arab partners despite possessing some considerable, albeit not unique, gaps in defense institutional capacity. This outcome potentially challenges my main argument in this book, which emphasizes the role defense institution building plays in overall military development.

In Chapter 7, I analyze more broadly the cultural and structural challenges of defense institution building both in Washington and in the Arab world. In Chapter 8, I conclude by identifying possible steps the United States and its Arab partners could take to develop Arab military capability more effectively. I also discuss the tradeoffs Washington might have to make as it seeks to build the military capabilities of its Arab partners, before tying the whole analysis to the important subject of the future of America's military presence in the Middle East, which is frequently in the US news headlines.

## Notes

1. All US national security strategies and national defense strategies since have put a premium on that objective. US Department of Defense, *Quadrennial Defense Review Report*, February 6, 2006, https://history.defense.gov/Portals/70/Documents/quadrennial/QDR2006.pdf?ver=2014-06-25-111017-150.

2. CIP Security Assistance Monitor, "Security Assistance Database," Center for International Policy (CIP), accessed December 17, 2020, https://securityassistance.org/security-sector-assistance/.

3. Sangar Khaleel and Jane Arraf, "Rocket Attack in Iraq Kills a U.S. Military Contractor," *New York Times*, March 3, 2021; Jane Arraf and Eric Schmitt, "Iran's Proxies in Iraq Threaten U.S. with More Sophisticated Weapons," *New York Times*, June 4, 2021.

4. Tom Bowman and Monika Evstatieva, "The Afghan Army Collapsed in Days. Here Are the Reasons Why," NPR, August 20, 2021.

5. Craig Whitlock, "The Afghanistan Papers: A Secret History of the War," *Washington Post*, December 9, 2019.

6. Brad Plumer, "The U.S. Gives Egypt $1.5 Billion a Year in Aid. Here's What It Does," *Washington Post*, July 9, 2013.

7. Ben Hubbard and Shuaib Almosawa, "Biden Ends Military Aid for Saudi War in Yemen. Ending the War Is Harder," *New York Times*, February 5, 2021.

8. Human Rights Watch, "Yemen Events of 2019," accessed February 25, 2021, https://www.hrw.org/world-report/2020/country-chapters/yemen#.

9. *NBC News*, "Splitting the Check: When Allies Helped Pay for Middle East War," September 14, 2014; Youssef M. Ibrahim, "Gulf War's Cost to Arabs Estimated at $620 Billion," *New York Times*, September 8, 1992.

10. Ibrahim, "Gulf War's Cost to Arabs."

11. Andrew Shapiro, Assistant Secretary for the Bureau of Political-Military Affairs, "Ensuring Israel's Qualitative Military Edge," Remarks to the Washington Institute for Near East Policy, Washington, DC, November 4, 2011.

12. Karen DeYoung and Dan Lamothe, "Qatar to Upgrade Air Base Used by U.S. to Fight Terrorism," *Washington Post*, July 24, 2018.

13. Glenn Kessler, "Trump's Claim the Saudis Will Pay '100 Percent of the Cost,'" *Washington Post*, October 21, 2019.

14. United Arab Emirates Abu Dhabi, "2004 Report to Congress on Allied Contributions to the Common Defense: UAE Submission," WikiLeaks cable 03ABUDHABI5390_a, December 23, 2003, https://wikileaks.org/plusd/cables/03ABUDHABI5390_a.html.

15. David Axe, "Iran Is Close to Getting an Atomic Bomb—but It Could Still Choose to Stop," *Forbes*, February 9, 2021.

16. Bilal Y. Saab and Michael Elleman, *Precision Fire: A Strategic Assessment of Iran's Conventional Missile Program* (Washington, DC: Atlantic Council, September 2016); Douglas Barrie, "Iran's Drone Fleet," *Iran Primer* (United States Institute of Peace), August 20, 2020, https://iranprimer.usip.org/blog/2020/aug/20/irans-drone-fleet.

17. Claire Parker and Rick Noack, "Iran Has Invested in Allies and Proxies Across the Middle East. Here's Where They Stand After Soleimani's Death," *Washington Post*, January 3, 2020.

18. Kate O'Flaherty, "The Iran Cyber Warfare Threat: Everything You Need to Know," *Forbes*, January 6, 2020.

19. Rick "Ozzie" Nelson and Scott Goosens, *Counter-Piracy in the Arabian Sea: Challenges and Opportunities for GCC Action* (Washington, DC: Center for Strategic and International Studies, May 2011).

20. Anthony Cordesman, *The Iranian Sea-Air-Missile Threat to Gulf Shipping*, with Aaron Lin (Washington, DC: Center for Strategic and International Studies, February 2015).

21. Joseph Trevithick, "Russia Is Extending One of the Runways at Its Syrian Airbase," *War Zone*, February 5, 2021.

22. Michael Crowley, "Israel, U.A.E. and Bahrain Sign Accords, with an Eager Trump Playing Host," *New York Times*, November 11, 2020.

23. Lee Lescaze, "Hill Battle Looms as Reagan Proposes Sale of AWACS to Saudis," *Washington Post*, August 25, 1981.

24. Dan Williams, "Israel Will Not Oppose U.S. Sale of F-35 to UAE," Reuters, October 23, 2020.

25. Aaron Mehta, "After Reshuffling, Israel Could Create 'Opportunities' for Regional Military Cooperation," *Defense News*, February 8, 2021.

26. Zack Beauchamp, "The Syria War: A History," *Vox*, September 21, 2015.

27. Joby Warrick, "More Than 1,400 Killed in Syrian Chemical Weapons Attack, U.S. Says," *Washington Post*, August 30, 2013.

28. Bilal Y. Saab, "What a New Iran Nuclear Deal Really Requires," *Foreign Policy*, January 27, 2020.

29. Bilal Y. Saab, "Integrated Air and Missile Defense Will Enhance Security in the Middle East," *National Interest*, October 30, 2021.

30. Gordon Lubold, "U.S. Works Up New Effort to Shift Military's Focus to Asia," *Wall Street Journal*, October 23, 2019.

31. *Economist*, "How America and Its Allies Are Keeping Tabs on Iran at Sea," January 2, 2020.

32. Winston Churchill, "Give Us the Tools," broadcast, London, February 9, 1941, International Churchill Society, https://winstonchurchill.org/resources/speeches/1941-1945-war-leader/give-us-the-tools/.

33. For more on military capability as defined by the US military, see Ashley J. Tellis et al., "Measuring Military Capability," in *Measuring National Power in the Postindustrial Age* (Santa Monica: RAND, 2000), 133–158.

34. Chairman of the Joint Chiefs of Staff Instruction, "Guidance for Developing and Implementing Joint Concepts," August 17, 2016, https://www.jcs.mil/Portals/36/Documents/Doctrine/concepts/cjcsi_3010_02e.pdf?ver=2018-08-01-134826-593.

35. Kenneth M. Pollack, *Armies of Sand: The Past, Present, and Future of Arab Military Effectiveness* (Oxford: Oxford University Press, 2019) and *Arabs at War: Military Effectiveness, 1948–1991* (Lincoln: University of Nebraska Press, 2002); Norvell B. De Atkine, "Why Arabs Lose Wars," *Middle East Quarterly* 6, no. 4

(December 1999); Jessica L. P. Weeks, *Dictators at War and Peace* (Ithaca, NY: Cornell University Press, 2014); Caitlin Talmadge, *The Dictator's Army: Battlefield Effectiveness in Authoritarian Regimes* (Ithaca, NY: Cornell University Press, 2015); George Gawrych, *The Albatross of Decisive Victory: War and Policy Between Egypt and Israel in the 1967 and 1973 Arab-Israeli Wars* (Westport, CT: Greenwood Press, 2000).

36. For a good study on the importance and requirements of Arab defense reform, see Zoltan Barany, "Reforming Defense: Lessons for Arab Republics," *Strategic Studies Quarterly* 7, no. 4 (Winter 2013): 46–69.

37. Charles F. Wald, "New Thinking at USEUCOM: The Phase Zero Campaign," *Joint Forces Quarterly* 4, no. 43 (2006): 72–73.

38. Stephen Biddle and Robert Zirke, "Technology, Civil-Military Relations, and Warfare in the Developing World," *Journal of Strategic Studies* 19, no. 2 (June 1996): 171–212; Risa A. Brooks and Elizabeth Stanley, *Creating Military Power: The Sources of Military Effectiveness* (Stanford, CA: Stanford University Press, 2007); Risa Brooks, "Civil-Military Relations in the Middle East," in *The Future Security Environment in the Middle East: Conflict, Stability, and Political Change*, ed. Nora Bensahel and Daniel L. Byman (Santa Monica, CA: RAND, 2004): 129–162; Risa Brooks, "Making Military Might: Why Do States Fail and Succeed? A Review Essay," *International Security* 28, no. 2 (Fall 2003): 149–191; Risa Brooks, "An Autocracy at War: Explaining Egypt's Military Effectiveness, 1967 and 1973," *Security Studies* 15, no. 3 (July–September 2006): 396–430.

39. Nathan W. Toronto, *How Militaries Learn: Human Capital, Military Education, and Battlefield Effectiveness* (London: Lexington Books, 2018).

40. For an excellent overview of UAE military effectiveness, see Kenneth M. Pollack, *Sizing Up Little Sparta: Understanding UAE Military Effectiveness* (Washington, DC: American Enterprise Institute, October 27, 2020).

41. Brooks, "An Autocracy at War."

42. The Correlates of War Project, a large scholarly data set, estimates 500,000 Iraqi dead and 750,000 Iranian dead. See the Correlates of War Project at https://correlatesofwar.org.

43. For more on this subject, see Pollack, *Armies of Sand*; Brooks and Stanley, *Creating Military Power*.

44. De Atkine, "Why Arabs Lose Wars."

# 2

# US Military Assistance: Old vs. New Model

NO ONE REVIEWING THE HISTORY OF AMERICA'S EFFORTS to help its Arab partners create military capability should be faulted for skipping altogether the era preceding 9/11 or the 2003 Iraq War. Throughout that period, neither side really bothered to seriously invest in that goal. US-Arab security cooperation was a mirage more than anything else.

That said, it is still important to describe the key elements of the old, transactional model of US-Arab defense and security cooperation because they remain largely the same to this day. The only factor that has changed in more recent years is Washington's incorporation of defense institution building practices into some, but certainly not all, of these US military assistance programs in the region.

Arms transfers, military advising, joint training and exercises, and professional military education constitute the core of US military assistance programs, not just in the Middle East but around the world. These tools have been very helpful for the US pursuit of various foreign policy goals in the region, including strengthening bilateral ties with partners, gaining access and influence in Arab countries, selling arms to Arab friends, and preserving Arab-Israeli peace agreements.

Yet when it comes to the US goal of boosting Arab military power, these instruments have been neither very harmful nor very helpful. They can best be described as necessary but insufficient for the goal of building full-spectrum military capability.[1] Consider this tennis analogy:

An amateur player has been practicing and playing with friends for many years, gaining some experience, learning a few tricks, and even winning a few matches along the way. But ultimately, they fail to truly elevate their game and reach their full potential because they never acquired proper training on tennis techniques and fundamentals from a professional coach. They never managed to build a solid tennis foundation to be able to play consistently at a high level and compete in tournaments. In the universe of military capability development, defense institutional capacity represents that foundation and those fundamentals.

## Arms Transfers

Nothing in US defense policy in the Arab world has been more sizable, persistent, controversial at times, and thus scrutinized than Washington's provision of increasingly modern and lethal weapons to its Arab partners. This old habit constitutes the spinal cord of America's military assistance programs in the region and in many ways the glue to hold US relations with Arab partners together. And it has hardly ever abated.

Regardless of who pays for those arms transfers, be it Washington or the Arab partner, the amount of weapons that has been shipped to the Middle East since the late 1970s and the amount of money that has been spent by both sides has been absolutely astronomical and unmatched by any other set of allies or partners around the globe. It is hard to come up with an exact number, but we are talking several trillions of dollars.

Much of the criticism of US weapons sales to the Middle East focused in more recent years on President Trump. Such condemnation was understandable given the role his administration (and that of his predecessor) played in sending American bombs to the Saudis for their disastrous war in Yemen. While weapons sales to the region under the Trump administration did soar—averaging $51 billion a year during the first three years of Trump's presidency[2]—such an inflation, relatively speaking, was hardly unique in the history of US military transfers to the region.

Eager to stem the negative effects of the boom in global weapons sales on international security, President Jimmy Carter pushed for arms restraint in a May 1977 policy. "Because we dominate the world market to such a degree," he said, "I believe that the United States can and should take the first step" in reducing arms sales.[3]

However, Carter's eminently moral outlook and sincere interest in weapons limitation and even disarmament would soon face the reality of global weapons sales competition, the crises of the Middle East, and the exigencies of the Cold War, leading Foreign Military Sales (FMS) under his administration to go up and land primarily in developing countries—mostly in pre-1979 Iran.

The ink on Carter's arms sales policy was barely dry when he signed multibillion-dollar deals with Egypt, Iran, Israel, and Saudi Arabia, all in the first year of his presidency. It was the shah of Iran, viewed by Washington as a key partner in its Soviet containment policy and a strong barrier to Moscow's access to Persian Gulf oil, who would receive the lion's share with the US transfer of a fleet of sophisticated airborne warning and control system (AWACS) planes in 1977 as part of a $5.7 billion arms package that included 160 F-16 fighter jets.[4]

President Reagan took things to a higher level, with deals throughout his two-term presidency reaching record numbers.[5] Eschewing any US endorsement of restraint in US arms sales, he shipped to the region some of the most modern weapons in the US arsenal, including F-15 and AWACS aircraft as well as air-to-air Sidewinder and antiship Harpoon missiles to Saudi Arabia; Cobra attack helicopters to Jordan; M48A5 tanks, armored personnel carriers, and ammunition to Lebanon; M60 tanks and military transport C-130 aircraft along with other reconnaissance and intelligence tools to Morocco; F-5E fighter aircraft and M60 tanks to Tunisia; and various types of scientific and technical equipment to Iraq.[6]

Much of Reagan's shift, articulated in his May 1981 arms transfer policy, was driven by changes in geopolitics and the international threat environment, including the Soviet invasion of Afghanistan in 1979, communist inroads into Africa and Latin America, the Iran-Iraq War, Tehran's rising ideological influence in the Arab heartland, and a drastic military buildup of the Warsaw Pact in Central Europe. But he also personally believed that arms sales to allies and partners were a critical instrument in the strategic quest to counter the ambitions of the "evil empire" across the globe.[7]

While President George H. W. Bush was consumed with the 1990–1991 Persian Gulf War, he too maintained a steady flow of arms to Arab partners and preserved the policy of his predecessor. On October 2, 1989, he called for the sale of US military equipment to "help friendly regional states meet their legitimate defense requirements, so long as such sales do not present a security threat to Israel."[8] A couple of months earlier, Bush authorized the transfer of 150 tanks, 24 F-15 fighter jets, and 200 antiaircraft missiles to Saudi Arabia in a $2.2 billion deal, which he would follow up shortly after with a $21 billion package of tanks, aircraft, and missiles to the kingdom (although those sales would arrive two years after the Persian Gulf War was over).[9] Had his presidency not been limited to one term, Bush could have supplied more weapons to Arab partners and possibly beaten Reagan's numbers given the immense gratitude the Gulf Arab states owed him for securing Saudi Arabia and liberating Kuwait.

President Bill Clinton assumed power with thoughts of reviewing US arms sales policy and reducing the proliferation of weapons around the world.[10] Ultimately, however, he stayed the course, except for one important twist (which would reappear vigorously under Trump): he formally emphasized the economic argument of those sales, stating that "all arms transfer decisions [would] take into account the impact on U.S. industry and the defense industrial base."[11]

It only took Clinton one year in office to achieve a record $36 billion in sales.[12] And of course the Middle East was a prime destination of US equipment. He authorized the transfer of $46.5 billion worth of advanced military hardware to the region in 1993–2000, most of which went to Saudi Arabia, receiving 72 advanced F-15 Eagle planes, 150 M1A2 Abrams tanks, 12 Patriot air-defense missile batteries, and thousands of missiles of various types. Kuwait and the UAE were not that far behind, obtaining 6 Patriot missile units, 256 M1A2 Abrams tanks, and 16 AH-64 Apache attack helicopters as well as 10 AH-64s and 80 F-16 fighter aircraft, respectively.

President George W. Bush further cemented the United States as the region's top arms exporter, and the Gulf Arab states were once again the most eager customers. Foremost on Bush 43's mind was the 2003 US war in Iraq. But Iran's sectarian drive across the region concerned him, too, and he believed it could be contained in part through the sale of advanced military equipment to Gulf Arab partners. Bush 43 had a strong personal relationship with Saudi King Abdullah bin Abdulaziz Al Saud, which he leveraged to sell Riyadh and its smaller neighbors a large number of US weapons. In January 2008, Washington sent $20 billion worth of high-tech weapons to the Saudis, including satellite-guided Joint Direct Attack Munitions (JDAM).[13]

President Obama might have had little affinity for the Gulf Arab states because he believed they were free riding on US regional security efforts and were suppressing their societies, but his administration in no way reduced the flow of US arms to them. Under Obama, US weapons made up almost half of all arms delivered to the Middle East from 2008 to 2011 and again roughly the same percentage between 2012 and 2015.[14] Some of this was the result of compensation for a US nuclear deal with Iran in 2015 that raised major concerns in Gulf Arab capitals given its failure to address Tehran's destabilizing behavior in the region.

Because of the fight against the Islamic State, Iraq also was a major recipient of US weaponry, receiving F-16 fighter aircraft, Apache helicopters, Abrams tanks, and many more items worth dozens of billions of dollars.[15] The Saudis got their handsome share too, acquiring equipment from Washington over the two terms of the Obama administration worth $115 billion,[16] much of it approved in a single deal in 2012. Those arms included bombs, F-15s, Apache and Black Hawk helicopters, missile interceptors, armed vehicles, and missile defense systems.

Like his predecessors, Trump viewed the Middle East as a prime target for US arms sales. In May 2017, he allegedly engineered a whopping $110 billion arms deal package for the Saudis, although what Riyadh actually agreed to and obtained was never certain.[17]

President Joe Biden has emphasized values and human rights in his foreign policy, much like Carter promised he would do. Yet in April 2021, he agreed to proceed with a weapons deal made with the UAE under the Trump administration that is worth more than $23 billion and includes F-35 fifth-generation aircraft and armed drones.[18]

The decades-long pattern of US arms sales to the region over successive administrations, both Democratic and Republican, shows that US weapons, despite the increasing concerns of some in Congress, will most likely continue to be shipped in abundance to the Middle East for a host of strategic, political, and economic reasons. To be clear, the Arab partners do need arms from the United States to fulfill many of their legitimate military and security needs, but because all Arab partners do not have proper defense planning processes and defense acquisition policies, many are unable to effectively utilize, integrate, and sustain those arms.

## Military Advising

Perhaps no great power appreciates the strategic value of military advising by friendly foreign forces better than the United States. After all, it was a small group of Prussian and French military advisers who helped the Americans gain their independence from British rule by enhancing the military capabilities and professionalism of the militias that would later form the Continental Army.[19] Over the years, the United States has used various mechanisms, vehicles, and forums to try to train and advise its Arab partners on a host of technical, tactical, operational, and to a lesser degree, strategic issues that concern the two sides. Two of the more high-level advising constructs the United States relies on in Washington (and sometimes in the region if it happens on a rotating basis) are joint military commissions and defense resourcing conferences.

Joint military commissions are bilateral forums in which senior US and Arab defense officials discuss US military assistance and develop plans for strengthening security ties. These conversations tend to be a bit more substantive and detailed than the bilateral strategic dialogues. But it is unclear if they are more impactful because they tend to be divorced from higher-level policy matters governing relations between the two countries. The United States has several such commissions with Arab partners including Jordan, Lebanon, Morocco, and the UAE.

Defense resourcing conferences, which in principle overlap with and take a cue from the joint military commissions, are annual meetings between senior US and Arab defense officials to address the core security requirements of the Arab side. At present, Washington has defense resourcing conferences with Egypt, Jordan, and lately Lebanon,[20] and the main objective of these engagements is to help the Egyptian, Jordanian, and Lebanese military leaderships match their US arms procurement decisions to their strategies and resources and encourage them to do joint threat assessments, strategic analyses, and capability planning with US counterparts. However, in the case of Cairo and to some extent Amman, little of that actually happens, and it is uncertain if the conferences have succeeded in positively influencing the defense choices of these two partners. (It has worked better in Lebanon's case, but only because the country has minimal if any leverage, which means that it is a lot more respectful of US preferences.)

## Joint Training and Exercises

CENTCOM provides training to all Arab partners on a regular basis through various constructs and organizations. For example, in Saudi Arabia, USMTM, OPM-SANG, and Ministry of Interior–Military Assistance Group (MOI-MAG) all train and advise the Saudi military and internal security forces on a range of technical, tactical, doctrinal, leadership, and personnel defense issues.

In Lebanon, the United States has trained the Lebanese army for more than a decade on how to better conduct border security, maritime security, and counterdrug operations. Despite Lebanon's small size, the US military training program in the country remarkably is one of the largest in the Middle East, underscoring its significance to CENTCOM's leadership.

The Jordan Operational Engagement Program (JOEP) is one of the more serious US military training programs in the region, with Jordanian and American officers and personnel jointly addressing issues of doctrine, strategy, and tactics and oftentimes conducting, for consecutive weeks, live-fire exercises, including battle drills and training for sniper contingencies, improvised explosive device reactions, map reading, land navigation, and tactical first aid.

The UAE's fighter pilots and special operations forces perhaps train more rigorously and aggressively with their American counterparts than those of any other Arab partner, both in the country and "on the sands of the Mojave Desert and in the skies over Nevada."[21] The UAE was involved militarily in Afghanistan for a little less than two decades, chiefly to get a taste of live warfare and seize the opportunity to train with US forces operating in the country.

The UAE is not the only Arab partner to send troops to Afghanistan—Jordan had a small security and humanitarian presence from 2002 to 2015 (Jordan Armed Forces Task Force 300B in Helmand province)[22]—but it is the first to have done so, and its 250 elite forces are the only Arab ones to have undertaken "full-scale operations" in support of US objectives.[23]

Oman, Bahrain, and Kuwait have their own training programs with the US military too, but they do not match the complexity, intensity, scope, and duration of those of Jordan and the UAE. Inferno Creek engages various units of the Omani and US militaries in a training exercise to build interoperability and develop shared understandings of each other's tactics, techniques, and procedures (TTPs). Manama's navy often conducts joint reconnaissance, surveillance, and search-and-rescue operations with US Naval Forces Central Command (NAVCENT), and the Bahrain Defense Force learns from the US Army techniques for protecting its own troops and responding to improvised explosive devices planted by Bahraini militants loyal to Iran. Neon Defender, in which the American and Bahraini militaries participate, is a useful joint maritime security training construct given its priorities of explosive ordnance disposal and minefield clearance, two big problems for multinational navies in the waters of the Persian Gulf caused by the navy of the Islamic Revolutionary Guard Corps (IRGC).

Kuwait regularly conducts training exercises with the US military, both on the ground and at sea, simulating attacks across the country's border as well as naval smuggling operations. It also has gone through a training regimen with the US Army on military police activities, learning how to better pursue crowd and riot control, detention and confinement operations, convoy security operations, urban operations, and first aid.

In addition to these bilateral training activities, the United States conducts more high-profile, joint exercises with several Arab partners, although the military utility of some is not entirely convincing. Eager Lion, an annual exercise involving the US and Jordanian militaries as well as several thousands of military personnel from land, naval, and air forces across a few dozen nations from around the world, is the most significant in the region.

The King Abdullah II Special Operations Training Center (KASOTC), the pride of King Abdullah II of Jordan who himself has more than thirty-five years of military experience, hosts many of the drills of Eager Lion. Using both light and heavy weapons, the exercise trains on multiple terrains over a period of roughly two weeks for realistic contingencies. The general purpose of Eager Lion is to promote interoperability, exchange military expertise, and develop joint planning techniques among the Jordanian and US militaries as well as other international partners. The program conducts various live-fire exercises, including air assaults, long-range bomber missions, maritime security operations, coordinated mortar and artillery strikes, unit-level training, sniper training, battlefield trauma training, mine-clearing training, riot control, and combat marksmanship.

Operation Bright Star is Egypt's flagship operational and tactical exercise with the United States and several other international partners including European and Gulf Arab nations. Conducted every two years, it has roughly similar purposes to Eager Lion. While Bright Star is significantly larger than Eager Lion (and is reportedly the largest multinational military exercise in the world), its training practices seem less intense and realistic—indeed, often planned and scripted to be as risk-averse as possible—and its US participation is noticeably smaller, ranging from 200 to 800 soldiers in each exercise, compared to Eager Lion's 3,700 American sailors and Marines.

Bright Star has been taking place since 1980, but it was suspended in 2011–2017 due to political turbulence in Egypt and tensions in US-Egypt relations. A long-standing symbol of the partnership between Egypt and the United States, this event carries great political significance for both countries, albeit questionable military value.

Despite or maybe because of its size, which has grown almost every year, Bright Star has not allowed for more focused maneuvers tailored for Egypt's fight against terrorism and insurgency in Sinai. CENTCOM often tries to steer Bright Star in the direction of combined urban assault, counterinsurgency tactics, and helicopter search-and-rescue missions. Egypt's generals, however, prefer air-to-air combat and naval drills. (In the latest iteration of the exercise—Bright Star 2021—American special forces operators did teach Egyptian counterterrorism units from the Ministry of Interior how to deal with casualties during combat. That said, the course was far from comprehensive or integrated into a broader and realistic unconventional contingency.) Because the Egyptian military is still postured primarily to fight conventional wars with Israel and its arms procurement policy—to the extent that a coherent one is discernible—reflects that reality, Bright Star is unlikely to achieve its true potential.

Native Fury is another biennial exercise tying the militaries of the United States and the UAE. With its real-life simulations including the seizure of Arab-looking cities, it has some resemblance to Eager Lion. In March 2020, despite the Covid-19 crisis and the limitations the pandemic had placed on CENTCOM's training with partners in the region, the exercise "saw 4,000 U.S. troops from the Army, Marines and Navy position armored vehicles and other equipment from Kuwait and the island of Diego Garcia in the desert, some 125 miles southwest of Abu Dhabi."[24]

In addition to Native Fury, since 2016, American and Emirati soldiers have trained together on Kuwaiti territory in dust storms and heat as part of annual exercises called Iron Union.[25] They have practiced better communication, coordination, live fire, strategic movement, and logistical support all during battle. At sea, the Emirati and American navies conduct various maritime patrols in the northern Gulf of Oman to disrupt smuggling by Iran and its proxies. They also run routine interoperability exercises to advance secure information sharing and maritime domain awareness.

In short, all Arab partners have air, land, and naval joint exercises with the United States, but some are not regular and all fail to match the political significance of Bright Star or the relative military utility of Eager Lion and Native Fury.

## Professional Military Education

The State Department provides professional military education to its Arab partners through several tools, including its International Military Education and Training (IMET) program. IMET is a grant program established by Congress as part of the Arms Export Control Act of 1976. It allows foreign military personnel to take US courses offered annually at the dozens of US military schools across the country, acquire observer or on-the-job training, and/or receive orientation tours.

It is hard to find senior personnel in the US military who do not appreciate the value IMET brings to US-Arab military relations. CENT-COM's leadership, for one, absolutely loves the program. In a public testimony before the Senate Armed Services Committee in February 2019, CENTCOM commander Gen. Joseph Votel described IMET as "dollar for dollar, perhaps one of the best tools that the Department of Defense and Department of State can wield in building our partnerships throughout the region."[26]

In CENTCOM's view, IMET helps build deep and long-term personal relations with Arab officers who come to the United States to study military, governance, and human rights topics and pursue technical training in US military schools. Years later, many of these officers supposedly rise to positions of leadership in their countries and contribute to the strengthening of military ties with the United States.

For all the returns IMET generates, it is remarkably a very low-cost program compared to all the other mechanisms the United States uses to train, advise, equip, and educate its Arab partners. For example, Washington's entire annual budget of global IMET programs, around $110 million in 2018, is roughly the same as that of a single F-35 fighter plane, which, depending on the model, could cost more than $105 million.[27]

In the Arab world, Jordan, Lebanon, Morocco, and Oman seem to have most committed to and benefited from IMET. Jordan has received nearly $19 million for IMET since 2014, making it one of the largest US global allocations, with graduates of the program including King Abdullah II and most of his closest military advisers.[28] Bahrain's king, Hamad bin Isa Al Khalifa, also is a graduate of the US Army's Command and General Staff College. Morocco's more recent numbers regarding IMET graduates are not available (from 2002 to 2005 the program trained 458 Moroccan security forces),[29] but the country has received a little more than $10 million for IMET since 2016 (a steady $2 million each year).[30] Lebanon and Oman have received around $13 million and $11 million, respectively, since 2014. Over 6,000 members of the Lebanese army have trained in the United States since 1970, including 310 members in 2019,[31] and over 927 members of the Omani Armed Forces, including 47 of them in 2018.[32]

## Limitations of the Old Model

For Washington, the fact that US military assistance programs in the pre-9/11 era were not generating more effective Arab military capability was not viewed as detrimental because on balance other more important foreign policy objectives at the time were met. Also, the shortcomings of these programs were more or less tolerated so long as hostile actors didn't launch major wars in the region and military contributions from Arab partners were not really needed.

Of course, wars and invasions in the Middle East did happen and Washington did need the military help of its Arab partners on several occasions. No example demonstrates the significant drawbacks of America's military assistance programs in the Arab world better than the 1990–1991 Persian Gulf War. Desert Storm exposed the Arab partners' military weaknesses and ineffectiveness on the battlefield like no other security crisis.

On August 2, 1990, Iraq, battered and bankrupt as a result of its devastating war with Iran during most of the 1980s, invaded and quickly occupied small and wealthy Kuwait next door. Six months later, the United States launched a major military campaign, the biggest since Vietnam, to restore the status quo ante. A little over a month after that, US troops achieved an overwhelming military victory, forever changing Iraq's future.

Though the decision to send hundreds of thousands of American soldiers overseas to fight a foreign war was not easy, Washington elected to intervene to prevent Saddam from moving his forces to Saudi Arabia, threatening Israel, and dominating the oil-rich region.[33] That the Arabs were in no position to deal with the crisis on their own and prevent it from escalating ultimately forced Washington's hand.

In Desert Storm, the United States deployed roughly 700,000 combat troops and 1,800 fixed-wing aircraft, flying over 116,000 sorties over an estimated forty-day period and striking various Iraqi targets.[34] In that massive US-led military campaign, the Arab partners (minus Jordan, whose King Hussein chose to politically align himself with Saddam for domestic political reasons)[35] played mostly a financial and logistical role.[36] However, this does not suggest they played no military role at all. Under the command of Saudi Lt. Gen. Khalid bin Sultan, Arab forces bombed Iraqi targets from the air, participated in ground attacks alongside the US Army, and performed various missions at sea that included minesweeping and naval gunfire support. (Command and control of coalition forces was established "with separate, but parallel lines of authority with [American and Saudi] forces remaining under their respective national command authorities.")[37]

But the truth is that most of the Arab states' war-fighting contributions were neither large nor crucial to the success of the overall operation (the Saudi Air Force's participation in multinational strike packages to attack airfields in western Iraq being one possible exception).[38] The numbers support this conclusion. In terms of air power, the Arab air forces flew roughly 8,077 sorties, which amounts to less than one-tenth of the total number of sorties by American airmen (the Saudis flew 6,852 sorties, the Kuwaitis 780, the Bahrainis 293, the Emiratis 109, and the Qataris 43).[39] Of all the Arab members of the coalition, the Saudis deployed the most air power, including 24 Tornados and 87 F-5s.[40] The Arab partners' contributions of ground troops were even more modest, with the Saudis committing five independent mechanized brigades and smaller units; the Egyptians the Fourth Armored Division, Third Mechanized Division, and Twentieth Special Forces Regiment; the Kuwaitis three independent brigades and smaller units; and the Bahrainis, Emiratis, Omanis, and Qataris chipping in too but with much smaller amounts.[41]

In short, in Desert Storm, all the operational planning and the crushing majority of the fighting was done by the Americans. All the critical battles that flanked, cut off, and degraded the Iraqi military and ultimately ejected Iraqi forces from Kuwait were waged by US troops. All the major operations that destroyed Saddam's command and control capabilities, suppressed his air defenses, established sea control and air dominance, and defeated the elite Iraqi Republican Guard units were conducted by American soldiers, airmen, and sailors.

The Arabs' military contributions slightly amplified some US operations and reduced the overall military and economic costs of the coalition, but what Washington cared about more at the time was their provision of financial resources and legitimacy to the intervention, which fed the perception among regional and world publics that Arabs, not just Westerners, were participants in the war effort.[42] Desert Storm was an opportunity for the Arab partners to go all-in with the United States against a mortal enemy. After all, this was an act of aggression of the most serious kind, one directed against not just one Arab neighbor but the entire Arab state system and regional order. Every Arab leader knew that Saddam's land grab wasn't going to stop in Kuwait City. And yet, the Arab partners failed to muster enough—or more importantly *effective*—military power in defense of their most critical security interests, preferring instead to pass the buck to the Americans. That their military contributions to such an existential fight were lackluster was an omen of things to come.

## Transitioning to a New Model

Since 9/11, more American officials and lawmakers have come to realize that providing more money and more arms to partner forces in the Middle East and other regions where the United States was putting out fires has not made those forces more militarily effective. In a Middle East beset by violence and constantly prone to crisis, resisting the temptation of tolerating more immediate tactical and operational gains is incredibly hard, but it is also vital for US long-term interests. The United States has pursued a whack-a-mole strategy in the Middle East for far too long. No doubt a lot of good has come out of it, including neutralizing threats and saving lives, but it is about time Americans realize that this approach is not enough to achieve their strategic objectives.

Because Washington has focused on short-term gains, it has settled for training and equipping the armed forces and security services of its Arab partners on how to counter immediate enemies. However, the key to more lasting security is having partners who are able to *sustain* their military abilities by developing the strategic, institutional, organizational, and programmatic fabric of their defense and security sectors. At the heart of this process is what the Department of Defense calls defense institution building or institutional capacity building.

Let me address one final point on US training, equipment, education, and doctrine (which I will come back to in Chapters 7 and 8) before I move on to address defense institution building. A big part of the problem with these enablers is that the United States provides them to its Arab partners with little sensitivity to their local contexts. It is training, equipment, education, and doctrine fashioned for *American* men and women, *American* organizations, *American* schools, and *American* commanders. It is how *Americans* do things, not how *Arabs* do things.

This bad habit isn't unique to the United States. The Soviets, and later on the Russians, had/have it too, for example. Americans, Russians, and Europeans assume that their system is the best, and they just give it to their allies expecting them to be as good with it as they are. What one finds almost everywhere in America's web of partnerships across the world is that those partner militaries that performed well did so because they took US and other foreign methods and adapted them to their own styles, systems, and institutions, and to their ways of doing things—in other words, *their* culture. That is what the Japanese and the Australians have done, as well as the Cubans, the Georgians, the Colombians, the East Germans, and the Chinese.

Of course, there is one problem on the Arab partners' end, which is that they want the United States to offer them the exact same training it provides to its own troops—mostly because they don't know any better, assume that is the best, and want the best. Many Arab partners probably would get infuriated if the United States told them that it was going to provide a version of its methods tailored to their needs/military/society because they would think that Americans were giving them something less than the best. It would hardly ever occur to them to do what, for example, the Israelis do, which is learn everything the Americans have to teach and then just incorporate the parts that work for them into their own approach to warfighting.

These systemic Arab and American problems together frustrate well-meaning American military officers sent to the Middle East to help build Arab partners' capabilities. These officers typically spend the first three to four months of their tour trying to get those partners to do it the American way, failing over and over again, at which point they get completely disillusioned, stop trying, and just count the months until they can return home. In many respects, this represented the old model of US military assistance in the Arab world.

## Definition and Background

Defense institution building is the process through which countries lay the organizational, behavioral, and normative foundations of defense. At least at its embryonic stage, this process is part and parcel of state building, and it hardly ever stops. Throughout history, nations typically have had to engage in some form of defense organization after they achieved their political independence and began to formulate plans to stand up an organized military force to protect the newly formed polity from internal and external threats.

For example, the Americans began their journey of defense reform in the early 1900s as they sought to create a reserve guard and a national guard. Others, like Chile for example, pursued military development much earlier. In 1818, the newly independent state of Chile requested the help of French military advisers to build up its armed forces. Sixty-seven years later, the Prussians stepped in too at the request of the Chilean government. Led by the famous Captain Emil Kôrner of the Imperial German Army, they turned the Chilean army in 1910 into "the best equipped land fighting force and the best educated officer corps in Latin America."[43] During that period, the Colombians, led by President Rafael Reyes (1904–1909), were engaged in an effort to professionalize their armed forces through revamped training and educational opportunities with the help of the French and later on the Chileans and the Swiss.[44]

In the 1930s, the Philippines embarked on a major military restructuring effort with the support of the Americans. Gen. Douglas MacArthur and his aide Maj. Dwight Eisenhower (who later became president of the United States) would help the Philippine army develop a comprehensive military school system, an air force, and large reserve forces.[45]

The policy prominence of and reliance on defense institution building rose after the Cold War and in many ways became synonymous with the European concept of security sector reform (SSR). Rooted in NATO's 1994 Partnership for Peace program, SSR sought to reform the governance mechanisms of the defense and security sectors of former Warsaw Pact states after the fall of the Soviet Union.[46]

Like SSR, institutional capacity building is inextricably linked to governance, though not necessarily to *political* governance or power sharing. "The professionalism and effectiveness of the defense and security sector," noted one comprehensive SSR study, "is not just measured by the capacity of the security forces, but how well they are managed, monitored and held accountable."[47] This to a large extent applies to defense institution building as well.

While there is philosophical congruence between SSR and defense institution building, they tend to part ways on the issues of scope and expectations. The former implicitly assumes that the process aids and ultimately leads to not only conflict resolution and postconflict reconstruction but also democratization in the host country, with the supplier or adviser nation often seeking, directly or indirectly, to push things in that direction. In contrast, defense institution building, at least the way the United States conceives of and approaches it with its foreign partners, does not necessarily hold such assumptions and is more concerned with the narrower task of supporting a partner's efforts to effectively employ and sustain US tactical and operational assistance. To be sure, this is still an enormous undertaking that requires a high degree of commitment by the supplier and a vast array of reforms by the recipient, but no concerted effort is made by the former to actively promote democracy or enhance political governance in the latter.

SSR tends to be more ambitious in part because it is influenced by the relative success of several post–Cold War experiences in Eastern Europe and more recently in Sierra Leone and South Africa where all these countries, having turned to the discipline to improve their security and governance abilities, ultimately became more politically open.[48] Defense institution building on the other hand has been shaped by the United States to generally fit its own goals and preferences with regard to security assistance and cooperation. Ever wary of nation building and democracy promotion in the Middle East given its deeply problematic experiences in Afghanistan and Iraq, the United States has sought in more recent years to develop its regional partners' defense and security capabilities without trying to reorient their politics. The term *security sector reform* has appeared in some Department of Defense directives on defense institution building, but on both macro and micro policy levels, it is evident that the United States has no intention of promoting that process in the same way the Europeans have in fragile and post-conflict environments.[49]

## In Practice

The United States needs its Arab partners to attain an ability to achieve specific military operational objectives—for example, stage an amphibious landing like the UAE military did in the spring of 2015 in Yemen to combat Houthi fighters; clear a town or village of insurgents like the Iraqi Counter Terrorism Service (CTS) did many times throughout its campaign against the Islamic State; interdict Iranian smuggling at sea like the Bahrainis have done in their territorial waters; or strike terrorist targets from the air as a number of Arab air forces did in several parts of the region with their US-made fighter jets. But what is even more important for Washington is that its Arab partners capably and responsibly perform such functions *over and over again* with little or no help from the United States. Defense institution building can help these countries install processes and bureaucratic structures to provide the direction, guidance, and resources through which tactical-level units and capabilities are conceived, created, improved, and sustained.

To illustrate this point, imagine that the United States has embarked on a program to help Qatar, for example, create rapid reaction forces, defined as an elite group of soldiers or commandos that could swiftly and effectively respond to emergencies. The following are some of the key steps that generally would have to be taken to achieve that objective:[50] The selected Qatari infantry battalion would have to develop secure communications, among other things. This would require purchasing secure radios, encryption equipment for commercial telecommunications, and satellite ground stations. It sounds relatively easy, especially for a wealthy nation like Qatar, but this is only the beginning. Purchasing secure radios also means acquiring their spare parts; building warehouses for all that equipment; training repair technicians, radio operators, and warehouse clerks; and conducting unit training. None of this can happen without building a school and creating a training curriculum to educate Qatari personnel and developing the necessary managerial infrastructure for centralized maintenance, supply, and distribution. And yet, more often than not, this is precisely what ends up lacking in US military assistance programs in the Middle East. Neither the United States nor the Arab partner commits to a comprehensive process of military capability development that guarantees the desired capability does not considerably weaken or disappear the moment the United States pulls the plug on the financial assistance or ends its operational involvement.

Here is another example, though this one reflects current reality. The United States supplies many of its Arab partners, particularly the Gulf Arab states, with some of the world's most modern fighter aircraft and helicopters. These weapons systems have served various purposes, including protecting the skies and, when necessary, striking terrorists and insurgents. But all of these Arab partners have underdeveloped systems for force employment, integration, and sustainment, and some do not have them at all.[51]

Both sides—that is, the supplier and the recipient—are guilty of wrongdoing. The United States often sells or helps finance these sophisticated and expensive weapons to its Arab partners without insisting on and helping with effective employment and sustainment. Most Arab partners tend to prioritize possession of the US equipment above all else. After they acquire it, either they rely exclusively on the United States to maintain it for them or they omit maintenance altogether, opting instead to simply replace the old with the new.

Sometimes Washington instructs American personnel to man and operate the purchased equipment for the Arab partner (with the latter's blessing), construct facilities on its territory, and do all the maintenance for it (while of course getting handsomely compensated for its services). For example, the United States has financed Jordan's acquisition of F-16 fighter jets for roughly two decades, but Amman has yet to make a serious effort to sustain these aircraft on its own or effectively plan and budget for necessary periodic upgrades, forcing the US military to perform all these essential functions for the Jordanians and Washington to keep subsidizing them through the State Department's Foreign Military Financing (FMF) account.

This is not just to pick on the Jordanians. Many other Arab partners do it too, including Iraq and several Gulf Arab states. Baghdad secured its own fleet of F-16 planes from the United States in 2011 as part of a $4.3 billion deal. Today, few Iraqi pilots are combat-ready, and most of those planes are grounded mostly due to improper maintenance and lack of spare parts.[52]

To give an idea of how critical and difficult it is to consistently maintain modern fighter jets, consider this: high-technology fighter aircraft must always be inspected before and after take-off and partially over-hauled and refurbished immediately following landing.[53] That is, of course, assuming major technical problems did not occur and nothing broke down during flight time, which if it did would necessitate an almost total rebuild of the plane. Depending on its type and specifications, each jet would have to possess 1.5–2 well-trained pilots (and the cost of training one F-16 pilot costs around $5.6 million).[54] A typical US fighter squadron, which on average contains between 18 and 24 airplanes, will have around 400–500 support personnel when operating from its home station and half of that during expeditionary operations.[55] The more modern and sophisticated the plane, presumably the costlier it is to maintain it.

Saudi Arabia's air war in Yemen against the Houthis clearly shows the effects of deficient institutional capacity on operational effectiveness. To understand why the Saudis have not been able to shoot straight, at least more consistently, and avoid such massive collateral damage, one has to look at the small but very important factors that seldom get looked at by the media. The Saudi air force has vastly underperformed in Yemen not just because of bad or insufficient training, but also because throughout its campaign it has not benefited from sound strategic guidance, it has regularly run out of fuel and ammunition, and it has lacked good intelligence—all because the human, strategic, and technological systems needed to support these requirements are suspected to be either inadequate or absent.

The attack against the kingdom's oil facilities in September 2019 is another glaring example. The Saudis might have been able to better defend against the Iranian missile assault had they programmed their missile defense batteries to protect both their military installations and oil infrastructure, but they failed to do so because all these years they had not engaged in proper defense planning and threat assessment, which are core elements of defense institution building.

## Multiple Levels and Functions

In the defense sectors of postindustrialized nations, including those of the United States, Japan, Australia, South Korea, and several NATO allies, institutional capacity is almost a given. When an individual joins the US military, for example, he or she is immediately provided a number of tools and benefits: a training plan; educational opportunities; tax-free room, board, and allowances; comprehensive health insurance; special home loans and discounts; and a career path. The effective formulation, distribution, management, and oversight of all these privileges require a solid bureaucratic infrastructure in national defense that is able to communicate and coordinate with other government agencies and possibly the private sector. Furthermore, each US military service has trained personnel to maintain equipment as well as policies, educational systems, and budgets to ensure that more trainers can be brought on board. But America's Arab partners have different traditions, norms, structures, and processes in place, many of which are less than effective.

Defense institution building typically is a long-term process. A single program, depending on its scope and the recipient's institutional capacity baseline, often is planned over a period of not months but many years and sometimes even decades. The effort is most rewarding, as former deputy assistant secretary of defense for security cooperation Thomas Ross rightly noted, when it's conducted at multiple levels, including the ministerial, joint or general staff, and military service headquarters levels.[56] Institutional capacity building can target numerous functions, but some of the more important ones include (1) policy, strategy, and planning; (2) oversight of policy implementation; (3) force development; (4) defense resource management; (5) human resource management; (6) logistics and acquisition; (7) rule of law; and (8) intelligence policy, organization, and professionalization.[57]

### Policy, Strategy, and Planning

Ideally, it all starts with a national security policy, defined as a principle of action or statement of intent formulated by the partner that generally covers *ends* (what needs to be achieved) as well as *ways* and *means* (how and with what resources those ends are to be achieved). The policy is supposed to set national security objectives and priorities and identify present and future threats. The strategy refers to the main elements that are needed to pursue the policy. A strategy also can be viewed as a plan, adopted by defense officials to formally communicate how they wish to fulfill and align policy objectives with planned activities and ultimately create a defense budget.[58]

Planning consists of the concrete steps that must be taken incrementally to achieve the elements of the strategy. In the defense institutional context, this trilateral process allows the partner to "develop and oversee defense and military strategies, plans, and policies that identify and prioritize defense objectives; direct when and how to commit military forces; provide for the management and oversight of both military and civilian elements of the defense sector; and develop plans that align available ways and means to desired ends."[59]

Once strategic guidance is set and given, planning translates this guidance into specific activities aimed at achieving strategic and operational-level objectives and attaining the military end state. This level of planning ties the training, mobilization, deployment, employment, sustainment, redeployment, and demobilization of joint forces to the achievement of military objectives that contribute to national security goals. Operational planning is similar to a blueprint for building a house from bricks. Like the other functions, it too requires institutional support to allow for the participation of various centers of influence and sources of expertise.

## Oversight of Policy Implementation

The partner may have the best ideas on defense and security reform and come up with the best policies, but if it has no well-resourced, independent, and effective oversight mechanisms to ensure that those ideas and policies are being executed in accordance with the law and top-level guidance, then strategic goals are less likely to be met. Proper civilian oversight on both the executive and legislative levels of government guides, harmonizes, professionalizes, regulates, enables, and constantly reforms the entire national security system. Even in the United States, a nation committed to the principle of civilian oversight of the armed forces, there have been questions in recent years about the lack of effective civilian oversight in the Pentagon, as the bipartisan, congressionally mandated National Defense Strategy Commission warned in 2018.[60]

In the Arab world, parliamentary oversight over the functions of defense and internal security ministries is vastly underdeveloped and mostly symbolic given the omnipotence of the executive branch. And even within the executive branch, Arab militaries often plan, budget, and operate independently, without the guidance, supervision, or input of officials in the defense ministry (assuming the latter exists).

## Force Development

This process generally provides a means within the partner's ministry of defense to organize, employ, and prioritize its military forces' activities and purposes across the operational environment. Force development is "an organizing construct of processes, policies, organizational information and tools that informs senior leader decision making on how to organize, train, equip, and provide forces to [military] units and commanders in support of defense strategy within allocated resource limits to accomplish [military] missions."[61]

## Defense Resource Management

Defense resource management seeks to achieve a cost-effective alloca-tion of resources toward national security objectives. This process helps the partner's defense ministry, not its military, analyze overall national security requirements and allocate the available funds to most effec-tively meet the ministry's strategic needs.[62] It then ensures that those funds are spent pursuant to the budget plan.[63]

## Human Resource Management

The US Army defines human resource management (HRM) as a process to "determine human resource requirements based on defense require-ments and force plans . . . and to manage and develop people."[64] In a nutshell, this is about getting the right people in the right place and training them to the right standard to perform the right functions. HRM is expected to organize and classify personnel; recruit and retain quali-fied personnel; train and develop personnel to make sure they have the skills and capabilities needed to effectively perform the roles as defined by the force structure; provide compensation and benefits in order to incentivize enlistment and job performance; and effectively utilize per-sonnel by assigning them to specific roles in the organization that would be a good fit for them.[65]

## Logistics and Acquisition

Like strategy, logistics can mean different things to different people depending on the context. In NATO, it often refers to materiel (the equipment militaries need and use), movement (the means by which militaries move people and materiel from where they are to where they are needed), infrastructure (the facilities required to train, deploy, sus-tain, and redeploy forces), services (the nonmateriel support forces require), and health (medical and health service support).[66] The acqui-sition and logistics policies within a country's ministry of defense are supposed to organize activities related to supplying and equipping the military forces.

## Rule of Law

This process seeks to ensure the necessary legislation and systems exist for the use of force to respect the law of armed conflict and human rights norms. According to the US military, the rule of law should include "just legal frameworks, public order, accountability to the law, access to justice, and a culture of lawfulness," all of which require effective governance and functioning institutions.[67]

Defense institution building seeks to help the partner improve the way it provides not just safety and security but also justice and accountability. This means developing legitimate and accountable structures and law enforcement agencies, including military and police, intelligence services, border guards, courts, and corrections systems, all in accordance with the rule of law. Whether it is in peacetime, during military and stability operations, or in postconflict reconstruction environments, the rule of law is absolutely critical to maintaining order and ensuring the legitimacy of the whole defense apparatus.

### Intelligence Policy, Organization, and Professionalization

Infamous for their omnipotent police states, Washington's Arab partners do not always have a good understanding of the real capabilities of their external adversaries because their ability to effectively collect, analyze, and distribute intelligence is relatively weak. This includes both tactical/operational intelligence, necessary for all phases of war and various military contingencies, and strategic intelligence, which seeks to inform long-term policy planning, identify evolving threats and opportunities, assess enemy capabilities and intentions, and reduce the risks and uncertainties of the future. All of this requires not only talent and funds but also institutionalization.

Even though it is at the higher levels where defense institution building is most needed and plays the most vital role, Ross correctly argues that the joint- and general-staff levels also could be improved through holistic institutionalization. The goals of capacity building at the operational level are to "ensure that a [partner's] military units are able to plan for, mobilize, deploy for, sustain, assess, [and conduct] military campaigns and major operations, and to demobilize and recover from such operations."[68]

As wide-ranging as this overview of defense institution building might appear, it barely scratches the surface. The universe of institutional capacity building includes various other legal, procedural, organizational, technical, and human aspects. Importantly, there is no one way to engage in this process, and different countries, even those sharing the same values and habits, pursue it differently depending on their strategic cultures, priorities, abilities, and constraints.

## US Security Cooperation Reforms

Although the United States has pursued a measure of defense institution building in the region since 9/11, those activities have been rather scattered and unsystematic. The new model of US military assistance would truly reach an inflection point, at least officially, in late 2016. Introduced by Senator John McCain on December 23, 2016, and published in the Fiscal Year 2017 National Defense Authorization Act (NDAA),[69] a set of security cooperation reforms recognized for the first time the strategic importance of defense institution building by codifying a stand-alone authority for the Department of Defense to conduct it—Section 332 of Title 10 of the US Code of Law. The reforms also consolidated the train-and-equip authority—Section 333—which calls for the pursuit of institutional capacity building with international partners. And finally, they recommended that Washington systematically assess, monitor, and evaluate its security cooperation programs to ensure they were meeting their targets.

To help achieve those ends and establish civilian oversight over security cooperation, the reforms created a new Office of the Deputy Assistant Secretary of Defense for Security Cooperation. A single US official, holding the position of deputy assistant secretary of defense, would seek to supervise security cooperation on behalf of the under secretary of defense for policy. In January 2022, an organizational change in the Department of Defense allowed for the creation of a new entity called the Office of the Deputy Assistant Secretary of Defense for Global Partnerships, which incorporated the security cooperation shop. According to the department, this new office will seek to prioritize, integrate, and evaluate bilateral and multilateral security cooperation activities.

McCain's role in the formulation of the reforms was instrumental. For years he had been warning about some of the pitfalls of US military aid in the region, including American weapons being misused, getting lost, or ending up in the hands of terrorists and enemies of the United States, but it was what happened on October 16, 2017, in Iraq that broke the camel's back. That day, Baghdad dispatched troops to the oil-rich city of Kirkuk with the goal of retaking it from Iraq's Kurds, who had plans of creating an autonomous state in the northern part of the country. Not only did Iraq's security forces, trained and equipped by Washington, assault a crucial US ally in the fight against the Islamic State, they did it with the help of Qassem Soleimani, Tehran's top operative in the Middle East (killed by American drones in January 2020),[70] who reveled in seeing Iraqi militias under his control use American Abrams tanks and Humvees in pursuit of their mission.

McCain, who was the chairman of the influential Senate Armed Services Committee at the time, threatened to push for the termination of the US train-and-equip program in Iraq if the Iraqis did not stop clashing with the Kurds and allowing Iran-backed local forces to employ US arms. "Make no mistake," he stated, "there will be severe consequences if we continue to see American equipment misused in this way."[71] A week later, in an opinion for the *New York Times*, he called the Kirkuk episode "totally unacceptable" and called for a new Middle East strategy, which of course has yet to come.[72]

## Defense Institution Building Mechanisms

Outside the Pentagon, the Defense Security Cooperation Agency (DSCA), historically mandated to focus on US arms sales to international allies and partners, began in 2017 to incorporate defense institution building into its practices following a congressional directive. DSCA did have several institutional capacity building programs prior to the issuance of the security cooperation reforms, but it did not have much expertise, experience, or desire for that matter to fully leverage those programs.

Created in 2010, the Ministry of Defense Advisors (MODA) program sought to support US stabilization and sustainment efforts in Afghanistan. However, all such efforts in the country were immediately shut down following the US military withdrawal in August 2021. MODA programs have been used outside Afghanistan also, in places including Montenegro, Kosovo, Bosnia, Ukraine, Georgia, Colombia, Iraq, and lately Saudi Arabia. MODA has deployed senior US personnel from the Defense Department to the defense and interior ministries of these partners to exchange expertise directly and regularly and build long-term personal and institutional connections.[73]

Two sister institutional capacity building programs belonging to DSCA are the Defense Institute of International Legal Studies (DIILS), which is intended to help the partner develop the legal and human rights aspects of national defense as well as the norm and practice of civilian control of the military, and the Defense Institution Reform Initiative (DIRI), which as its name suggests seeks to assist the partner in reforming various elements and functions of its defense establishment. To help it execute its relatively new institutional capacity building mission, DSCA brought expert help from the Defense Governance and Management Team, the Center for Civil-Military Relations, and the International Defense Acquisition and Resource Management program. In April 2019, these three entities became part of the new, Monterey-based Institute for Security Governance (ISG), which is tasked with overseeing all capacity-building efforts for DSCA. At the time of writing, DSCA is undergoing a process of major reorganization in which ISG would fall under a new School for International Training and Advising, itself part of a new Defense Security Cooperation University.

## Notes

1. Daniel Byman makes a similar point in the counterinsurgency context. See Daniel L. Byman, "Friends Like These: Counterinsurgency at the War on Terrorism," *International Security* 31, no. 2 (Fall 2006): 83.

2. Michael LaForgia and Walt Bogdanich, "Why Bombs Made in America Have Been Killing Civilians in Yemen," *New York Times*, May 16, 2020.

3. Emma Rothschild, "Carter and Arms Sales," *New York Times*, May 10, 1978.

4. Stephen McGlinchey and Robert W. Murray, "Jimmy Carter and the Sale of the AWACS to Iran in 1977," *Diplomacy & Statecraft* 28, no. 2 (2017): 254–276. US military focus on Iran actually started with Carter's predecessors—Richard Nixon and, following his resignation over the Watergate affair, Gerald Ford—who opened the floodgates of American weapons to the shah.

5. Claudia Wright, "Reagan Arms Policy, the Arabs and Israel: Protectorate or Protection Racket?" *Third World Quarterly* 6, no. 3 (July 1984): 638–656.

6. Daniel E. Price, "Presidential Power as a Domestic Constraint on Foreign Policy: Case Studies Examining Arms Sales to Saudi Arabia," *Presidential Studies Quarterly* 26, no. 4 (1996): 1099–1113.

7. Andrew Glass, "Reagan Brands Soviet Union 'Evil Empire,' March 8, 1983," *Politico*, March 8, 2018.

8. The White House, *U.S. Policy Toward the Persian Gulf*, National Security Directive 26, October 2, 1989.

9. Michael T. Klare, "Fueling the Fire: How We Armed the Middle East," *Bulletin of Atomic Scientists* (January–February 1990): 20.

10. Lora Lumpe, "Bill Clinton's America: Arms Merchant of the World," *Nonviolent Activist* (May–June 1995).

11. The White House, "Statement by the White House Press Secretary on Conventional Arms Transfer Policy," February 17, 1995.

12. William D. Hartung, "Nixon's Children: Bill Clinton and the Permanent Arms Bazaar," *World Policy Journal* 12, no. 2 (Summer 1995): 25.

13. NPR, "Bush Announces $20 Billion Arms Deal for Saudis," January 14, 2008.

14. Clayton Thomas, *Arms Sales in the Middle East: Trends and Analytical Perspectives for U.S. Policy* (Washington, DC: Congressional Research Service, October 11, 2017).

15. Ibid.

16. Marcus Weisgerber and Caroline Houck, "Obama's Final Arms-Export Tally More Than Doubles Bush's," *Defense One*, November 8, 2016.

17. Bruce Riedel, "The $110 Billion Arms Deal to Saudi Arabia Is Fake News," *Markaz* (blog), Brookings Institution, June 5, 2017, https://www.brookings.edu/blog/markaz/2017/06/05/the-110-billion-arms-deal-to-saudi-arabia-is-fake-news/.

18. Patricia Zengerle, "Biden Administration Proceeding with $23 Billion Weapons Sale to UAE," Reuters, April 14, 2021.

19. Remi Hajjar, "What Lessons Did We Learn (or Re-Learn) About Military Advising After 9/11?" *Military Review* (November–December 2014): 63–75.

20. US Department of State, "Inaugural U.S.-Lebanon Defense Resourcing Conference," May 21, 2021.

21. Rajiv Chandrasekaran, "In the UAE, the United States Has a Quiet, Potent Ally Nicknamed 'Little Sparta,'" *Washington Post,* November 9, 2014.

22. Ibrahim Alharahsheh, "Jordanian Contributions to Afghanistan," *UNIPATH*, February 20, 2015; *Jordan Times*, "Military's Afghanistan Mission Completed," January 5, 2015.

23. *BBC News*, "Muslim Troops Help Win Afghan Minds," March 28, 2008.

24. Jon Gambrell, "US, UAE Troops Hold Major Exercise amid Virus, Iran Tensions," Associated Press, March 23, 2020.

25. Daniel Sanderson, "Exclusive: Inside the 'Iron Union' as US and UAE Troops Train for Combat," The National, December 23, 2019.

26. Joseph L. Votel. *Testimony Before the United States Senate Committee on Armed Services.* 116th Congress, February 5, 2019.

27. Valerie Insinna, "In Newly Inked Deal, F-35 Price Falls to $78 Million a Copy," *Defense News*, October 29, 2019.

28. US Department of State, "U.S. Security Cooperation with Jordan, Fact Sheet," Bureau of Political-Military Affairs, April 8, 2020, https://www.state.gov/u-s-security-cooperation-with-jordan/.

29. Government Accountability Office (GAO), *Security Assistance: Lapses in Human Rights Screening in North African Countries Indicate Need for Further Oversight* (Washington, DC: GAO, July 31, 2006).

30. Congressional Research Service (CRS), *Morocco: Background and U.S. Relations* (Washington, DC: CRS, October 26, 2018).

31. US Department of State, "U.S. Security Cooperation with Lebanon, Fact Sheet," Bureau of Political-Military Affairs, May 1, 2020, https://www.state.gov/u-s-security-cooperation-with-Lebanon/.

32. US Department of State, "U.S. Security Cooperation with Oman, Fact Sheet," Bureau of Political-Military Affairs, last modified June 15, 2021, https://www.state.gov/u-s-security-cooperation-with-oman/.

33. Richard N. Haass, "Desert Storm, the Last Classic War," *Wall Street Journal*, July 31, 2015.

34. For more precise data on Operation Desert Storm, see Thomas A. Keaney and Eliot A. Cohen, *Gulf War Air Power Survey*, Summary Report (Washington, DC: US Air Force, December 22, 1993); Shannon Collins, "Desert Storm: A Look Back," US Department of Defense, January 11, 2019, https://www.defense.gov/News/Feature-Stories/story/Article/1728715/desert-storm-a-look-back/; Oriana Pawlyk and Phillip Swarts, "25 Years Later: What We Learned from Desert Storm," *Air Force Times*, January 21, 2016.

35. Alan Cowell, "War in the Gulf: Jordan; Jordanian Ends Neutrality, Assailing Allied War Effort," *New York Times*, February 7, 1991.

36. Michael R. Gordon, "1991 Victory over Iraq Was Swift, but Hardly Flawless," *New York Times*, December 31, 2012.

37. Associated Press, "War in the Gulf: Military Briefing; Transcript of Briefing in Riyadh by the American Commander," February 25, 1991; US Central Command, *Operation Desert Shield/Desert Storm,* Executive Summary, July 11, 1991.

38. Peter Hunt, "Coalition Warfare: Considerations for the Air Component Commander," Thesis, Department of the Air Force, Air University Press, March 1998, 27.

39. Keaney and Cohen, *Gulf War,* 184.

40. Ibid., 199.

41. US Department of Defense, *Conduct of the Persian Gulf War: Final Report to Congress*, April 1992, 500; Anthony H. Cordesman and Abraham R. Wagner, *The Lessons of Modern War, Volume IV: The Gulf War* (Boulder: Westview Press, 1996), 95.

42. Rick Atkinson and David S. Broder, "U.S., Allies Launch Massive Air War Against Targets in Iraq and Kuwait," *Washington Post*, January 17, 1991.

43. Frederick M. Nunn, "Emil Korner and the Prussianization of the Chilean Army: Origins, Process, and Consequences, 1885–1920," *Hispanic American Historical Review* 50, no. 2 (May 1970): 300–322.

44. Paul J. Angelo and Olga L. Illera Correal, *Colombian Military Culture* (Miami: Steven J. Green School of International & Public Affairs, Florida International University, 2020).

45. Eric Setzekorn, "Eisenhower's Mutual Security Program and Congress: Defense and Economic Assistance for Cold War Asia," *Federal History*, no. 9 (2017): 9.

46. Bilal Y. Saab, "Broken Partnerships: Can Washington Get Security Cooperation Right?" *Washington Quarterly* 42, no. 3 (Fall 2019): 81.

47. Mark Sedra, "Introduction: The Future of Security Sector Reform," in *The Future of Security Sector Reform,* ed. Mark Sedra (Waterloo, ON: Centre for International Governance Innovation, 2010), 16.

48. For a good study on security sector reform in Sierra Leone, see Adedeji Ebo, "The Challenges and Lessons of Security Sector Reform in Post-conflict Sierra Leone," *Conflict, Security and Development* 6, no. 4 (2006): 481–501. For a perspective on security sector reform in South Africa, see Sandy Africa, *The Transformation of the South African Security Sector: Lessons and Challenges,* Policy Paper No. 33 (Geneva: Geneva Centre for the Democratic Control of Armed Forces [DCAF], March 2011).

49. US Department of Defense, *Defense Institution Building (DIB)*, DOD Directive 5205.82, January 27, 2016.

50. This example is inspired by Aaron Taliaferro's study on defense management entitled *IDA's Standard Model: Defining the Defense Management Domain* (Alexandria, VA: Institute for Defense Analyses, August 2019).

51. Alexandra Kerr, "Defense Institution Building: A New Paradigm for the 21st Century," in *Effective, Legitimate, Secure: Insights for Defense Institution Building,* ed. Alexandra Kerr and Michael Miklaucic (Washington, DC: National Defense University Press, 2017), xiii.

52. Hollie McKay, "Billions Wasted? Iraqi Pilots Claim Pricey F-16 Program Is Falling Apart," *Fox News*, August 26, 2020.

53. Author's interview in Manama with a US Air Force F-16 technician who wishes to remain anonymous, November 18, 2016.

54. Niall McCarthy, "The Cost of Training U.S. Air Force Fighter Pilots," *Forbes*, April 9, 2019.

55. Michael Moran, *Modern Military Force Structures* (New York: Council on Foreign Relations, October 26, 2006).

56. Thomas W. Ross Jr., "Defining the Discipline in Theory and Practice," in Kerr and Miklaucic, *Effective, Legitimate, Secure,* 21–46.

57. US Department of Defense, *Defense Institution Building.*

58. Martin Neill, Aaron C. Taliaferro, Mark E. Tillman, Gary D. Morgan, and Wade P. Hinkle, *Defense Governance and Management: Improving the Defense Management Capabilities of Foreign Defense Institutions* (Alexandria, VA: Institute for Defense Analyses, March 2017).

59. Ross Jr., "Defining the Discipline in Theory and Practice," 38.

60. National Defense Strategy Commission, *Providing for the Common Defense: An Assessment and Recommendations of the National Defense Strategy Commission* (Washington, DC: United States Institute of Peace, November 13, 2018).

61. Neill et al., *Defense Governance and Management.*

62. US Army, *Advising at the Senior Level: Lessons and Best Practices,* Handbook 19-06 (Fort Leavenworth, KS: Center for Army Lessons Learned, January 2019).

63. Ibid., 55.

64. Ibid.

65. Taliaferro, *IDA's Standard Model*, 16.

66. Ibid., 18; Senior NATO Logisticians' Conference Secretariat, *NATO Logistics Handbook* (Brussels: NATO Headquarters, October 1997).

67. US Joint Forces Command, *Handbook for Military Support to Rule of Law and Security Sector Reform*, February 19, 2016, 5; United States Institute of Peace and United States Army Peacekeeping and Stability Institute, *Guiding Principles for Stabilization and Reconstruction* (Washington, DC: Endowment of the United States Institute of Peace, 2009).

68. Ross Jr., "Defining the Discipline in Theory and Practice," 43.

69. National Defense Authorization Act for Fiscal Year 2017, Public Law no. 114-328, 130 Stat. 2000 (2016), https://www.congress.gov/114/plaws/publ328/PLAW-114publ328.pdf.

70. Karen Zraick, "What to Know About the Death of Iranian General Suleimani," *New York Times*, January 3, 2020.

71. Joe Gould, Tara Copp, and Shawn Snow, "Pentagon Says Iraqi Train-and-Equip Mission Could End if Attacks on Kurds Continue," *Defense News*, October 16, 2017.

72. John McCain, "We Need a Strategy for the Middle East," *New York Times*, October 24, 2017.

73. Hugh F. T. Hoffman, "Lessons from Iraq," in Kerr and Miklaucic, *Effective, Legitimate, Secure*, 329–358.

# 3

## Saudi Arabia: Rebuilding Everything

ITS IMMENSE WEALTH AND HIGH-TECH MILITARY ARSENAL notwithstanding, Saudi Arabia has one of the most underwhelming armies in the world. Its inability to leverage its extensive national assets is what makes the Saudi army so incredibly disappointing.

Perhaps unsurprisingly, also substandard is Saudi-US defense cooperation, despite Riyadh being the largest arms sales customer of the United States in the world, with more than $100 billion in active FMS cases.[1] Washington has sought since 2018 to readjust several aspects of its military assistance to the kingdom to make it more effective, more responsive to emerging security threats and requirements, and more mutually beneficial. But prior to that, Saudi Arabia was an exemplar of everything that was wrong with America's military assistance programs in the region. This bilateral defense relationship, anchored in the broader oil-for-security covenant since World War II, was highly imbalanced and limited in more ways than one.

The implicit understanding in Washington and in Riyadh was that a Saudi military that was able on its own to protect the kingdom against all threats and make military contributions to regional security was not an urgent priority. The United States was willing to play the role of guardian, and Saudi Arabia was happy to offer generous compensation in the form of cheap oil, money, and military access.

This quid pro quo suited both countries for decades, until Saddam invaded Kuwait in the summer of 1990. All of a sudden, the shortcomings of Washington's military assistance to Saudi Arabia were on full display. The Saudis, much like the rest of the Gulf Arab states, were helpless in the face of the battle-tested Iraqi war machine.

In Desert Storm, the Saudis barely engaged in direct combat, but when they did, they mostly underachieved. Even in their supposedly finest hour in Al Khafji, they could not finish the job on their own. In January–February 1991, Iraqi units led by the 5th Mechanized Division, 3rd Armored Division, and 1st Mechanized Division attacked the Saudi town of Al Khafji in a desperate attempt to draw Riyadh into the war and coalition troops into ground combat.[2] The 2nd Saudi Arabian National Guard (SANG) Brigade and the Qatari Brigade performed much better than anticipated. But ultimately they couldn't repel the invaders by themselves and had to frantically call for US air and artillery fire support to liberate the city.[3]

Roughly two and a half decades later, the Saudis would be at war again, and their military capabilities would be put to the test in Yemen. No doubt, they were able to field a better-trained force with more powerful arms and sustain a much longer fight than in Desert Storm. But they still would face tremendous challenges on the battlefield and, to this day, fail to reverse the territorial and strategic advances of the Iran-backed Houthis, all the while greatly contributing to Yemen's humanitarian catastrophe.

## Goals of US Military Assistance

Washington's military assistance to Saudi Arabia serves four main US goals: First, maintain a close relationship with the Saudi king and influence his decisionmaking, especially on energy production and pricing matters, in ways that contribute to US interests. Second, ensure US military access, basing, and overflight in a country whose geopolitical importance due to its deep oil reserves is massive and whose strategic location—sitting between Europe, Africa, and Asia and serving as a unique hub for global trade—is critical for Washington's projection of US power and influence on the world stage. Third, support the US economy through mega weapons sales to the kingdom. Fourth, enable the Saudi military to secure its own borders, counter transnational terrorism, and deter Iranian conventional aggression. This fourth goal became more urgent and important only a few years ago.

## Train and Equip

Until Yemen, there wasn't a whole lot of serious joint training between the American and Saudi militaries, be it on Saudi soil or in the United

States. The terrorist attacks of September 11, 2001, strained relations between Washington and Riyadh a great deal, drastically limiting military cooperation.

Two years after 9/11, the United States withdrew most of its troops from the kingdom. Although Riyadh wanted the Americans out due to political sensitivities to the US presence, its worst fears about their departure would soon materialize. Right as the United States was invading Iraq in 2003, al-Qaeda leader Osama bin Laden ordered from his hideout in Afghanistan the launch of a deadly homegrown insurgency against the House of Saud. It would take the Saudi security services many months to end the armed, widespread, and well-organized insurrection.

Critical to Riyadh's counterterrorism achievement was US training and equipment. In his memoirs, former CIA director George Tenet recalled how the CIA under his leadership provided "unprecedented assistance" to the Saudis from the spring through the summer of 2003, tipping them with precious intelligence about the most dangerous plots al-Qaeda was planning inside the kingdom, including attacks with chemical weapons.[4] In addition, US special forces provided operational and tactical support to the Saudi counterterrorism services, training them on how to more effectively fight in urban and densely populated environments.[5]

Sixteen years later, the US military would return to Saudi Arabia, and specifically to Prince Sultan Air Base, to help address what was perceived to be a growing Iranian threat to the region. CENTCOM would not have the same tools it once had during and after Desert Storm, but Washington still would provide it with significant assets to pursue its new mission, including two fighter squadrons, one air expeditionary wing, two Patriot missile defense batteries, one Terminal High Altitude Area Defense (THAAD) system, and more than 3,000 personnel.[6]

Since 2019, CENTCOM has taken steps to help the Saudi military try to integrate its air and missile defense architecture, build its maritime interdiction capabilities, and combat the persistent terrorist threat posed by al-Qaeda and the Islamic State. With the Saudis launching their campaign in Yemen in 2015, naturally all US military assistance gravitated toward that war effort. The US Army's elite units provided intelligence, training, coordination, and logistical support to the Saudis. How much of that is ongoing is unclear, though US refueling of Saudi aircraft did halt in November 2018 following the Saudi authorities' murder of US-based Saudi journalist Jamal Khashoggi in Turkey.[7]

In 2016, "between 50 and 60 U.S. military personnel provided coordination and support to the Saudi-led coalition. . . . And six to ten Americans worked directly inside the Saudi air operations center in Riyadh."[8]

Through a multiyear program worth $750 million, US military lawyers also have trained their Saudi counterparts on how to reduce collateral damage and ensure that the Saudi air strikes are in accordance with international law.[9]

The United States has provided all this assistance to the Saudis through three organizations that have been based in the kingdom for several decades: USMTM, OPM-SANG, and MOI-MAG. Operational since the early 1950s, USMTM works closely with the Saudi general armed forces, taking advantage of both the Pentagon's Title 10 and the State Department's Title 22 authorities.

OPM-SANG has been advising the SANG since a memorandum of understanding was signed in 1973 by US Ambassador to Saudi Arabia Nicholas Thacher and SANG Commander Prince Abdullah Ibn Abdul Aziz stipulating that the United States would train, equip, and develop the military, logistics, administrative, and management capabilities of four battalions of mechanized infantry and one battalion of light artillery within the SANG.[10] As for MOI-MAG, created as a result of a 2008 agreement between US Secretary of State Condoleezza Rice and Saudi Minister of Interior Nayef bin Abdulaziz Al Saud, it advises and trains the kingdom's internal security and counterterrorism forces.[11]

USMTM, OPM-SANG, and MOI-MAG advisers are in Saudi Arabia not to fulfill operational duties, serve on Saudi staffs, or integrate into the Saudi armed forces' daily operations, but rather to strictly offer advice. Even at the brigade level, the Saudis have made it a point of emphasis that they are the ones who drive the process of cooperation, not the other way around.[12]

Although US military assistance to Saudi Arabia has always centered on equipment transfers more than anything else, it would be a mistake to dismiss the tactical/operational training that has taken place between the two sides over the years. For example, since 2008, the US Army has helped train the Saudis' security forces on countering terrorism and protecting critical infrastructure by providing "security assistance training to include marksmanship, patrolling perimeters, setting up security checkpoints, vehicle searches at entry control point, rules of engagement toward possible threats and personnel screening."[13] US Army personnel also have provided their Saudi counterparts with training courses on flight, firing range, and military police,[14] although some of the more operational training activities have been suspended since December 2019 due to a shooting by a Saudi military student at a US Navy base in Florida.[15]

For many years, the Royal Saudi Land Forces (RSLF) have conducted various drills with US soldiers to improve both readiness and interoperability levels, help develop Saudi command and control processes during operations, and unify joint military concepts. One of those joint US-Saudi exercises is Falcon Claws, which is now in its fourth iteration.

At sea, Saudi and American sailors have participated in Nautical Defender, a bilateral and sometimes multilateral maritime exercise meant primarily to build and sustain the war-fighting capabilities of the Royal Saudi Naval Forces (RSNF) and enhance military interoperability with the US Navy. The latest version of Nautical Defender, held in January 2021 with the participation of the British, was the largest exercise to date.[16] It trained on multiple simulated scenarios, coastal harbor defense, counter-unmanned aerial systems, shipboard gunnery, high value unit escort, small arms, and diving and mine clearance skills.

In April–May 2020, the RSNF and the US Navy conducted joint, two-phased sustainment training as part of Sentinel Shield. The design of the exercises, geared more toward the Americans than the Saudis, was meant to help develop capabilities to "rapidly deploy aviation, maritime, and ground combat elements—all from over the horizon—at a moment's notice."[17]

In the air, the Royal Saudi Air Force (RSAF) and the US Air Force engage in bilateral drills with various mission sets on a fairly regular basis. For example, the Saudis are regular participants in the famous US Red Flag exercise in Nevada. In March 2019, they unveiled their new F-15SA Advanced Eagle fighter jets and carried out more than 800 sorties during the two-week, advanced training.[18]

In May 2021, two US Air Force F-16 Fighting Falcons along with two US Marine Corps F/A-18D Hornets conducted the third iteration of a joint drill with Saudi F-15 Strike Eagles called Desert Mirage. The training was designed to enhance the interoperability and air defense capabilities of the two sides.[19] A few months before that, Saudi and American pilots held a joint exercise called Dragon that sought to improve tactical interception training, combat training, counterattack, and suppression of enemy air defenses.[20]

In December 2020, the RSAF, the RSNF, NAVCENT, and US Air Forces Central (AFCENT) conducted combined joint air operations in support of a maritime surface warfare exercise in the Persian Gulf. The exercise marked the fifth joint and combined aviation integration operation that year. Importantly, it included joint terminal attack controllers (JTACs) "directing a wide variety of platforms to conduct simulated fires against surface threats attempting to attack coalition forces."[21]

In September of that year, the American 378th Air Expeditionary Wing and RSAF participated in a joint training exercise called Desert

Eagle at Prince Sultan Air Base that focused on force integration and a joint emergency response to a simulated aircraft mishap on the flight line.[22] The Americans performed a hot pit refuel of Saudi F-15E Strike Eagles, following a large formation flight.[23]

## Institutional Capacity Building

Until a couple of years ago, the Saudi defense establishment, in both its civilian and military aspects, was not a source of pride for the kingdom's leadership. Not only was it costing the Saudis hundreds of millions of dollars every fiscal year, but it also was making them less safe. For a nation that consistently has been one of the world's largest military spenders, this outcome was as embarrassing as it was troubling.

Saudi Arabia had no ability to formulate a coherent national defense strategy or national military strategy. Strategic vision existed in the minds of one or two Saudi royals close to the king, and there were no clear and dependable procedures to effectively communicate strategic and policy guidance to the armed forces.

To the extent that it was preached, the Saudis did not engage in systematic defense analysis or rely on strategic planning processes. This meant that there was no method to prioritize, be it missions or capabilities, and no plan to achieve jointness and make full use of the various branches of Saudi armed forces. The Saudis had no clue how to properly identify their military requirements—which often meant that they bought expensive equipment they did not need or know how to operate—and were unable to monitor, assess, evaluate, and improve the readiness levels of their armed forces.

Military acquisition was a sham in Riyadh. To procure equipment, the Saudi armed services used to assess on their own what they believed they needed to accomplish their goals and go straight to either the defense minister himself or the ministry of finance to make their requests. There was no centralized control over or public transparency in this process, which inevitably introduced plenty of inefficiency and corruption, the ultimate Achilles' heel of the Saudi defense system.

The Saudis had no joint staff or doctrine, which meant that national defense missions were executed through the individual armed services. Both on the civilian and military side, they did not have enough skilled people to effectively run the Ministry of Defense (MoD) and operate and absorb the vast amount of sophisticated defense systems they periodically purchased from foreign powers, including the United States.

The MoD had no ability to systematically identify, train, deploy, and retain a technically capable force. There were no rules or credible organizational mechanisms to allow Saudi civilian and military personnel to more effectively communicate, analyze, plan, and operate together. Adherence to sound principles and practices of defense budgeting and programming was inconsistent at best. Finally, HRM policies, functions, and strategies—an HRM "system"—that allow for the recruitment, training, promotion, assignment, and retirement of personnel either did not exist or were seldom applied.

What is dispiriting is that many of these problems still exist to this day. What is encouraging, though, is that the Saudi leadership, under the command of MBS, recognizes those deficiencies and seems for the first time ever determined to address them in close partnership with the United States. Washington's military assistance program in Saudi Arabia, while still emphasizing arms sales, began to take on a more holistic approach in late 2017 when the Saudis communicated to US officials their desire to invest in defense governance and pursue defense transformation. To better organize and coordinate military assistance, the United States brought USMTM, OPM-SANG, and MOI-MAG together under the concept and unified authority of the senior defense official/defense attaché (SDO/DATT).[24]

Prior to the formulation of MBS's defense transformation plan, the United States was involved in very modest efforts to assist the Saudis in developing some measure of defense institutional capacity. Most of these activities, tactical in nature, were paid for by Riyadh through the FMS process and were primarily designed to help the Saudis better employ the arms they purchased from Washington.

Things started to transition in the fall of 2016 when most US-enabled defense institution building initiatives in the kingdom were placed under US funding. The goal then was to aid a group of Saudi colonels, working under the leadership of the brilliant Saudi assistant minister of defense Gen. Mohammed bin Abdullah Al Ayesh (who died from an illness in August 2020), to conduct basic capability development planning.

Ayesh's highly capable team possessed the specialized knowledge to perform such functions, but they lacked a formal tool set, which the American advisers were eager to provide. Initially, the United States had little to no visibility into the defense transformation plan because of Saudi infighting and/or disorganization. Indeed, not all senior Saudi military personnel endorsed the plan when it first came out. Ayesh for one was not the biggest fan, at least in the beginning, because he thought it did not do enough to promote jointness in the Saudi armed forces.

In January 2018, a meeting between then-DSCA director Lt. Gen. Charles Hooper and Samir Al Tabib—the head of the Saudi transformation management office—broke loose US access. Since then, it has been a full-blown US defense institution building program in Saudi Arabia, with American advisers conducting eight trips a year (though interrupted during the global Covid-19 pandemic) all funded under the Pentagon's Title 10 authorities.

Like most things MBS does, the US-inspired defense transformation plan is incredibly large and ambitious, consisting of 308 initiatives. The new MoD is divided into two parts, one civilian-led and tasked with fulfilling the duties of directing, enabling, and acquiring, and one military-led and responsible for generating and operating the force.

Tabib's assistant for executive affairs, Khalid bin Hussein Bayari, runs three separate offices, each with distinct functions (they somewhat resemble the Pentagon's various offices of the under secretaries of defense):

- one for strategic affairs (the "direct" part) that seeks to develop policies and strategies, planning procedures, intelligence systems, strategic communications, and legal affairs mechanisms;
- one for "centers of excellence" (the "enable" part) that runs issues related to information technology, finance, human resources, facilities and engineering, health services, and administrative support; and
- one for armament and procurement (the "acquire" part) that handles all aspects of acquisition (including programs, policy, planning, and budgeting), local industry development, projects, spare parts and maintenance, repair and overhaul, supplies and services, and research and development (R&D) and technology.

US advice has targeted four key areas in Saudi Arabia's defense transformation plan: (1) human capital development, (2) joint staff, (3) acquisition, and (4) force sustainment.

## Human Capital Development

No challenge to the defense transformation plan, and MBS's broader reforms in the kingdom, is more significant than human capital development. The Saudis struggle immensely in finding properly educated and sufficiently skilled individuals to join the armed forces and the new MoD; in training, developing, promoting, and retiring their military personnel; and in running their military schools.

Saudi Arabia has made a lot of progress in its civilian educational system over the past decade. Today, the adult literacy rate is approximately 95 percent, compared to 71 percent in 1992. The youth literacy rate is 99 percent.[25] The country has seen a dramatic increase in government spending on education (on par with that in high-income countries) and in university enrollment, but it still lags behind on key metrics, including academic performance (lower scores on international tests of science, math, and reading) and returns to education. One of the root causes of these educational challenges is the fact that there is no independent knowledge sphere in Saudi Arabia. Nor is there an inclusive environment that allows and encourages Saudi nationals to assemble freely, think critically, self-evaluate, and be creative and entrepreneurial.

Consistent with Prussian theory, stipulating that the military can be "the school of the nation,"[26] the Saudi army theoretically can be the vanguard of transformation in education, as the Emirati military is trying to be, but it cannot be the *only* agent that is transforming. Saudi society as a whole has to change too. It is not just the means at the disposal of the average Saudi citizen that are lacking when it comes to both civilian and military education, it is also the usually problematic mindset and approach, which are attached to societal culture. "Most militaries, and especially modernizing militaries like the Saudis, tend to think of professional military education like a polio shot," said David Des Roches. "They understand they need it, but once they get it from the best provider in the world they are set for life and never revisit it again."[27]

With regard to recruitment, Riyadh has always relied on volunteers to form a national army because there is no policy of national conscription. MBS might institute compulsory military service like MBZ recently did in the UAE, but a changed policy on conscription might bring with it a set of expectations by Saudi military personnel that reflect those of the average Saudi citizen: expectations of rights and empowerment, to which the royal family has always been sensitive. None of this means that Saudi Arabia cannot build a competent army without mandatory military service—many nations around the world do not have it and some like Jordan and Lebanon have dropped it—but the fact that the kingdom has not had conscription since its very inception in the 1930s suggests that its military development process will take even longer to mature.

Given that unemployment in Saudi Arabia is a serious problem—in 2020 it stood at an all-time high of 15.4 percent—one would think that military recruitment would not be very challenging.[28] After all, Saudis hailing from poor and underdeveloped regions are desperate for jobs, and the military is one important avenue for economic security. But the reality is that the Saudi government historically has neglected Jizan, Najran, and other parts of the southern region. These areas predominantly are inhabited by Saudi Shiites, who have a culture that is closer to that of Zaydi Yemenis and thus does not have much in common with the official Saudi culture that is based in Najd.[29] Saudi Ismailis have felt socioeconomically marginalized by Riyadh for decades. That they have little incentive to fight Yemenis and make the ultimate sacrifice for the House of Saud is not very surprising.

For the more ambitious or aspiring Saudis, military service generally is not viewed as a rewarding career. With the exception of the RSAF, social prestige and better economic opportunity are typically found in the oil business or private sector, not in the military. All of this, of course, MBS is trying to change.

Because recruitment has been such a chore, the Saudis have not been able to create a competent personnel corps. Many officers are promoted not because they are talented and deserving but because they are connected to someone in the large ruling family. Saudi Arabia's political leaders and military commanders, like all their Arab counterparts, emphasize and reward seniority, conformity, and personal loyalty much more than performance.[30]

The Saudi NCO corps has insufficient authority and even less leadership development. It is "largely untested and their enlisted men are drawn from the lowest rungs of Saudi society."[31] Many Saudi officers have as much skill, experience, knowledge, and depth of training as regular Saudi soldiers, which is never good. The British, who aided the Saudis' military development process in the 1930s and 1940s, knew all along that the officer corps was the biggest weakness of the Saudi defense establishment. Not only were there not enough officers, but those serving were "old, uninterested, untrained, and illiterate."[32]

As the Saudi educational system improved over the years, with more Saudis gaining their primary and secondary education, so did the quality of the Saudi officer corps. Military schools were created, and many Saudis were sent to Egypt for training purposes, which helped on some level. And as the Americans got more and more militarily involved in the kingdom starting in the early 1950s (often in competition with Cairo), Saudi military training and organization received an important boost. Yet, the challenges of incentivizing Saudi citizens and empowering Saudi officers remained all those years.

Saudi Arabia currently has five military academies all heavily influenced by the British experience: the King Abdulaziz Military Academy (Army), the King Faisal Air Academy (Air Force), the King Fahd Naval Academy (Navy), the King Abdullah Air Defense Academy (Air Defense), and SANG's own King Khalid Military Academy. The

King Fahd Naval Academy is almost a copy of its British counterpart, and many of the flight instructors at the King Faisal Air Academy are British nationals.

The Saudis also have a War College, an Armed Forces Command and Staff College, and a very recent, but probably not yet fully constructed, SANG Command and General Staff College—all three established with the help of the United States. The SANG Command and General Staff College is established very much like the US Army Command and Staff College at Fort Leavenworth.

Finally, the Saudis are in the process of building a National Defense College with the help of the Americans, though very little is currently known about its policies, programs, and procedures. With the exception of the Air Academy, which according to US Air Force advisers has produced competent Saudi air force officers, all these military entities require significant reform.[33] Although these academies are supposed to be educational institutions, it is not clear that they actually educate or produce Saudi leaders as they claim to do. Two tactical challenges of Saudi Arabia's military schools can be summed up as follows: there is neither an academic standard nor an objective evaluation of the performance of the Saudi students. The system does not punish underachievers—indeed, no Saudi royal ever fails—nor does it reward the high-level performers.

Because Saudi military schools are not accredited, Saudi officers often are unable to find employment after graduation. Granted, not everybody in the military needs a four-year college degree. The United States, for example, is in the minority even among postindustrialized nations in insisting on the prerequisite of a college degree to become a junior officer. Even Sandhurst, the prestigious British military academy, has canceled its undergraduate education entirely as it no longer combines academics with military training. Instead, it now offers courses only to students who have enrolled elsewhere.

That said, the complexity of military operations and weapons systems in the twenty-first century requires, among other things, specialized knowledge and systematized training, which can be achieved (though not exclusively) through an organized academic program. The academy route can be rewarding, but it should not be obligatory as there are many other ways to acquire the necessary professional development and education to become an officer.

Alongside its military academies, the United States, for example, has a federal program called the Reserve Officers' Training Corps (ROTC) that also produces officers—probably twice as many as those who attend the academies and at a fraction of the cost. There are not many alternative professional and intellectual development tools in Saudi Arabia, and even if the Saudis manage to create more technical and vocational training programs, on their own they will not address the broader challenge of the country's civilian education system.

The promising reality is that there is an acceptable amount of good young military officers in the kingdom. The problem is that they are not given many opportunities to thrive. As dozens of American advisers who have worked with Saudi military personnel attest, some are extremely knowledgeable about various subjects and have experiences that are more versatile than those of many NATO officers.[34] But these same American advisers also found that when it came to military issues, somehow the Saudi officers performed less well and lost much of their competence and zeal. "It's as if there's a psychological firewall or something. It's like you are dealing with two very different individuals," lamented one US senior officer who just finished his service in Riyadh.[35]

Retirement is another snag in the Saudi military system. The Saudis do not have what the Pentagon calls an "up-or-out" policy—that is, a policy that requires officers to achieve a certain rank within a certain period of time if they wish to stay in the force (although US military leadership is currently considering substituting "up-or-out" with "perform-or-out" to emphasize talent and skills rather than upward mobility).[36] Saudi officers are not required to be promoted within a certain period of time and are hardly ever asked to leave the service if they fail to get promoted. It's also difficult to groom the next Saudi military leaders if the path to generalship is riddled with tribal and political obstacles.[37]

Saudi senior officers retire very late and often block the promotion of younger, better educated, and more capable peers.[38] Anybody who hangs around long enough in the Saudi military becomes brigadier general, complained one young Saudi officer.[39] Because of that, the Saudis have ended up with a column in their personnel system instead of a pyramid. And inside that column, they have failed to build a virtual triangle that allows them to find the leadership that they need at the level where they need it (squadron commanders, group commanders, wing commanders, etc.) because they do not have the HRM policies to do that. "The Saudis want to turn their Land Forces academy into West Point," said one American military adviser supporting the effort to reform the Saudi academies, "but what's the point of constructing state-of-the-art facilities and formulating the best curricula if there's no merit-based system and attendance records are poor?"[40]

Of all the Arab partners, the Saudis probably benefit the least from American professional military education because, in the words of one US National Defense University senior staffer with administrative responsibilities for the Saudi program, "they don't know how to leverage their participation in IMET, unlike the Jordanians, for example."[41] The problem is not registration numbers. For example, in 2019, it was reported that the Saudis had 852 trainees in the United States, which is roughly 16.5 percent of the total of foreign students.[42] Rather, it's about attitude and diligence.

None of the above means that the Saudis are bad at developing, educating, training, and managing their military *across the board*. As is often the case, some agencies and units do it better than others, and in Saudi Arabia, the SANG, given the generous attention and resources it receives from top Saudi leadership, has been a bit more competent at recruiting and training Saudis from certain (but not all) regions of the kingdom.

Through OPM-SANG, the SANG has received a vast amount of US assistance in force development and benefited from the US Army's comprehensive advisory services over the years. The SANG has a military academy of its own in Riyadh and according to an older study by Saudi Col. Bandar Al Harbi, it graduates more than 500 officers (the numbers might be different and ideally higher today).[43] Qualifications for the academy require a high school diploma, and students spend three years of study before they graduate as second lieutenants.[44]

The SANG has three training centers for its three commands in Riyadh, the Western Region, and the Eastern Province, each able to accommodate as many as 4,000 people at once. Recruits go through a period of at least half a year of training before they join their units. Before Desert Storm, the SANG had a strength of about 35,000 active duty personnel and about the same number of irregulars. Active duty personnel were organized into two mechanized brigades and four light infantry brigades, supporting units, and schools. Since then, SANG has embarked on an ambitious force expansion initiative that will eventually create a nearly 100,000-man modernized force.[45]

The school system can accommodate more than 2,000 soldiers and officers training in multiple courses of different lengths at the same time. Examples of such courses include primary and basic NCO, intelligence, infantry, combined arms, personnel administration, equipment readiness, and medical specialist.[46] The SANG's schools have courses in English, and after reaching basic writing and speaking standards, Saudi officers are sent to the United States for advanced study. Upon graduation, they attend basic and advanced officer courses in the US Army officer school system.[47] To supplement the development functions of its academy, the SANG also creates opportunities for Saudi university graduates with more technical and scientific degrees by offering them military training and graduating them as officers.[48]

These improvements and processes notwithstanding, the Saudi rulers still insist on controlling recruitment when it comes to the SANG as they continue to emphasize regions and tribes that are traditionally more loyal to the House of Saud. This, naturally, has shrunk the pool of recruits and oftentimes led to the hiring of unskilled and uneducated personnel.

In 2016, US Maj. Gen. Frank Muth, former head of OPM-SANG in Saudi Arabia, sought to establish officer and NCO academies for the SANG in an attempt to create a stronger cadre of SANG leaders. "We're going to pull staff sergeants and sergeant first classes out of the [light-armored vehicle (LAV)] formations, put them through an intensive six-week training cycle, and we're focusing on some basic stuff," said Muth. He added, "I'm talking patrolling, weapons fire, communication, land navigation, physical training . . . and just basic skill sets."[49] It's unclear, however, if any of this has produced positive outcomes.

Perhaps the most exciting aspect about the human personnel reforms in the Saudi defense transformation plan is the leadership's commitment to recruiting Saudi females. One of Vision 2030's key goals in fact is to enable women to increase their participation in the Saudi workforce and the wider Saudi economy. Saudi women now can be considered for more senior ranks in the military such as lance corporals, corporals, sergeants, and staff sergeants.[50] Another bright spot in the transformation process is the Saudi youth's views toward MBS's reforms. Young Saudis, who make up the majority of the population, are the strongest believers in MBS because his Vision 2030 promises to aggressively tackle the unemployment challenge, which has hit them the hardest.[51] Yet neither youth nor female participation is sufficient to overcome the broader societal challenge of passive resistance. Saudi public servants can wholeheartedly support change and always say yes to MBS's reforms, but if they keep showing up to work late and leaving early, and taking multiple breaks during the day, it will not make much of a difference.

Although it is absurd to claim that all Saudis have a poor work ethic, it is not inaccurate to say that too many in the public sector and the military exhibit little drive and persistence. "The Saudi officers I worked with typically showed up to work at eleven in the morning and left at two in the afternoon, and sometimes they did not come at all," affirmed a US military adviser who had a tour in Saudi Arabia a few years ago.[52] Studies have shown that most Saudi government bureaucrats show little commitment to hard work, are not ambitious, and care more about allowances.[53]

With greater incentives, better education, and more training opportunities for Saudis, these norms can gradually change, but this has to start at an early age. Saudis have not been taught at the elementary and high school levels the importance of work ethic. This is unfortunate because this was not always the case. Not too long ago, Saudis, both young and old, worked industriously. They used to gladly perform a wide spectrum of jobs, from taking out the garbage and fixing the sewage system to maintaining schools, working at construction sites, and designing buildings.[54] Since the oil and economic boom of the 1970s and 1980s, however, it has been mostly foreign workers who engage in these activities, not only more effectively but for lower pay (about 90 percent of all private sector jobs in the kingdom belong to imported workers).

MBS has pushed for the "Saudization" of jobs, but for this initiative to work the overall Saudi attitude toward work needs to return to what it once was, and new Saudi entrants to the labor market have to be at least as skilled and productive as the foreign workers. This is an enormous challenge, and MBS is aware of it.[55]

Because the military is a microcosm of society, it is not unusual to see these issues play out among officers and soldiers too. All the generals nominally have embraced the defense transformation plan, but very few are actively pushing for change partly for fear of losing their traditional privileges, and even fewer are empowering younger officers who are eager to assume leadership positions. As a result, MBS does not have many enthusiastic or committed "transformation partners" in the armed forces, which is why he has had to rely on American, British, and other foreign nationals to help him execute several parts of the transformation plan.

The Saudis need their own version of the US Army Training and Doctrine Command (TRADOC), which upon its creation in 1973 fundamentally transformed the army. "It would have been nice to have a Saudi Gen. Depuy around here to push for and supervise change," said a senior American adviser involved in the Saudi transformation plan.[56] The general he was referring to is William E. Depuy who commanded a battalion of 90th Infantry Division in World War II and led the 1st Infantry Division in Vietnam. It was under his leadership that TRADOC was formed.[57]

With this many societal and cultural challenges, knowing where to start and what to fix first was very daunting for the Saudis and their American advisers. But MBS ultimately decided that a bold approach that totally breaks with the past and seeks to radically shake things up was the way to go. Relying on international best practices in defense management, American and foreign advisers have allowed the Saudis to come up with an entirely new HRM system for both civilian and military personnel that is technically based on qualifications and merit. That's the good news. The bad news is that little of it is applicable in the Saudi context.

The experts essentially recommended to the Saudis they build an MoD that is roughly the size of the Pentagon. Yet it is obvious that Saudi Arabia has nowhere near the amount of human resources that are necessary to competently staff such an incredibly large bureaucracy. To put it simply, Saudi Arabia has no defense professionals. They have to be "created" from scratch.

Saudi managers supervising the transformation process are currently recruiting private sector Saudi personnel with business degrees and entrusting them with defense duties. Because they have no national security backgrounds, however, these new employees oftentimes apply principles from the business world to critical national security questions. They look at radars used by the Saudi military, for example, and suggest holding off on repairs or enhancements until "tomorrow's better model comes out," which of course is an ill-advised approach that has detrimental effects on *current* operational needs.

One big challenge of the MoD's new human resources office is filling in those hundreds of positions while at the same time running this newly designed HRM system. That the new civilian recruits are responsible for human resources policies for both the civilians and the military despite the fact that they know very little about military personnel systems is a hindrance. More experience and better communication with the armed services will surely help, but it will take a long time to mature.

Some of the new HRM policies require the approval of other ministries including the Ministry of Interior and Ministry of Human Resources and Social Development, which can be very slow. With time and money—indeed a very long time and a ton of money—the hope is that such a large Saudi workforce can be created (assuming more people are going to want to work in the MoD and not in the oil sector), but the question is to what end and at what price? The focus here ought to be effectiveness and efficiency, not size or prestige. The Saudis are certainly better off building an HRM system that is tailored for them and takes into account their local capacities.

It is a similar human capital challenge in the armed forces. Despite their relatively low drive and mediocre competence levels, most Saudi service chiefs are still allowed to command troops. This might not change anytime soon because the bench of military leaders in the kingdom is not deep at all. There are many bright officers, as mentioned before, but they tend to be young and, again, insufficiently encouraged and empowered.

### Joint Staff

To help the Saudis build a truly joint staff, the United States proposed setting up two offices in the new Saudi MoD, one led by the chief of general staff of the Saudi armed forces (currently Gen. Fayyad Al Ruwaili) and another by the commander of the joint forces command (Lt. Gen. Mutlaq Al Azima, the deputy of Ruwaili, is currently serving in an acting capacity). The chief of the general staff will oversee all branches of the Saudi military, minus the SANG. This includes the RSLF, the RSNF, the likely-to-be-combined RSAF and Royal Saudi Air Defense Force (RSADF), and the Royal Saudi Strategic Missile Force (RSSMF). He also will serve as the director of a national defense university (which has yet to be created) and have a joint staff. The commander of the Saudi Joint Forces Command will have a joint force staff of his own as well as an operations center and theater joint forces commanders assigned to him, depending on the military missions.

One US source advising on the joint staff effort described it as the microcosm or cornerstone of all the other transformation plan's pillars.[58] This Saudi Joint Forces Command is modeled after the British Permanent Joint Headquarters in Northwood, which commands joint and multinational military operations and provides policy and military advice to the British Ministry of Defense in London.

### Acquisition

The Saudi acquisition process currently looks nothing like it once did. The biggest and most visible improvement is that there actually is a process. A fatal flaw in the past was to allow the Saudi service chiefs to pick the weapons they wanted. The outcome was disastrous for force posture planning but also not surprising: the navy chief always wanted a warship, the army chief a tank, and the air force chief a fighter jet. Nobody thought about how their own force could integrate with the others. So when the Saudis rolled into Yemen, they realized that most of their equipment was not a good fit, and most of the ground units could not communicate with the air assets.

Gone are the days when the Saudi armed services ran the show and, ultimately, ran the whole procurement operation to the ground. At least on paper, everything now runs through the MoD's Office of Armament and Procurement, which is led by Deputy Minister of Defense Ibrahim Al Suwayed and seeks in theory to identify capability gaps in accordance with the US formula of DOTMLPF-P.

Of course, it's not all perfect. Some old Saudi habits linger and some weapons purchases are made to satisfy *political* rather than military priorities. Take the recent Saudi acquisition of the US THAAD missile defense system, for example. No doubt the Saudis could use it to protect against a host of long-range Iranian missiles, but it is probably overkill.

Instead of acquiring THAAD, the Saudis would have been better off making the most out of their already formidable US-purchased missile defense infrastructure by integrating it with their own air assets and those of their Arab neighbors. They have yet to do that because they probably do not see that task as a priority and they still do not fully trust Qatar, which hosts powerful US missile defenses and radars too.

With a price tag of $15 billion and probably more, THAAD is not the wisest military investment for Saudi Arabia, which needs every penny to transform its economy, attract foreign direct investment, and reform its bureaucracy. Riyadh simply cannot afford to keep buying expensive US weaponry that it does not necessarily need and that will cost a lot to sustain.[59]

The US-inspired defense acquisition reforms also led to the creation of two new entities, the General Authority for Military Industries (GAMI) and the Saudi Arabian Military Industries (SAMI). GAMI seeks to "regulate, enable, and license" the Saudi defense industry. It essentially exercises a policy oversight role over any weapons procurement above $100 million and encourages weapons standardization to facilitate sustainment.[60] SAMI is a national holding company for domestic military manufacturing. Although Western defense firms used to be the primary suppliers to the Saudi armed services, SAMI now hopes to make a modest contribution by delivering smaller and unsophisticated equipment, often via partnerships or joint ventures with other international companies.[61]

GAMI and SAMI, both Saudi government–owned, are responsible for developing a domestic defense industrial base that is able to localize half of the kingdom's military spending by 2030 according to Vision 2030 (though the roles and responsibilities of the new acquisition office in the MoD and those of GAMI and SAMI need to be further clarified in order to avoid redundancies and turf battles). No doubt, it is an aggressive and probably unrealistic target, but "even if they reach 10 percent," argued one American adviser presently involved in the Saudi acquisition reform process, "it would be a huge win for the Saudis."[62]

## Force Sustainment

The United States has pursued a number of initiatives with Saudi Arabia to help it tackle the issue of sustainment, which is the most enduring and profound weakness of its armed forces and defense establishment. Indeed, what the Saudis need perhaps more than anything else is a force sustainment system that supports their war plan(s) to defend the kingdom from Iranian conventional aggression and Islamic insurgency at home (assuming such operational plans actually exist).

Given how the issue of sustainment touches almost all elements of national defense, US advice has been both wide and deep, starting with the basic or foundational issue of strategic planning. The result of that effort is an internally published Saudi national defense strategy, a first in the history of the kingdom. Riyadh also has started to develop an ability to monitor, assess, and evaluate readiness and is on the path to coming up with joint capability development plans—other feats it had never accomplished before.

Recognizing that joint capability development plans can only get the Saudis to a "program" and a budget (which then allows them to buy weapons), American advisers are helping the Saudis with ideas on how to convert the defense budget into combat power through the installment of a force sustainment system. Such a system ideally would have four critical elements: (1) a force presentation process (how forces are presented to the joint forces commander); (2) a force readiness process (how to meet the demands of assigned missions mainly through maintenance and training); (3) a force generation process (how to provide suitably trained and equipped forces, including their means of sustainment, deployment, and recovery); and (4) a force management process (how to determine requirements, allocate resources, and assess employment of the resources).

That the Saudis ended up with the majority of their national force fighting in Yemen is precisely why they need a force sustainment system. For example, they could not effectively rotate their troops. Several units were stuck in Yemen for more than four years mainly because the Saudi military does not have force rotation policies. It is no wonder those troops were exhausted and ultimately less capable in combat operations.

If the Saudis can find a way to combine joint force utilization (which essentially means how their Joint Forces commander employs his troops) with joint force management (which is how their chief of General Staff manages the force that the Joint Forces commander needs at any given moment) and then add a force sustainment process, then they would have something that resembles and does the absolutely vital work of the Pentagon's Joint Strategic Planning System (JSPS). The JSPS is the formal method through which the US chairman of the Joint Chiefs of Staff conducts strategic planning and offers military advice and direction on a range of issues to the president, the secretary of defense, and the National Security Council (NSC). Without something that performs the functions of this system, it does not matter what the Saudis fix on the front end if the back end is not working.

There are two reasons why a so-called "Saudi JSPS" would be far simpler than the American one (beyond the obvious fact of the United States being a global power with global interests and Saudi Arabia being a regional power with fewer national security worries and aspirations). First, the Saudis, unlike the Americans, do not build (significant) weapons systems or conduct (large-scale) R&D. This makes acquisition a lot more straightforward. They are simply purchasing, not developing. In the Saudi case, joint capability development and acquisition can be done *jointly from the beginning* through the joint capability planning (JCP) process with the (yet-to-be-formed) Saudi joint staff in the lead. Saudi acquisition planning within JCP also would use a different approach given that, unlike their American counterparts, the Saudi services do not get to make acquisition decisions (at least not anymore). This would terminate the need for the laborious and lopsided US Joint Capabilities Integration and Development System (JCIDS), which defines acquisition requirements *after* the services have their say, and the US Joint Requirements Oversight Council, which reviews and validates the work of the JCIDS.

Through their simplified system, the Saudis have an opportunity to avoid the Americans' great flaw of conducting service-centric capability planning and to instead do it all in accordance with the defined mission. The end result is an operational planning and execution system that can limit its focus to joint force generation, joint force management, and joint force employment. This type of emphasis is tailored to defending the Saudi homeland rather than, as the United States does, projecting power globally.

Second, the center of the new Saudi joint staff structure, now run by the chief of the General Staff, is technically strong, unlike in the American case. All the service chiefs in Saudi Arabia, minus the SANG (for now), currently answer to the chief of the General Staff, who in principle has more power and authority than his US equivalent, the chairman of the Joint Chiefs of Staff. (Despite the latter's direct line to the US president, the chairman has little actual budget or statutory control.)

This new centralized system shaves many layers and reduces the complexity of the American JSPS. Once again, none of these force sustainment elements are relevant if the Saudis do not have a coherent war plan for protecting the kingdom from the threat posed by Iran. Joint force presentation should be keyed to such a plan. So should force generation and force readiness. Otherwise, what are the Saudis generating and preparing for?

If the Saudis do have a war plan, the responsibility of Washington would be to better understand what steady-state activities Riyadh is pursuing to defend the kingdom and how many of those Saudi assets American commanders can rely on to help with the execution of the operational plan.

## Outcomes

US arms sales to Saudi Arabia have allowed Washington to (1) wield significant political influence in Riyadh, (2) acquire critical military access in an oil-rich country that sits between three continents and is the home of two of Islam's holy sanctuaries, and (3) generate trillions of dollars of revenue to the US economy. Those are *not* small US returns.

But if one were to evaluate that assistance on the basis of creating Saudi military capability, then it is hard not to see it as one giant failure. The amount of money spent by both sides on trying, though never seriously until recent years, to enhance the capabilities of the Saudi armed forces is precisely what makes it all seem so inadequate. It hasn't *all* been bad, of course. The Saudis have improved some, but certainly not all, of their air force and missile defense capabilities over the past few years as their intervention in Yemen shows. Let's very briefly recall what happened during that conflict.

In the beginning, Saudi Arabia and its allies quickly dominated Yemen's skies by effectively grounding fighter planes and neutralizing air defense batteries the Houthis had seized from the Yemeni military in previous years. Saudi pilots proceeded to methodically destroy various military installations, weapons depots, and ballistic missile forces belonging to the Houthis in the first few days of the aerial campaign. "By any objective standard," said one US military adviser based in Riyadh, "it was an impressive and pleasantly surprising accomplishment."[63]

It's true that the Yemeni air force was minuscule and the country's air defense assets—SA-2 Guideline and SA-3 Goa surface-to-air missile batteries—were dated and no match to the state-of-the-art aerial capabilities deployed by the Saudis. However, if you were to ask anybody in the US military if the Saudis could have achieved those same feats in Desert Storm, their answer would be no.

The Saudis also surprised many with their ability to sustain a high volume of air strikes. Over a period of twenty-nine days or so, the RSAF executed over 2,400 strike sorties, averaging 100 per day and releasing at least 1,000 air-to-surface weapons.[64] Saudi pilots were able to maintain operational tempo for another year.[65] But once that initial list of stationary targets was more or less exhausted, things started to unravel for the Saudis. Aerial targeting became incredibly more difficult either because the Saudis were not taught by the Americans how to hit mobile targets or because they did not know how to effectively apply their training.

Also, the Houthis made the job of the Saudis a lot harder. Protected by caves and mountains, they improved their hiding tactics. They learned from Lebanese Hezbollah how to operate from urban areas and use civilians to shield themselves. They stored many of their weapons in schools and hospitals.[66] And like the Taliban and the Islamic State, their leaders often moved with their wives and children and used public buses for transport.[67]

The Saudis sometimes got played by the Houthis. Their own intelligence on more mobile targets has been bad, and they have relied a little too much on Yemeni sources that lack credibility or have deliberately misled. The Saudis at first were either too lazy to vet their sources and confirm the intelligence or they had little capability to do those things.

Problems with targeting did not start with Operation Decisive Storm, however. In 2009–2010, for example, the RSAF had to abort an air strike on a target the Yemeni government helped identify because it turned out to be a rival to then-president Ali Abdullah Saleh.[68] Perhaps the most embarrassing and tragic incident resulting from poor targeting happened in October 2016 when the Saudis bombed a funeral, killing at least 140 people and wounding another 600.[69] Earlier that year, the UN reported that Saudi air strikes were responsible for two-thirds of the 3,200 civilians who had died in Yemen then, or approximately 2,000 deaths.[70] That number has risen significantly since.

Many air forces around the world, including those of NATO, struggle with dynamic targeting, especially in combat operations near or inside urban centers. The issue with the Saudis, however, is that they did not even try, at least in the beginning, to adjust to this kind of aerial warfare and adopt the necessary measures. The Saudi pilots kept flying at higher altitudes and dropping the same payloads. (Ultimately, they did transition to a lower-intensity, close-air-support campaign with the help of their American Apache and Black Hawk helicopters, but not fully, as they still overwhelmingly prefer to rely on their fixed-wing aircraft.) Despite the fact that the number of Yemeni civilians killed was increasing dramatically, the Saudis' rules of engagement remained loose for many months.

Unlike the Emiratis, the Saudis do not have JTACs on the ground, which is a huge shortcoming. "You can have the world's best pilots dropping bombs," said a Riyadh-based American officer with years of military service in the Middle East, "but if you don't have a good visual of what you're really bombing the chances are you won't hit your target."[71] What the Saudis used was proxy JTACs who not only were inadequately trained (it wasn't much more than a regular guy with a video camera) but sometimes transmitted information that suited their own personal agendas.

JTAC training is very hard to secure and even harder to sustain. This is not a one-time investment like learning how to shoot a rifle. To stay current with their JTAC training, soldiers require a systemic program or an academy, neither of which the Saudis have.

Would more aerial exercises in the United States, more sustained training with mandatory monthly flying hours, and better eyes on the ground have helped the Saudis shoot with greater precision and reduce the collateral damage? In theory, yes.

The Saudis have started to fill some of those gaps by, among other things, forming in August 2016 a new Saudi Joint Incident Assessment Team to "investigate the facts, collect evidence, and produce reports and recommendations on claims and accidents during coalition operations in Yemen."[72] They also established in April 2019 an Air Warfare Center at the King Abdulaziz Air Base in the Eastern Province to further combat training of Saudi pilots and improve the readiness and capabilities of the RSAF.

To take full advantage of these new tools and facilities, there has to be some measure of defense institutional capacity. The RSAF lacks the TTPs, nested in organizational processes, that are necessary to operate proficiently.[73]

It's a similar bureaucratic shortcoming with Saudi intelligence, for example. The Saudis still do not have a streamlined institutional infrastructure to effectively collect intelligence on their enemies, credibly analyze it, and promptly disseminate it to the military services and the broader national security bureaucracy. The Saudis, like all other Arabs, put a premium on human intelligence and in-person briefings but often-times at the expense of systematic analysis.

Similar to many other developing countries, Saudi Arabia does not have a so-called "intelligence community." Until the launch of MBS's defense transformation plan, everything was rigidly stovepiped when it came to intelligence, and Saudi princes ran their own intelligence shops and staffed them with loyalists. These agencies rarely talked or cooper-ated with each other (although things began to improve during and fol-lowing al-Qaeda's insurgency in the kingdom in 2003–2004).

Command and control is another issue in Riyadh's air campaign and the broader Saudi war effort, although it has gotten much better since the first phase. In the United States and virtually all NATO countries, if the pilot is going to take out a high-value target, such as a key Houthi leader in Yemen's case, there is a very rigid process whereby the com-mander and sometimes even top political leadership authorize engage-ment. Initially, the Saudis did not have that process, and the pilots ended up deciding by themselves which strategic targets they were going to hit. Inevitably, tragic mistakes were made, such as the bomb-ing of schools and hospitals.

With regard to Saudi Arabia's air and missile defense capabilities, one would assume that they are terrible given the fact that the Houthis repeatedly have attacked Saudi cities and infrastructure inside the king-dom. However, that would be incorrect. With the help of US training and equipment, the Saudis have done relatively well against the hun-dreds of higher-altitude, longer-range missile attacks.[74]

It is useful to remember that no matter how potent and integrated a country's air and missile defense architecture is (and Saudi Arabia's is not), there is no such thing as a perfect defense. Inevitably, there will be leaks, especially when missiles are fired, like in Saudi Arabia's case, at a rate possibly unseen in the history of ballistic missile warfare.[75] And the question is not necessarily how many but what impact those pene-trating missiles have had on Saudi Arabia's national security.

Not all projectiles are equally deadly or precise. There's little point in shooting down a flying object that is about to harmlessly crash in the middle of the desert, especially when the interceptor missile costs immensely more than the relatively cheap attacking missile. The draw-back, of course, is that this efficient, deliberate approach by the Saudis unavoidably feeds misperceptions and skews the statistics in favor of "noninterceptions."

There have been important misses, of course, although some are hard to corroborate. In March 2018, the Houthis bombed Riyadh with seven missiles and caused casualties there for the first time (at least one person was killed).[76] In June 2019, they attacked the Abha International Airport near the southwest border, wounding twenty-six people. Two months later, they fired ten ballistic missiles at Jizan airport.[77] In the summer and fall of 2020, they hit Riyadh a couple more times and aimed a number of drones at the Abha airport again, putting it out of action for several hours.[78]

Yet the most devastating conventional attack against Saudi Arabia without a doubt occurred in September 2019 when the kingdom's energy installations in Abqaiq and Khurais were struck, causing the largest rise in crude oil prices in a single day. The Houthis claimed they were behind the assault, but US defense officials determined that Iran launched those weapons from its own territory.

The effective Iranian strike was proof that Saudi Arabia was unprepared for low/slow-flying drones and cruise missiles. It succeeded partly because the Saudis did not have the right assets to guard against that type of threat. In addition, their missile defense architecture was oriented toward Yemen, not Iran, which is where the attack originated from.[79] It remains unclear if the shorter-range US-built missile defense systems that the kingdom owns are now operational.[80]

However, here again, it's not just better or the right kind of hardware that the Saudis need to counter the various threats. They need better defense organization. No weapons system, no matter how powerful, can fix the Saudis' problem of having multiple and often competing entities for air and missile defense.[81] To more effectively coordinate countermeasures, Saudi air and missile defense units need proper command and control procedures, which currently they do not seem to have.[82]

Last but not least, the Saudi air and missile defense force is not integrated with the RSAF, which hampers overall military effectiveness. The Saudis cannot rely exclusively on a defensive strategy to protect against Houthi missiles because it is simply unsustainable both financially and operationally. They have to incorporate the element of deterrence, which itself requires a measure of offensive counterair that seeks to destroy and/or disrupt the Houthis' missile capabilities not only before but after launch.[83] A shared feed of the incoming missile to the defense batteries and the attack assets is a must. This is how NATO does it in peacetime, crisis, and conflict.[84]

Unfortunately, that is not how the kingdom's air force and air defense force are postured. The Saudi armed services have always functioned as silos and thus have never worked with and talked to each other effectively. This is an issue that clearly goes beyond the lack of proper tactical communications equipment. This is about politics.

As mentioned previously, the SANG has a distinct chain of command and human resources, intelligence, training and education, communications, and health departments that are also separate from those of the MoD. Various Saudi princes have treated the national security ministries over which they have presided as their own fiefdoms and money-making machines. MBS has acknowledged the major, self-inflicted weakness that is caused by this unintegrated Saudi military structure, and he seems to be addressing it by deemphasizing the traditional independence and powers of the SANG and the Saudi Ministry of Interior (MOI) and giving the green light to create greater synergies among all military and internal security agencies.[85]

With US help, the SANG and to a lesser extent the MOI currently are undergoing a process of restructuring to more effectively align their visions and strategies with those of MBS's broader defense transformation plan (the MOI's counterterrorism duties have now been transferred to the Presidency of State Security, which MBS created in 2017).[86] If MBS manages to effectively incorporate the SANG into the RSLF—which is no simple matter because these two entities' processes to organize, train, equip, deploy, employ, and sustain do not match at all—it might show that he is more serious about creating a joint force than he is about absorbing the SANG into the new defense architecture under his command (though one does not necessarily preclude the other).

The consensus among Riyadh-based American military watchers of the Saudi military is that the SANG tends to fight more competently and train harder than all other Saudi ground units, though there is no conclusive public evidence of its superior performance in Yemen.[87] The SANG allegedly runs its internal processes, including planning, budgeting, and management, better than any other in the Saudi military. Unlike other Saudi armed services, seldom does the SANG procure large weapons systems that it does not need or cannot effectively operate.

Effective combined arms for the Saudi military currently is a long shot and will not be achieved until the Saudis' distinct military services first learn how to better communicate among themselves and effectively pursue basic kinetic operations. "The performance of the Saudi ground and special forces was not just consistently disappointing in Yemen, it was humiliating for the Saudi leadership," said a retired US special operations flag officer who worked closely with the Saudis. "Over and over again, the Emiratis had to pull the Saudis' chestnuts out of the fire."[88]

One recently retired American general with seventeen years of experience in the region recalls that in the very early days of the war in Yemen, the Saudis attempted ground operations. Yet the first troops they dispatched initially got lost and could not reach their destination. Regardless of what could have caused this outcome—bad maintenance of their vehicles along the way, poor land navigation, or timidity on the part of Saudi soldiers who just were not excited about joining the fight in Yemen—it was utterly embarrassing.

This unfortunate early experience implies that if the Saudis could not make a simple administrative move from one country to another over a virtually nonexistent border, the prospects of them engaging in skillful maneuvers in battle were not encouraging. Military evaluations by retired American officers of the RSLF's performance along the southern border judge that the Saudis have had a hard time fulfilling even the most basic military functions such as locating the enemy, understanding and using military equipment, and standing guard.

For example, artillery, considered to be a relatively easy-to-use piece of equipment, has presented significant challenges for the Saudi army. Saudi soldiers have not been able to effectively identify Houthi batteries and provide warning to their fellow infantrymen. Counterbattery radars, which the Saudis did not possess for years, would have helped tremendously but would have been unlikely to fix the fundamental problem of not knowing how to accurately fire the artillery after detecting that of the enemy.

In that same vein, battlefield surveillance technology, which can be used to watch threats emerge in real time, also would have helped the Saudis in their mission to protect the southern frontier, but neither more men nor better hardware will make a big difference if they are not accompanied by credible Saudi investments in doctrinal development, which the US military assistance program seems not to have emphasized. There's no point in deploying more soldiers to defend the border if they are not skilled in guerrilla or unconventional warfare and specifically if they are not trained in mountain warfare given Yemen's northern terrain.

To systematically incorporate that kind of specialized training into the doctrine of the RSLF, who all along have been programmed to fight in the open desert against a conventional enemy coming from Iraq, requires processes, procedures, and a high level of defense organization that currently does not exist in the Saudi military and ministry of defense.

There is a problem of Saudi discipline too. Even if the Saudis secure the best training manuals, they still need to consistently show up and commit to the training exercises. In recent years, the United States helped develop a state-of-the-art range complex for live-fire training for the SANG. This expensive and highly advanced urban facility—which the Saudis paid for in full and the Americans believe is even better than Jordan's much-touted, US-funded KASOTC—has barely been used. Although very few ambitious Saudi soldiers do sporadically attend, their training is not serious or realistic.

The Saudis set up a joint forces command in Yemen, but it was neither effective nor sufficiently empowered. The job of a joint forces commander is to synchronize the war effort, seamlessly communicate with all the separate units, and share accurate intelligence to whoever needs it. The Saudis have had weaknesses on all three fronts.

Prince Fahd bin Turki, who was the Saudi commander of Joint Forces until he was sacked in September 2020 by MBS, "had the right instincts but he did not have the right resources and supporting organization,"[89] said a retired CENTCOM commander. The Saudis currently do not have an ability to achieve any measure of jointness and are not likely to develop one for many years to come. "The reason why the Saudis can't fight their way out of a paper bag despite having spent an excess of a trillion dollars over the last 40-plus years," argued one American military source based in Saudi Arabia, "is because they have not absorbed and developed the human qualities to allow those US-purchased weapons to be wielded to the fullest extent of their technical and tactical capability."[90]

Readiness is not the Saudis' strong suit, to put it mildly. What they fail to realize—and this learning process is in no way unique to them among Washington's Arab partners—is that just because they bought fifty M1A1 tanks, for example, does not mean that they actually can deploy all fifty of them. Some of these vehicles might be in repair, others used for training.

Air and missile defense is another example. If the Saudis buy twenty Patriot batteries, what they once again seem to miss is that they will not be able to defend all twenty targets on their critical assets list. And even when they try to do that, they ultimately run readiness rates into the ground, which hampers overall sustainment, ultimately allowing them to defend only five strategic facilities.

This is one of the major downsides of US weapons sales to the Saudis and other Arab partners. Washington hardly ever helps them understand the true capability inside the weapon system that they are buying. As a result, they struggle in determining how many units they actually can field or deploy for a particular mission. (And because the latter is often ill-defined, it negatively impacts the readiness equation— i.e., are those fifty tanks too few or too many for that specific mission?)

The Saudis also do not know how much it costs to sustain the equipment. Readiness is expensive, difficult, and time-consuming. It is impossible to overstate its significance and impact on planning and fighting. Yet the Saudis have a poor understanding of and inadequate approach to readiness, which seldom is mission-based.

Not unlike other Gulf Arab militaries, the Saudis have overinvested in their air force at the expense of building up their army and navy. Decades of indefensible, ad hoc weapons acquisition practices in Saudi Arabia have led to the creation of a force that has a relatively strong air and air defense force but major weaknesses in both land and naval power.

One American senior adviser in Riyadh nicely summed up this predicament: "The Saudis built an armored force capable of fighting in the open desert with modern American weapons that can shoot a mile and a half away and kill another tank, and they took that to the mountains of northwest Yemen and southwest Saudi Arabia and basically said we're going to do the same thing down here. They realized immediately it's not the same fight and they were not prepared for it."[91]

No readiness, no matter how high its levels, can fix the problem of fighting the wrong war in the wrong way. The United States' deep scars from Afghanistan and Iraq can attest to that. The Saudis have been fighting in Yemen with the capabilities they have, which are not based on any kind of serious threat analysis or requirements-based plan. The sins of Saudi procurement of the past have come to life in Yemen in the most visible and painful way.

All in all, compared to how countries like Jordan, the UAE, and lately Lebanon have been able to leverage the train-and-equip part of US military assistance, the Saudis are far behind, unable to prosecute even the most basic land-based missions, secure their territorial waters, and engage in combined arms. The US effort to train and equip the Saudi military has produced very uneven results because of significant American missteps too. Until very recently, this whole US operation in the kingdom wasn't integrated. USMTM, OPM-SANG, and MOI-MAG functioned autonomously and there was almost no intersection between them.

It's true that the Saudis preferred it that way, and Washington could not force them to stop treating their distinct military branches and national security ministries as rivals. But the Americans did feed into this flawed Saudi mindset and approach by too easily accepting the status quo and failing to point to better practices. To his credit, Secretary of Defense Robert Gates tried to change the structure in 2008–2009, but he was met with stiff resistance from CENTCOM leadership at the time.[92]

There is still a chance the Saudis can turn things around because for the first time in their history, there's someone at the top deeply invested in changing the way things are run not only in the defense space but in the entire country. The Americans seem to be invested too. They have realized that a weak Saudi Arabia that cannot defend itself against Iranian aggression presents a growing challenge to their priorities in the region and elsewhere.

That said, the Saudis are at the very beginning of a very long and arduous journey of defense reform. MBS's defense transformation plan, engineered with the help of the Americans, offers hope for the future, but societal culture, human capital, and administrative capacity will pose the biggest challenges to success.

Whenever the word *culture* is mentioned negatively in any analysis of defense reform or military effectiveness, the immediate reaction is that the country undergoing such reform is doomed given how incredibly difficult it is and how long it takes to change culture. But it's not impossible. Some like the UAE, as I will discuss later, have done it. For the kingdom, MBS's aggressive push for change helps, but it is only through consistent adherence to an established process of implementation of the transformation plan that the Saudis can gradually learn new methods, let go of bad habits, and create new norms.

Ideas matter a great deal, but process matters just as much. The Saudis have a plan, which is an achievement, but to effectively execute it, they need a fairly clear and relatively easy-to-use process. They do not have it, at least not yet.

The expectation is that implementation mechanisms will be agreed upon, developed, and refined as the plan moves forward. But the longer there is uncertainty about those processes, the less likely the Saudis will reach their targets on time. Hadi Fathallah correctly argues that what Riyadh lacks in the broader Vision 2030 is not strategies—it has plenty of those—but processes that help get them from point A to point B.[93] The same problem exists with the defense transformation plan.

With an army of American and foreign consultants advising Riyadh, it is not surprising that different execution ideas and methods have been presented to the Saudis. Even within the same country—the United States, for example—advisers from separate agencies have promoted their own strategies for defense management and sometimes found it difficult to reach common ground. What makes this problematic for the Saudis is that they are for the most part incapable of evaluating by themselves the various recommendations of the international advisers and determining which make sense and which do not.

One typical flaw in the Saudi defense transformation plan is that its creators first built an organizational chart and then they started thinking about processes for execution, when it should be the other way around. The lack of such processes was not an issue in the past because abundant Saudi money used to lubricate Riyadh's internal operations and make problems magically go away. But those financial resources have declined and will continue to do so as the world transitions to a low-carbon future. The absence of rigorous implementation processes has exposed all of the Saudis' military inadequacies. It is like the low tide showing clearly all the wreckage under the water line.

Because Saudi Arabia has not adopted a comprehensive and inclusive approach to state building, it has not pursued bureaucratic rationality processes that are so central to overall military development. To put it simply, Riyadh cannot effectively execute its defense transformation plan if the Saudi bureaucracy as a whole is malfunctioning. To put it in even starker terms, the country's future economic development is contingent upon a marked improvement in the state's bureaucratic capacity.[94]

The Saudis now get to start with a clean sheet of paper. It is disadvantageous because the Saudis are building almost everything from scratch, which is an insanely heavy lift. It is advantageous because they can build a new system that hopefully works for them without having to worry too much about legacy policies, programs, and procedures that did not work in the past.

Also, this is all taking place in a relatively permissive security environment, despite the war in Yemen. This is nothing like Iraq or Afghanistan, where the United States essentially tried to rebuild both countries' military and security forces while countering existential threats to their societies.

Last but not least, there is a ton of strategic and economic pressure to realize these reform objectives, and it is arguably a good kind of pressure. Riyadh fully understands that the United States will not have a robust presence in Saudi Arabia or the region for much longer. So to the extent possible, the Saudis have to rely on themselves to pursue their national security objectives. Meanwhile, the changing nature of the global energy market has forced the Saudi economy like never before to become more diversified and sustainable, which means that both Vision 2030 and the defense transformation plan *have to succeed.* There is no Plan B.

The concern, of course, is that MBS might be biting off more than he can chew, and the risk is that by trying to attack everything at once he might end up accomplishing very little if anything at all. This is why a gradual approach is key and why unsexy processes of implementation are as important to success as the ideas of the plan themselves. The trick for well-intentioned American advisers involved in the transformation effort in the kingdom is to get the Saudis to stop treating the plan as the be-all and end-all and to instead get them to work on essential processes they desperately need to defend the kingdom *today* and to work on adequate plans for the future.

## Notes

1. US Department of State, "U.S. Relations with Saudi Arabia," Bureau of Near Eastern Affairs, December 15, 2020, https://www.state.gov/u-s-relations-with-saudi-arabia/.

2. Rebecca Grant, "The Epic Little Battle of Khafji," *Air Force Magazine*, February 1, 1998.

3. James Titus, *The Battle of Khafji: An Overview and Preliminary Analysis* (Maxwell Air Force Base, AL: Air University, September 1996), 15; William P. Head, "The Battle for Ra's Al-Khafji and the Effects of Air Power January 29–February 1, 1991," *Air Power History* 60, no. 1 (Spring 2013): 12; Paul W. Westermeyer, "The Battle of al-Khafji," in *U.S. Marines in Battle: Al Khafji, January 28–February 1, 1991* (Washington, DC: US Marine Corps History Division, 2008).

4. George Tenet, *At the Center of the Storm: My Years at the CIA* (New York: HarperCollins, 2007), 366–367.

5. Author's interview on June 2, 2020, via phone with an American diplomat serving in the consulate at the time. The person spoke on the condition of anonymity because of the sensitivity of the conversation.

6. Gordon Lubold and Nancy A. Youssef, "U.S. Military Returns to Saudi Arabia in Response to Iran," *Wall Street Journal*, July 18, 2019.

7. Todd South, "Senators Want to Know if US Military Advisers in Yemen Are Helping or Hurting the Conflict," *Army Times,* April 18, 2018; Helene Cooper, Thomas Gibbons-Neff, and Eric Schmitt, "Army Special Forces Secretly Help Saudis Combat Threat from Yemen Rebels," *New York Times*, May 3, 2018.

8. Angus McDowall, Phil Stewart, and David Rohde, "Yemen's Guerrilla War Tests Military Ambitions of Big-Spending Saudis," Reuters, April 19, 2016.

9. Eric Schmitt, "Saudi Arabia Tries to Ease Concerns over Civilian Deaths in Yemen," *New York Times*, June 14, 2017.

10. James D. Smith, *Saudi Arabian National Guard Modernization Through U.S. Army Project Management* (Carlisle Barracks, PA: US Army War College, August 25, 1975).

11. Richard Bumgarder, "MOI-MAG Advise and Train in Saudi Arabia," US Army, November 6, 2019, https://www.army.mil/article/229552/moi_mag_advise_and_train_in_saudi_arabia.

12. Lance Brender, "What Am I Doing in Saudi Arabia?" *Armor* (April–June 2016): 52–58.

13. Richard Bumgarder, "MOI-MAG Advise and Train in Saudi Arabia," US Army, November 6, 2019.

14. Ibid.

15. Patricia Mazzei and Eric Schmitt, "Pentagon Restricts Training for Saudi Military Students," *New York Times*, December 12, 2019.

16. US Naval Forces Central Command Public Affairs Office, "Saudi, UK, U.S. Forces Complete Exercise Nautical Defender 21," US Naval Forces Central Command, Combined Maritime Forces–US 5th Fleet, February 4, 2021.

17. Melissa Heisterberg, "U.S., Saudi Forces Conduct Joint Military Exercises on Saudi Islands," US Marines, May 29, 2020, https://www.marines.mil/News /News-Display/Article/2201371/us-saudi-forces-conduct-joint-military-exercises -on-saudi-islands/.

18. *Arab News*, "Saudi Air Force Completes 'Red Flag' Military Exercise in US," March 23, 2019.

19. Rachel Buitrago, "PSAB Hosts Joint Air Defense Training with RSAF Forces," US Air Forces Central, May 22, 2021, https://www.afcent.af.mil/Units /378th-Air-Expeditionary-Wing/News/Article/2626794/psab-hosts-joint-air-defense -training-with-rsaf-forces/.

20. *Arab News*, "Saudi and US Air Forces Begin Joint Training Exercise," February 28, 2021.

21. US Naval Forces Central Command Public Affairs Office, "Saudi, U.S. Forces Conduct Joint Aviation Integration Exercise in Arabian Gulf," US Navy, December 21, 2020.

22. Cary Smith, "378 AEW, RSAF Partner Together in Training Exercise," US Air Forces Central, September 12, 2020, https://www.afcent.af.mil/News/Article /2345817/378-aew-rsaf-partner-together-in-training-exercise/.

23. Cary Smith, "USAF, RSAF Conduct Exercise Desert Eagle in CENTCOM AOR," US Air Forces Central, September 14, 2020, https://www.afcent.af.mil /Units/378th-Air-Expeditionary-Wing/News/Article/2346303/usaf-rsaf-conduct -exercise-desert-eagle-in-centcom-aor/.

24. US Department of Defense, DOD Directive 5105.75, December 21, 2007.

25. Jennifer Bell, "Now Read This: How Saudi Arabia Is Aiming to End Illiteracy by 2024," *Arab News*, November 21, 2018.

26. For more on this, see Ronald R. Krebs, "A School for the Nation? How Military Service Does Not Build Nations, and How It Might," *International Security* 28, no. 4 (Spring 2004): 85–124.

27. Author's interview by phone on November 3, 2020.

28. Davide Barbuscia, "Saudi Unemployment Spikes as Virus-Hit Economy Shrinks by 7% in Second-Quarter," Reuters, September 30, 2020.

29. Eleonora Ardemagni, "The Saudi-Yemeni Militarized Borderland," *Sada* (Carnegie Endowment for International Peace), January 9, 2020.

30. Anthony H. Cordesman and Nawaf Obaid, "The Saudi Security Apparatus: Military and Security Services—Challenges and Developments" (paper presented at the DCAF Working Group on Security Sector Governance and Reform in the Middle East and North Africa [MENA] Workshop on Challenges of Security Sector Governance in the Middle East, Geneva, July 2004).

31. Mark Perry, "US Generals: Saudi Intervention in Yemen a 'Bad Idea,'" Al Jazeera America, April 17, 2015.

32. Stephanie Cronin, "Tribes, Coups and Princes: Building a Modern Army in Saudi Arabia," *Middle Eastern Studies* 49, no. 1 (January 2013): 13.

33. Author's interview via audiovisual communications technology with four current US Air Force officers with oversight responsibilities for the Middle East on June 12, 2020. The officers spoke on the condition of anonymity.

34. Author's interview by phone on July 3, 5, and 6, 2020. The sources spoke on the condition of anonymity.

35. Author's interview by phone on July 3, 2020. The source spoke on the condition of anonymity.

36. Meghann Myers, "'Up or Out' Is on Its Way Out, and It's Time for 'Perform or Out,' Army Secretary Says," *Army Times*, January 24, 2019.

37. Mehran Kamrava, "Military Professionalization and Civil-Military Relations in the Middle East," *Political Science Quarterly* 115, no. 1 (Spring 2000): 67–92.

38. Anthony Cordesman and Nawaf Obaid, *Saudi Military Forces and Development: Challenges and Reforms* (Washington, DC: Center for Strategic and International Studies, May 30, 2004).

39. Author's interview by phone on August 8, 2020. The source spoke on the condition of anonymity.

40. Author's interview by phone on August 22, 2020. The source spoke on the condition of anonymity.

41. Author's interview in Washington, DC, on October 3, 2020. The source spoke on the condition of anonymity.

42. Shawn Snow, "Pentagon Eyes Big Expansion of Foreign Military Training Program," *Military Times*, December 3, 2019.

43. Bandar O. Nahil Al Harbi, *Saudi Arabia National Guard (SANG)* (Carlisle Barracks, PA: US Army War College, March 27, 1991).

44. Ibid.

45. Office of the Program Manager–Saudi Arabian National Guard. Data presented are found on the official website of OPM-SANG, www.army.mil/opm-sang, accessed on October 13, 2020.

46. Al Harbi, *Saudi Arabia National Guard*.

47. Ibid.

48. Ibid.

49. Joseph Trevithick, "Houthi Rebels Trounce Saudi Force amid Concerns over the Kingdom's Military Competence," *War Zone*, September 30, 2019.

50. *Arab News*, "Saudi Women Invited to Join Ranks of the Armed Forces," October 3, 2019; *Saudi Gazette*, "Ministry of Defense Opens Doors for Women in Four Key Sectors," October 4, 2019.

51. World Bank, *Unemployment, Youth Total (% of Total Labor Force Ages 15–24) (Modeled ILO Estimate)—Saudi Arabia* (Washington, DC: World Bank, June 21, 2020).

52. Author's interview by phone on August 17, 2020. The source spoke on the condition of anonymity.

53. *Saudi Gazette*, "Studies Show Need for Intensive Work Ethics Training in Saudi Arabia," February 27, 2016.

54. Abdulateef Al-Mulhim, "Saudi Youth, the Issue of Unemployment and Work Ethic," *Arab News*, March 9, 2013.

55. Andrew England and Ahmed Al Omran, "Saudi Arabia: Why Jobs Overhaul Could Define MBS's Rule," *Financial Times,* February 28, 2019.

56. Author's interview via web conferencing technology, August 12, 2020. The source spoke on the condition of anonymity.

57. US Army Training and Doctrine Command, Home page, accessed November 10, 2020, https://www.tradoc.army.mil.

58. Author's interview via web conferencing technology, September 3, 2020. The source spoke on the condition of anonymity.

59. Amanda Macias, "Saudi Arabia, US Take a Significant Step Toward Closing $15 Billion Deal for Lockheed Martin's THAAD Missile Defense System," *CNBC*, November 28, 2018.

60. General Authority for Military Industries, Home page, accessed on November 7, 2019, https://gami.gov.sa/en.

61. Saudi Arabian Military Industries, Home page, accessed on November 8, 2019, https://sami.com.sa/.

62. Author's interview by phone, November 6, 2020. The source spoke on the condition of anonymity.

63. Author's interview on April 16, 2020. The source spoke on the condition of anonymity.

64. Michael Stephens, "Mixed Success for Saudi Military Operation in Yemen," *BBC News*, May 12, 2015.

65. Nabih Bulos and David S. Cloud, "As Top Allies Scale Back in Yemen, Saudi Arabia Faces Prospect of an Unwinnable War," *Los Angeles Times*, August 11, 2019.

66. Mariano Castillo, "U.N. Rep Accuses Saudi-Led Coalition of Violating International Law," *CNN*, May 11, 2015.

67. Author's interview with two CENTCOM officers based in Doha, Qatar, August 11, 2020. The sources spoke on the condition of anonymity.

68. McDowall, Stewart, and Rohde, "Yemen's Guerrilla War."

69. *The Times*, "Saudi Bombs Kill 60 After Yemeni Peace Plan Fails," October 31, 2016.

70. McDowall, Stewart, and Rohde, "Yemen's Guerrilla War."

71. Author's interview on August 23, 2020. The source spoke on the condition of anonymity.

72. Human Rights Watch, *Hiding Behind the Coalition* (New York: Human Rights Watch, August 24, 2018).

73. Ralph Shield, "The Saudi Air War in Yemen: A Case of Coercive Success Through Battlefield Denial," *Journal of Strategic Studies* 41, no. 3 (2018): 461–489.

74. Barbara Opall-Rome, "Raytheon: Arab-Operated Patriots Intercepted Over 100 Tactical Ballistic Missiles Since 2015," *Defense News*, November 14, 2017.

75. Ian Williams and Shaan Shaikh, *The Missile War in Yemen* (Washington, DC: Center for Strategic and International Studies, June 2020); Ian Williams and Shaan Shaikh, "Lessons from Yemen's Missile War," *Defense One*, June 11, 2020.

76. Marwa Rashad, Sarah Dadouch, and Abdulrahman al-Ansi, "Barrage of Missiles on Saudi Arabia Ramps Up Yemen War," Reuters, March 26, 2018.

77. Al Jazeera, "Houthis Claim Attack on Military Target in Saudi Capital Riyadh," August 26, 2019.

78. Reuters, "Saudi-Led Coalition Starts Military Operation Against Yemen's Houthis," July 1, 2020; Reuters, "Yemen's Houthis Say They Fired Drones at Saudi Arabia's Abha Airport," September 7, 2020; Reuters, "Yemen Houthis Say Attacked 'Important Target' in Riyadh with Missile, Drones," September 10, 2020.

79. Sebastien Roblin, "Why U.S. Patriot Missiles Failed to Stop Drones and Cruise Missiles Attacking Saudi Oil Sites," NBC, September 23, 2019; Tim Lister, "The Billions Saudi Arabia Spends on Air Defenses May Be Wasted in the Age of Drone Warfare," CNN, September 19, 2019.

80. Stephen Kalin and Sylvia Westall, "Costly Saudi Defenses Prove No Match for Drones, Cruise Missiles," Reuters, September 17, 2019.

81. Helene Cooper, "Attacks Expose Flaws in Saudi Arabia's Expensive Military," *New York Times*, September 19, 2019.

82. Natasha Turak, "How Saudi Arabia Failed to Protect Itself from Drone and Missile Attacks Despite Billions Spent on Defense Systems," *CNBC*, September 19, 2019.

83. Craig R. Corey, "The Air Force's Misconception of Integrated Air and Missile Defense," *Air & Space Power Journal* 31, no. 4 (Winter 2017): 81–90.

84. NATO, "NATO Integrated Air and Missile Defence," accessed on November 4, 2020, https://www.nato.int/cps/en/natohq/topics_8206.htm.

85. Author's interview with a Saudi general in the RSLF in Riyadh, July 25, 2017. He spoke on the condition of anonymity.

86. See the official website in Arabic of the SANG, accessed on November 11, 2020, https://mngdp.sang.gov.sa/?page_id=8713. See also Neil Partrick, "Saudi Defense and Security Reform," *Sada* (Carnegie Endowment for International Peace), May 31, 2018.

87. As the king's personal army, or at least as it used to be, the SANG played a seminal role in uniting Saudis and forming the Saudi state between 1901 and 1932. Ever since, it has received the utmost care and attention of the Custodian of the Two Holy Mosques, which has allowed it, a little bit like the Egyptian military, to dabble into civilian areas that have nothing to do with war fighting, including construction, education, and health care.

88. Author's interview via web conferencing technology, October 30, 2020. The source spoke on the condition of anonymity.

89. Author's interview with a retired CENTCOM general, October 2, 2020. The source spoke on the condition of anonymity.

90. Author's interview over the phone with an American general based in Riyadh, September 23, 2020. The source spoke on the condition of anonymity.

91. Author's interview over the phone with an American general based in Riyadh, September 23, 2020. The source spoke on the condition of anonymity.

92. Author's interview by phone with a former senior Pentagon official, November 1, 2020. The source spoke on the condition of anonymity.

93. Hadi Fathallah, "Challenges of Public Policymaking in Saudi Arabia," *Sada* (Carnegie Endowment for International Peace), May 22, 2019.

94. Consult this source for a broader perspective on the importance of bureaucratic capacity: Abdelrahman Al-Hegelan and Monte Palmer, "Bureaucracy and Development in Saudi Arabia," *Middle East Journal* 39, no. 1 (Winter 1985): 48–68.

# 4

# Jordan:
# Still Falling Short

UNTIL THE RISE OF THE UAE MILITARY IN RECENT YEARS,
Jordan fielded one of the more capable armies in the Arab world. More
operationally sound and tactically proficient than many of its Arab peers,
the Jordanian Armed Forces (JAF), much like the Emirati military, has
pockets of excellence: the Royal Jordanian Air Force (RJAF), the quick
reaction forces (QRF), and the special operations forces (SOF). The SOF
developed an ability lately to train not only their own personnel but also
other friendly forces inside and outside Jordan—in Yemen, Syria, and
Iraq—for various counterterrorism and security missions.[1]

The JAF has leveraged US training and equipment better than most
other Arab partners. Its commitment to professional training, developed initially with the help of British troops based in the country until
1956–1957 and from then on with the US military; its adherence to
higher (but still lacking) standards of equipment maintenance (at least
of its air assets); and its reasonable ability to absorb US advice on
some but not all doctrinal, tactical, and operational matters all make it
one of the better students and counterterrorism partners of the US military in the Arab world.

In terms of military contributions to collective security interests,
Jordan, a major non-NATO ally since 1996 (thus earning it special benefits from Washington in the areas of defense trade and security cooperation), is the only Arab country to have directly committed military
assets to all US-led coalition operations in the region since 2001,

87

including Operation Enduring Freedom, Operation Iraqi Freedom, Operation Unified Protector, and Operation Inherent Resolve.

From 2002 to 2015, Jordan had a small security and humanitarian presence in Afghanistan—JAF Task Force 300B in Helmand province— as part of the NATO mission to stabilize the country.[2] Jordanian SOF elements are believed to be presently deployed in Syria, working with the US military. They are also stationed in Mali along with a Jordanian QRF contingent, assisting UN activities on the ground. Finally, the RJAF has flown with the Saudis in Yemen (though it is unknown if this continues to this day) and provided training for the air forces of the Kenyans, the Pakistanis, and the Turks in Mafraq Air Base.[3]

That said, despite Washington pouring dozens of billions of dollars into the JAF for several decades, the Jordanians have important deficiencies in their human capital, their force development, their defense management systems, and their strategic-level institutions. This makes them vastly incapable, now and for the foreseeable future, of sustaining and ultimately graduating from US military assistance, which is the Achilles' heel of all US military assistance programs in the Arab world.

## Goals of US Military Assistance

US military assistance in Jordan serves three main US goals: (1) foster close and enduring political ties with the country's top political leadership (i.e., King Abdullah II, who's also the Supreme Commander of the JAF) and influence their decisionmaking in ways that suit US interests; (2) maintain access, basing, and overflight for the US military (as illustrated by the defense agreement made public by Jordan in March 2021 that allows free entry of US forces onto the kingdom's territory);[4] and (3) help the JAF defend the country's borders against outside threats, disrupt terrorist groups operating on its own soil, and contribute to external counterterrorism operations with the United States and other coalition members. But US foreign assistance to Jordan does not just contribute to collective security interests and enable stronger military cooperation; it also helps ensure the very survival of the Hashemite Kingdom, accounting for approximately 4 percent of Jordan's gross domestic product and quadrupling in historical terms over the past fifteen years.[5]

Jordan receives at least $1.275 billion per year under the current 2018–2022 Memoranda of Understanding, which includes a minimum of $350 million of FMF each year, making Jordan the third largest recipient of annual US foreign aid in the world, after Afghanistan and

Israel.[6] However, this is separate from US humanitarian assistance and Defense Department funding, which amounts to hundreds of millions of dollars per year. Of note, Jordan receives more Section 333 train-and-equip money from the Pentagon than any other US partner *across the globe*—to the tune of a quarter of a billion dollars since 2017 (roughly $50 million each year).[7]

The stability of Jordan is a major concern of Washington in the region in large part because it directly impacts the security of Israel, an enduring US Middle East policy priority. Having a trusted partner in Amman who is willing and able to sustain the 1994 peace treaty with the Jewish state, engage in extensive military and intelligence cooperation with the Israel Defense Forces (IDF), and promote a peaceful resolution of the Israeli-Palestinian conflict is a vital US interest in the region (it's estimated that more than half of the 6.3 million population of Jordan is of Palestinian origin).[8]

While numerous Arab partners have had to deal with the challenge of violent Islamic fundamentalism for decades, Jordan has faced a more imminent threat in recent years due to its shared borders with both Syria and Iraq, where al-Qaeda and Islamic State militants have had a menacing presence. That is why since 2014 US military assistance to Jordan has focused on helping the JAF secure the Hashemite Kingdom's frontiers and conduct military operations mainly against Islamic State fighters.

For these main reasons, and the fact that Amman has barely any national funds to spend on defense, Washington finances almost all of Jordan's military needs and requirements. Unlike Saudi Arabia, the UAE, and Qatar, who pay for American weapons and a range of advisory and training services with their own money, the vast majority of Jordan's defense budget is supported by programs belonging to the State Department (FMF, IMET, and the Counterterrorism Partnership Fund [CTPF]) and the Defense Department (mainly Section 333 and since 2014–2015 various mechanisms to fund and reimburse for expenses related to border security and the fight against the Islamic State).

This key distinction in military funding source—US versus Arab—is not small with regard to US purposes. It makes the goal of evaluating the efficiency and effectiveness of US military assistance to Jordan all the more important and necessary. It is not that Washington should not or does not care how other wealthy Arab partners run their defense budgets or what US weapons they purchase, but there's a limit to how much US preferences can dictate or influence their judgment. At the end of the day, it is their own money and they have a sovereign right to use it in ways they think are most beneficial to their interests.

With Jordan, though, just like with Lebanon, Bahrain, Oman, and other recipients of US military aid, Congress has the right, and certainly the responsibility, to ask whether US taxpayer money is being properly used to advance US national security goals in the country and the region. That at least is the theory. In reality, hardly ever have members of Congress exercised this right because many sincerely (but wrongly) believe that any attempt at honestly reviewing the US-Jordan security partnership will have adverse effects on relations with King Abdullah II—who carries weight on Capitol Hill—and on Jordanian stability and, thus, Israeli security.

## Train and Equip

The United States is reported to have roughly 3,000 troops in Jordan, tasked with advising, equipping, and training with the JAF.[9] American service members are stationed in several camps and bases across the country, including Muwaffaq Salti Air Base, KASOTC, Camp Titin, Camp QRF-Zarqa, King Abdullah II Air Base, Safawi Air Base, and Tower 22 along the Jordanian-Syrian border.

Washington has pledged to support Jordan's military modernization goals for all the reasons I listed above. However, from the outset CENTCOM made it very clear to the country's political and military leaders that it had no interest in helping them build a large army focused on fighting conventional wars and, more specifically, on repelling an unlikely Syrian invasion from the north. (The Syrians once invaded Jordan, but that was during the events of Black September in 1970 when the Hashemite Kingdom was in a state of civil war and Palestinian leader Yasser Arafat instructed his militias to overthrow the Jordanian monarchy. The chances of this happening again are so remote, given Syria's own domestic conflict since 2011, the dilapidated state of Assad's army, and the much-improved self-defense capabilities of the Jordanians, that it is not worth prioritizing.) What the US military has done with the Jordanians instead is help them restructure their force to make it smaller, lighter, more flexible, and able to effectively deal with complex security threats including terrorism and insurgency.

The US-based doctrinal focus of the JAF (it used to be, and many parts remain, mostly British), to which the Jordanians consented several years ago, shifted from the number of battalions and platforms (90 percent of the JAF's equipment is American) to the delivery of a timely and successful response led by QRF and SOF that are able to communicate, coordinate, and fight jointly with air assets. That is the JAF's vision for the future, and this is where it is investing the most.

As part of this US-enabled restructuring effort, the JAF's armor battalions are believed to have been reduced from twelve to eight. Two new antitank systems were incorporated to retain a sufficient capacity for counterinsurgency operations. And it is estimated that six heavy artillery battalions, along with four multiple launch rocket system battalions, were created. The border regiment security force was completely revamped and is now supported by a state-of-the-art electronic security and surveillance system. Older aircraft were phased out, some were modified, and new ones were purchased, all to improve operational capability and interoperability with US and coalition forces. Finally, three heavy boats were retired and replaced by two medium-sized boats for coast-guarding purposes.

Washington has used three main vehicles to help strengthen the JAF and more specifically enhance its counterterrorism, counterinsurgency, and border-security capabilities: the JOEP, the Joint Border Security Program (JBSP), and a separate train-and-equip program with Jordan's SOF units. Founded in 2014, the JOEP seeks to provide the JAF's 77th Marines, Border Guard, SOF, and QRF with weapons, ammunition, communications, and tactical military training to enable them to conduct counterterrorism operations and defend the country's borders. This training program is one of the largest the Pentagon funds through its Section 333 account. It consists of fourteen-week training cycles between the US military and the JAF on "marksmanship, tactical first aid, map reading, land navigation, battle drills, [reaction] to improvised explosive devices, sniper training, and several other [soldier] skills."[10]

Until recently, as part of the JOEP, a US National Guard Infantry Battalion and about fifty US Marines were assigned to the Jordanian Border Guard and the QRF, respectively. Yet due to Washington's recent reallocation of US military resources to the Indo-Pacific region, the battalion had to be moved. This has forced the few remaining Marines to be responsible for advising and assisting both the Border Guard and the QRF. However, this reduced US troop presence wasn't all bad. It pushed the Jordanians to step up, expand their training, and ultimately become trainers themselves, though with US oversight.

That's exactly what happened in May 2020, when the JOEP began to transition from a peer-to-peer to a train-the-trainer model. Various units of the US military partnered with their JAF counterparts to "develop and execute the [Instructor Trainer Course], which certified JAF junior officers and [NCOs] as lead JOEP [instructors]."[11]

The JBSP was launched in 2009 to support the eleven battalions that are responsible for security along "the 160-mile stretch bordering Syria and another 115-mile demarcation line with Iraq."[12] The three-phased $100 million program was supposed to end in 2017, but it got extended to include a fourth phase in order to cover both the northern and eastern borders. It most likely will go on for the foreseeable future because the need to fix and maintain sophisticated equipment such as sensors, cameras, and computers is constant.

JBSP provides Jordan with an integrated surveillance detection and interdiction system comprised, among other things, of six watchtowers arrayed along the borders, all serving as observation posts with long-range optics, ground radars, day/night cameras, and a full command, control, and communications suite to provide early identification of any potential threat.

Operating under a centralized border security directorate, the border guard battalion is a mechanized unit supported by motorized assets as well as an antitank platoon, mortars, and artillery. It is sufficiently manned with trained personnel and competent leaders, and it is proficiently maintained with its own maintenance shop. Thanks to US communications equipment and training, the JAF is able to collect, consolidate, analyze, and share intelligence at the headquarters level to inform counterterrorism and border security plans and operations.

With respect to the SOF train-and-equip program, the United States has helped the JAF leverage its regional comparative advantage in this domain by investing in the 101st Special Forces Battalion, the 71st Counterterrorism Battalion, and the 82nd Airborne Battalion. (The 28th Prince Hussein bin Abdullah II Royal Ranger Brigade and the Prince Hashim bin Abdallah II 5th Aviation Brigade were absorbed into the QRF following the 2017 restructuring of the Joint Special Operations Command.)

Jordanian SOF personnel have served as liaison officers in US Special Operations Command (SOCOM), training on advanced techniques, expertise, and tactics. They have attended seminars and conferences with the US Joint Special Operations University in Florida, and through their participation in the international special operations cell they have worked with the special forces branches of multiple US geographic combatant commands (GCCs), including CENTCOM and Africa Command (AFRICOM).[13]

Washington spent approximately $100 million to construct KASOTC, which became operational in 2009. Located on the outskirts of Amman, this massive and state-of-the-art facility is an international hub for SOF and law-enforcement training on urban and counterterrorism operations. It is used by various countries around the world (thus generating much-needed economic revenue for Jordan) and reportedly has "a mock village, an embassy compound, driving and shooting ranges, and even an Airbus A300 with targets to simulate hostage scenarios."[14]

Paradoxically, KASOTC is seldom used by the JAF nowadays, and it is run by a private sector company. Even though it was built with American FMF money, the US military has to pay rent to use it, and the same goes for the JAF itself.

Doubling down on Jordan's SOF is a reasonable US investment. Though they are not better than their Iraqi or Emirati counterparts, they are modestly better than most in the Arab world, and they have key counterterrorism responsibilities that are crucial for Jordanian and US security interests. Founded in 1963, their numbers have catapulted since and are now anywhere between 7,000 and 8,000. They are grouped under the Jordanian Special Operations Command (whose headquarters was deactivated in 2017 following a set of reforms by the JAF commander partly aimed at cutting costs).[15] They receive the special care and attention of King Abdullah II, who as a Cobra pilot himself once commanded the SOF and reorganized them in 1996 to become a more modern force.

The QRF is a recent addition to Jordan's SOF family. It was born in 2014 to serve as a strategic mobile reserve force. Responsible for internal and external security operations, it is an air-mobile, combined-arms battalion with two permanent infantry companies and one rotational infantry company. It reports directly to the JAF commander.

The QRF is largely well-trained for complex operations including counterincursion, air mobility, and night operations, and it has integrated fire support and aviation support planners. Twice a month the RJAF's 8th Squadron, whose Black Hawk helicopter pilots are all trained in the United States and deemed by US airmen as reliable and professional, conducts training with the QRF on day/night air assault and air movement missions. JTACs organic to the QRF are integral to each mission for planning and execution.

The QRF is well organized and capable of sustaining operations for twenty-four hours against an irregular platoon-sized threat. Company-level QRF are vehicle mobile. Intelligence, surveillance, and reconnaissance (ISR) assets at the battalion level include long-range surveillance cameras and unmanned aerial vehicles (UAVs). Command and control of the QRF are exercised using multiple command and control (C2) nodes successfully for a forty-eight-hour period.

The QRF was operationally tested in live combat when on June 21, 2016, it was alerted that a tower was attacked along the Jordanian-Syrian border. Initial reports indicated that a vehicle laden with explosives was at the tower. Although no explosives ultimately were found in the suspected vehicle, the ability to swiftly and effectively move forces to the site and coordinate with the 8th Squadron was demonstrated.

For all the much-improved capabilities of the JAF's elite ground units in recent years, the country's ace in the hole and go-to source for protection and strategic deterrence remains the RJAF, which the United States single-handedly built almost from scratch. Washington has financed both the maintenance of Jordan's older F-16 squadrons and, very recently, the acquisition of sixteen new F-16s and various attack and tactical transport helicopters and UAVs. It also has provided training in support of the RJAF's efforts to establish NATO qualification for integrated air-to-ground combat operations, maintain an F-16 squadron capable of supporting the full range of coalition missions, and develop an ability to deliver ground forces anywhere inside Jordan, even at night. In February 2021, the State Department approved the transfer of a $60 million F-16 Air Combat Training Center to the RJAF to help it meet its maintenance and effective employment goals.[16]

Yearly participation in Falcon Air Meet since 2006 and Eager Lion since 2011 has helped the RJAF develop an ability to effectively plan, conduct operations, and develop a mission-oriented joint training cycle with significant emphasis on combined training with the United States and other coalition partners. Like the UAE Air Force, the RJAF has a small cadre of NATO-certified JTACs capable of supporting integrated air-to-ground combat operations. Through Eager Lion, the Jordanians hope to amplify their JTAC program.

Falcon Air Meet is an annual aerial exercise meant to improve cooperation and interoperability between the United States, Jordan, and regional partners. The US Colorado Air National Guard has been responsible for "setting up, coordinating, and officiating the series."[17] Missions include dog fights, maintenance, munitions handling, and close air support. In 2013, Falcon Air Meet was incorporated into the larger and more complex Eager Lion.

As discussed in Chapter 2, Eager Lion is a US-led, multinational exercise. It is unique in the region because all training operations are improvised and ad hoc. They are not set-piece battles, for which Arab armies are notorious. Rather, dynamic operations happen simultaneously and in multiple areas across the country.

To illustrate, SOF runs operations in the north, the QRF in the southern port city of Aqaba, and conventional forces in both the north and center of the country, but all on the same scenario with things rapidly changing depending on how events are unfolding in different theaters. "This wasn't like units would rehearse a visit-board-search-and-seizure mission down in Aqaba eight times before they did it in front of the king,"[18] said one Jordan-based senior US service member who watched the exercise. "This was legitimate training, and the Jordanians want to keep getting better at it."[19]

The RJAF also has an ISR wing with three squadrons, one composed of UAVs and two unmanned ISR assets. All squadrons support border and internal security missions. The relatively new 25th Squadron has six AT-802 Border Patrol Aircraft, provided to the RJAF by the UAE in 2013, and four AT-802 Longswords, delivered by the United States in 2016. The squadron provides the RJAF with a decent ISR platform with extended endurance (ten hours) and the capability to use live video feeds.

After a Jordanian fighter pilot was captured and burned to death by the Islamic State in 2015,[20] the JAF trained extensively on search-and-rescue operations, which are the hardest types of missions any military can do. In one seemingly effective training, with US personnel monitoring, the Jordanians put up an armed AT-802 air tractor for ISR, then they flew their Black Hawks in to pick up the pilot from the SOF, treated him on the ground, put him on an airplane, and flew him out. Then the AT-802 dropped bombs to simulate engaging enemy forces moving on them and instructed the SOF to get off the objective. The JAF did every step of this process, which was conducted at night and with live fire, with a degree of success (though US servicemen overseeing JAF training obviously have a strong incentive to say good things about its quality and output).

In real-life operations, the RJAF did well in Libya, deploying tactically for the first time in a multinational air campaign. For seven to eight months in 2011, "six RJAF F-16s escorted humanitarian aid flights and carried out combat air patrols during NATO operations."[21] The Jordanians were proud of what they accomplished, and the Americans were impressed.

In summary, many years of US advising, assisting, equipping, and training with the JAF have turned it into a more (though still insufficiently) professional and tactically capable force that can perform some combat and search-and-rescue operations and engage in less sophisticated versions of combined arms (certainly not up to NATO standards).

Also, the cultural sensitivities and religious backgrounds of Jordan's troops (and those of other Arab partners) are assets the US military can never replicate. Indeed, an American soldier, no matter how intellectually curious and well-versed, is simply unable to engage Muslim shaikhs and tribal leaders and understand the preconditions of conflict and traits of the enemy in the same way as his Jordanian counterpart.

Among the JAF's weaknesses is its peculiar inability to properly use radios, though this is not unique to the Jordanians in the Arab world. (The Jordanian troops' default is still the commercial messenger platform WhatsApp, which is extremely insecure, especially for the modern battlefield.) Keeping NATO certifications of the JAF's JTACs current also is a continual fight due to a general lack of commitment on the part of many Jordanian soldiers.

Although some Jordanian units have demonstrated some proficiency with combined arms in training exercises (they are simply not tested in live warfare), the very concept and practice of jointness is still very much deficient across the board, which also is not uncommon in the region. Integrated combat happens only in those previously mentioned small units or pockets of excellence. A conventional JAF unit cannot fight jointly. The JAF may not need to right now because neither the military vision of King Abdullah II and the JAF leadership nor the mission is conventional, but threats continue to evolve in the Middle East, requiring changes in doctrine and strategy. So having that joint conventional ability is never a bad investment.

With regard to logistics, partly because of its defensive doctrine and nonexpeditionary mindset, the JAF is incapable of organically deploying logistics teams to areas of operations and particularly along the borders. Not unlike other Arab partner forces, they have to resort to logistics bases that are dozens of miles away, which affects the speed and efficacy of operations.

## Institutional Capacity Building

The United States increasingly has been providing Jordan with advanced training and sophisticated military equipment since the latter's peace deal with Israel in 1994. Yet, American advisers only began to work with the JAF on institutional capacity building in 2016–2017. Since then, a small team of American experts has been making periodic trips to the country and running workshops to help the JAF develop its strategic planning and defense management capacities.

The US intent initially was to assist the JAF with a strategic defense review (SDR) to inform the structural reform process, help create a more organized defense governance architecture, and better utilize the generous US security assistance. This was not the first time the United States had worked with the JAF on an SDR. The first one took place in 2006–2007, though its findings were never implemented partly because the American team of specialists did not stick around and help with execution, and the second one was in 2012, a year after the onset of the civil war in Syria, which meant that its recommendations became less relevant or pressing due to the radical changes in the regional security environment.

The latest SDR also had to be shelved because in October 2016 the JAF, following the king's directive, was undergoing significant changes in its general-officer leadership, which forced many senior officers to retire, including the general charged with leading the SDR. As a result, the US focus shifted from overarching strategic planning to near- and mid-term strategic planning, mainly through the introduction of capability-based assessment tools that looked at priority capability areas. These tools feed the acquisition process and generally amplify resource management efforts.

Unlike in Saudi Arabia, there is presently no MODA program in Jordan. This is partly due to Amman's sensitivity to having foreigners serve as official advisers in administrative tasks at general headquarters (GHQ) after what happened with British brigadier general Alex Macintosh. In November 2019, the senior British officer was sacked because he was accused of becoming "too close" to the king and wielding too much political influence. Even though he was making changes that the king asked for, he was hated across the board by the JAF's rank and file, making his stay no longer welcome.[22]

Another reason for the absence of a MODA program in Jordan is US resources. CENTCOM would love to help the JAF create a joint staff in GHQ that is able to take on the functions of personnel, strategy, policy, plans, and so on, but Washington has determined it doesn't have the bandwidth for such an investment at the moment.

Because there is no US staff that's embedded in Jordanian national security organizations to consistently offer advice to their Jordanian counterparts, the US-supported institutional capacity building effort is more or less limited to the activities of the ISG specialists, who are not based in the country, and of the modest security cooperation team at the US embassy, whose members have little time for or true expertise in defense institution building.

That's a heavy lift, considering the fact that Jordan is starting from an almost nonexistent defense institutional foundation, which means that it needs a ton of support in that area. The country has no standing ministry of defense (instead, it has a civilian body called the Committee of Defense Resources and Management of Investments, which was supposed to form a nucleus for a future ministry of defense), and concomitantly, no civilian defense professionals. In 2007, King Abdullah II shared with Defense Secretary Robert Gates his desire to create a secretariat to perform the functions of a ministry of defense. But that interest never materialized. As a result, all of Jordan's national security thinking and processes happen at the JAF's GHQ and are mainly run by JAF army personnel. Current JAF commander Maj. Gen. Yousef Huneiti, who comes from the RJAF and is a fighter pilot by training, has sought to involve the navy and air force in GHQ operations to promote a more meaningful culture of jointness, but the organization remains army-centric.

Indeed, there is no real joint staff in GHQ, and there is very little intellectual and practical cross-pollination of air force and navy in the army-dominated GHQ. Most JAF senior staff are armor or field artillery officers. There are no senior Jordanian SOF officers, and there is currently only one navy officer. There is even discrimination, felt by many in the JAF, against the SOF, which sounds bizarre because as former SOF commander the king takes special interest in the organization. To some degree, this resembles America's experience in the 1970s prior to the formation of SOCOM, when joining SOF was considered a career killer.

To show how dysfunctional the joint staff in the JAF is, consider the combat search-and-rescue exercise I described earlier. Oddly enough, despite its remarkable success, it was not properly reported to the JAF commander even though it was one of the best exercises the Jordanians had ever done. The Americans had to brief Maj. Gen. Huneiti about it "because it died at GHQ," as one US service member said.[23] If it is not tanks or artillery, GHQ cares very little. That's the downside of having these clusters of excellence in the JAF: they don't get to have their own staff to run their operations better. Because of this considerable gap in GHQ's joint staff, joint operational concepts—be it for border security or internal security including counterterrorism, crisis management, and civil unrest—are poorly developed or downright nonexistent.

Although the US military will not have the chance any time soon to help the JAF create a joint staff, it benefits from a number of other institutional capacity building efforts that are engineered by ISG specialists and pursued in partnership with Jordanian personnel. Let's start with human capital, or HRM, which is the most critical initiative.

## HRM

This is the JAF commander's number-one priority. The United States is committed to supporting the JAF in this area, from how long enlistment in the JAF and what pay scales should be to how the overall force structure should look. Although they're early in that process, American ISG specialists are going deep into the human aspect of the JAF's force generation methods because the shared belief is that this reform experiment is what drives everything else.

The RJAF and the SOF are pursuing human capital development better than any other branch in the JAF largely because they have better-educated personnel and are the beneficiaries of stronger investments from the country's political and military leadership in addition to better-quality US advisory help. These two services, unsurprisingly, are the first two choices for enlisted Jordanian soldiers.

Jordan has a highly educated population and the military is socially high-ranked. Jordanian soldiers do not get paid very well due to national economic constraints, but joining the military is typically a good career choice. There is growing interest in the officer corps, especially with the more attractive jobs. For example, in Jordan's Air Academy, there were once 8,000 applicants for 50 slots, recalled one US officer based in Jordan. To be sure, a large number did not have proper qualifications, but with this many applying, getting a really good 50 was attainable.

JAF leadership hold students to higher standards in the country's military schools. In the RJAF, for example, senior managers flunk people out of flight school if they underperform. In terms of gender diversity, the JAF is more committed to that goal than most other Arab armies. It has female helicopter pilots and soon will have its first female F-16 pilot. The United States has helped nurture the JAF's interest in female participation through the active engagement of Lt. Amy Mitchell, the female air attaché at the US embassy who has been working in Jordan for the past few years and has been a constant source of advice for Jordanian female military recruits.

Despite having set up an NCO academy in recent years, the JAF's NCO education is rather weak, which again is not unusual among Arab armies. The JAF's officer culture is seniority-based. For example, a company commander does not get to question a battalion commander or a brigade commander, no matter how unwise or wrong the orders might be. The operating principle of the JAF is very much based on senior leadership giving both the "what" and the "how." In other words, the JAF does not have a mission-based culture where the soldiers determine, or at least have the opportunity to weigh in on, how to accomplish the mission and conduct operations.

While the British have taken the lead in JAF officer training and put a decent amount of money into this effort by supporting the Royal

Jordanian Command and Staff College, the United States is helping with NCO education restructuring by holding training sessions in Jordan and amplifying Jordanian officer participation in and graduation from the US military education system. US officials also have encouraged the JAF's leadership to tap into its FMF funds, rather than rely solely on IMET assistance, to further invest in its personnel development (the amount of $3 million per year from IMET, while substantial for IMET participation in the United States, is certainly not enough for the broader and critical goal of JAF human capital development).

The JAF created an NCO program in 2010 in part because JAF leaders recognized that one of the reasons why their troops struggled in Afghanistan was because of the lack of a professional NCO corps.[24] Since then, thanks to US assistance and mentorship, the JAF has been able to revamp "its evaluation system to determine the appropriate qualifications for NCO selections and promotions."[25]

From 2010 to 2016, the Jordan Basic Instructor Course, held in both Jordan and the United States, graduated more than 140 Jordanian NCOs.[26] When the US Warrior Leader Course at the NCO Academy in Fort Bliss began allowing international military students in October 2010, the Jordanians were the first to show up, eager to mingle with and learn from their American counterparts.[27]

As things progressed nicely and scores of Jordanian NCOs were receiving professional training in the United States, the plan was to move to the next step and help the JAF build its own NCO leadership course within Jordan. In December 2016, CENTCOM hosted a two-week-long "train the trainer" course in Amman that featured instruction from US Army NCOs and taught leadership to the JAF's enlisted leaders.[28]

A year later in November, NCOs from the JAF and the US Army worked to develop a "comprehensive overhaul" of the Jordanian training system for the JAF's leaders.[29] A few months after that, implementation began, with American soldiers observing and assessing the theoretical and practical training of the JAF's NCO Academy Squad Leader Course and Modern Operations on Urban Terrain exercise.[30] This US-inspired program of instruction is 70 percent hands-on and 30 percent classroom, which many Jordanians seem to appreciate.[31]

One of the goals behind the JAF's partnership with the US military was to produce an NCO guide similar to the US Army Blue Book that standardizes roles and responsibilities of the NCO.[32] Much progress toward that goal was made in July 2018 when a small team of US NCOs from the Colorado Army National Guard, who have been partners with the JAF since 2004 through the National Guard Bureau's State Partnership Program, visited Jordan and shared experiences and best practices with the commanders of various units of the JAF.

In April 2019, a team of American soldiers landed in Amman to conduct an NCO subject matter expert exchange with the JAF NCO Academy on the enlisted force structure, promotions, professional military education (PME), performance feedback, evaluation processes, and career developments for both armies.[33] Two months later, American instructors from the US Air Force Senior NCO Academy provided the first-ever senior NCO mobile education course in Amman. "The instructors partnered with [RJAF] translators to present the two-week course to 30 RJAF senior enlisted."[34] Inspired by a five-week course held at Maxwell Air Force Base in Alabama, the condensed course teaches issues in which the JAF has important weaknesses, such as officer empowerment, critical thinking, and problem-solving.

NATO has volunteered to help the JAF with NCO reform as well. For example, in September 2016, a team of five NCOs from Germany, Greece, France, the UK, and the United States visited Jordan's NCO Academy to deliver the NATO NCO leadership training to JAF personnel.[35]

The assumption is that as more Jordanian NCOs go through US, British, and NATO training, the JAF officer culture will gradually change. That said, mainly for cultural reasons, the JAF's generals are still hesitant to wholeheartedly buy into the NCO leadership development program and increase their trust in their subordinates. This attitude will continue to hamstring the NCO restructuring process.

At home, the Jordanians have two military academies, one for the air force, which is very good compared to others in the region, and one for the army, which is less impressive. There is no academy for the navy— Jordanians go to third parties for naval training, including Greece and Pakistan—or the SOF. Members of the royal family get to attend prestigious Western military institutions such as Sandhurst in the UK.

There is a Prince Hashem bin Al Hussein School for Special Operations, and it trains and qualifies Jordanian officers and NCOs as well as those of Arab and friendly countries, but it is more like the Fort Benning Army Base in the United States. It teaches the ranger course and some specialized training, but its courses are of short duration. It is not a four-year degree-granting school and it doesn't even offer the equivalent of an officer basic course.

Jordan's SOF school has gone through an evolution and several names and restructuring efforts since 1963 when the first ranger and airborne course was taught by American trainers and a ranger and airborne training wing was established in infantry school. SOF students are taught a range of courses that include Platoon Commanders' Basic Tactics Course, English Language Training Course for Officers/NCOs, Ranger Course, Airborne Course, Air Assault, and Fighting in Built Up Areas. Just like in the JAF, enrollment in the SOF is on a voluntary basis.

The King Hussein Air College in Mafraq, which recently has partnered with nearby Al al-Bayt University, teaches basic and more complex flying techniques to include solo flying and formation flying. In early 2021, King Abdullah II inaugurated the expansion of the college and the installment of a Technical University College for Aviation Sciences.[36] At the King Hussein Air College, students can get a bachelor's degree in aviation and major in subjects such as air traffic control navigation.

Founded in 1950 as a cadet school, the Jordanian Royal Military Academy, which is for the army, trains officer cadets for operational field combat for two years. Like the Prince Hashem SOF School, it trains cadets from other Arab nations, including Bahrain, Kuwait, Saudi Arabia, and the UAE. Aside from physical fitness, training stresses intellectual learning and includes courses on general science, math, and psychology. The academy caters to about 500 cadets, who are instructed by forty-five officers and fifty NCOs.[37] After receiving general infantry training at the academy, the cadets are passed on to specialist schools, where they learn basic skills of radio, artillery, commando operations, armored division tactics, and so on.

The follow-on schooling of Jordanian officers is respectable compared to peers in the region. The Royal Jordanian Command and Staff College was founded in 1954. Academically linked with Mutah University, a national institution for military and civilian higher education born in 1981 by royal decree, it educates Jordanian military personnel and officers from other Arab countries and awards bachelor's degrees in military science.

Although the United States, as mentioned previously, has ceded much of the JAF officer educational terrain to the UK, the US National War College has sought to partner with the Royal Jordanian National Defense College to try to improve its curriculum and, specifically, help it transition from memorization to critical thinking. Not all memorization is bad, of course. Seeing some amount of memorization among lieutenants and captains is acceptable, but seeing it among majors and colonels, which tends to be the case with the JAF, is not.

With US support, Jordan will build a new King Abdullah II Defense Academy, which would incorporate the Royal Jordanian National Defense College, the Command and General Staff College, and the Center for Strategic Studies. The latter was established in 1984 initially as the first security studies–focused academic center in the University of Jordan. It has expanded since to include topics related to politics, economics, and the environment, and it offers a professional diploma in refugee and forced migration studies. Within this new academy, a Joint Doctrine and Concepts Center will be created to further educate JAF officers on doctrine and equipment. Although it is Jordanians teaching Jordanians in Arabic at the Royal Jordanian National Defense College, the United States puts in an exchange officer every couple of years. It also encourages the Jordanian educators and administrators to move to a seminar model that Americans use in their war colleges. This is important because very little if any creative thinking or ingenuity takes place in those Jordanian schools, as evidenced by the fact, shared by American advisers based in Jordan, that many of the papers Jordanian officers write have the same subjects as those of their predecessors.

Some of the challenges the JAF faces in force generation are typical in Arab armies. Even though Maj. Gen. Huneiti has installed strict rules for SOF and RJAF enlistment, he is under a lot of pressure to recruit for the army from local tribes that are close to the king and politically influential. "Every time he goes to his office, there's a shaikh waiting for him and asking him to give a job to his idiot nephew," said one Jordanian F-16 pilot.[38]

Even though the king's vision for the JAF's future is "better and smaller," the latter part may not be possible any time soon because of reasons that have nothing to do with the military. Political considerations, partly informed by the revolt of military veterans in 2011–2013, and economic difficulties in the country, especially during Covid-19, have turned the JAF into a jobs program.[39]

This explains the latest change in JAF conscription policy (military conscription was scrapped after Jordan signed a peace treaty with Israel in 1994), where men and women aged between twenty-five and twenty-nine can join for one year. To be clear, this new rule is not meant to strengthen the military.[40] Rather, it is supposed to reduce national unemployment by paying conscripts $141 a month for three months and covering their salaries up to a minimum wage of $310 for the remaining nine months when they work in private companies.[41]

During that full year, the newly enlisted go through symbolic indoctrination and vocational training, but they receive no military training whatsoever. King Abdullah II had to freeze the program in 2021 because he understood it was not sustainable, but if the political costs of his decision continue to grow, he might have to reinstate it.

Legacy hires are another huge problem, which again is not unique to the JAF in the Arab world. To touch those would be politically explosive because it would upset key tribes that are part of Jordan's governance structure. It is also a twenty-year enlistment, so if the Jordanians graduate from the military academy or if they just enlisted as regular soldiers, they are guaranteed twenty years of salary until retirement. Similar to Saudi Arabia and other Arab countries, there is no "up or out" system in the JAF like in the US military, so it really limits the ability to get those nonperformers out, and pretty much everybody gets promoted on time.

English proficiency in the JAF is an issue that hampers stronger cooperation with the US military. Jordan wants to use Jordanian English language instructors because it all goes back to the JAF's jobs program. American advisers are trying to get their Jordanian partners to go with a contracted solution to this problem. Some branches, like the RJAF, have endorsed and benefited tremendously from it. The army, however, has retained its own instructors largely because it wants to keep the jobs program. SOF personnel and very few NCOs do speak English because they have deployed and regularly interacted with American soldiers in Syria and elsewhere. The result is a mixed bag, with some fluent and the vast majority unable to speak English at all, despite participation in IMET classes in the United States.

## Capability-Based Assessments

As their name suggests, capability-based assessments, which have served as an alternative to an SDR since 2016, are meant to assess the state of the JAF's various capabilities. They also seek to inform the JAF's restructuring and planning decisions and ultimately create an in-house capability to manage defense resources. These completed assessments are followed by plans to *implement* the recommendations of the assessments.

Led by American advisers, the first two such assessments focused on ground forces mobility and border security—two very high priorities for the JAF, especially since Syria's civil war in 2011 and the Islamic State's rapid regional expansion shortly after—followed by combined arms and tank development. These analytic exercises were extremely useful not only for the JAF but also for the US embassy security cooperation team. They helped inform some critical decisions across the DOTMLPF-P and answer some really hard defense resourcing questions for the JAF.

The relatively successful outcome of these products prompted additional assessments that focused on targeted airlift and mobility operations and long-range precision strike capabilities. The latter was particularly instrumental in helping guide the recapitalization or restructuring of the JAF's F-16 fleet, leading to the decision to purchase sixteen new planes rather than fix old ones, which would have cost more over the long run and been less effective from a capability and interoperability standpoint. This required more US funding up front, but with the expectation that sustainment savings would be generated over a fifteen-year timeframe.

## Acquisition

Supported by those capability-based assessments, the JAF's acquisition process is largely driven by the United States, but the Jordanians have taken it as their own and they get a vote in prioritization. Through a five-year security assistance roadmap (FYSAR), the United States and Jordan go through a rigorous five-year budgeting process to determine what capabilities the JAF needs to meet the country's security objectives. The current memorandum of understanding expires in 2022, but once again will be renewed.

Led by the SDO/DATT, the US embassy security cooperation team works directly with the JAF commander and his chief of procurement, who now better understand the strategic logic and economics of the acquisition process. The king's military adviser at the palace is far less knowledgeable about the numbers, but he is willing to listen and, more importantly, keep his boss in line.

Although there's rigor in this interactive process, not all of it is good on the American side, partly due to a desire by high-level US officials to always support the American defense industry (in other words, provide it with opportunities to sell specific hardware). However, "what works for Lima, Ohio, doesn't always work for Amman, Jordan," said one US service member based in Jordan. He added, "We often have to play the role of honest broker to make sure the JAF gets what it truly needs."[42]

One example of a misguided procurement choice is the high mobility artillery rocket systems (HIMARS), which the JAF doesn't necessarily require given its ongoing restructuring effort and move away from a conventional posture. HIMARS typically engages enemy artillery, air defense assets, and armored personnel carriers—capabilities the JAF will not be dealing with, be it from Syria or any other neighbor, for the foreseeable future. Furthermore, each HIMARS missile is worth $100,000, which the JAF simply cannot afford.

Jordan's army has been getting the short stick lately when it comes to procurement because of the RJAF's strategic needs. When the Americans and the Jordanians hold FYSAR discussions, roughly $200 million is immediately taken off the top and going to F-16 sustainment. The rest of US funding is divided across the JAF's programs. To some degree, this is defensible because the RJAF's F-16s are the only deterrent against conventional aggression and invasion, no matter how unlikely those might be.

### Intelligence

Very recently, US intelligence specialists have begun work with the JAF on how to create a professional and dependable intelligence service for the latter's Directorate of Military Intelligence. This initiative is the result of a comprehensive US assessment that found the JAF's intelligence collection, analysis, and management capabilities to be suboptimal and heavily focused on human intelligence, a weakness shared by the country's highly competent and CIA-trained General Intelligence Directorate.[43]

### Logistics

The JAF's logistics enterprise is incredibly stovepiped and inefficient. Both the United States and NATO have provided logistics assistance to the JAF since 2016 to ultimately enable it to develop a networked, economical, and more responsive system with a larger supporting capacity. In support of that long-term plan and through a comprehensive logistics capability-based assessment that cuts across all of the JAF's services, including its GHQ, US logisticians have helped their Jordanian counterparts pursue a total restructuring process to create, among other things, a professional logistics staff, stock holdings, and warehouses and to retire old equipment that's less efficient, economical, and serviceable.[44]

In addition, the US military has offered logistics courses and practical training to the JAF. For example, in September 2017, units from the US Army completed a three-phased training with the JAF at the Royal Jordanian Supply and Transportation School in Amman on tactical logistical sustainment operations as part of an effort to boost interoperability between the JAF and the US military in that domain.[45] The training, which featured seminars and hands-on activities, offered a shared understanding of how the US Army thinks about logistics and provides the essential supplies, personnel, and equipment required to sustain CENTCOM's operations. By the end of the training, more than forty JAF logisticians had "graduated."[46]

## Rule of Law

Legal advisers from the US military have provided modest technical assistance to the JAF to enhance its ability to ensure legal compliance during border security and peacekeeping operations. The target of reform is Jordan's Military Justice Directorate, and the US-led initiative ultimately seeks to create a Jordanian operational legal adviser corps.

## Outcomes

The JAF has an opportunity to become more effective in its operations and more efficient in its defense management in large part because King Abdullah II is fully behind this vision and not interested in micromanaging this transformation project (for now at least), like other Arab autocrats are prone to do. In the words of one senior American military observer currently based in Jordan, "The king actively monitors the JAF's restructuring, but he doesn't control it. He has empowered the JAF commander to do it."[47]

Much good has come out of the institutional capacity building effort in Jordan, including the JAF's enhanced ability to engage in strategic planning, prioritize, and think about future needs and requirements. The capability-based assessments have been so useful for the JAF that its leadership has decided to create a Capability Development Department to develop an in-house capacity to plan and implement. Also, some progress has been made toward the cause of efficiency through the creation of "train the trainer" programs, smarter logistics philosophy and practices, and various other cost-saving measures.

These important achievements notwithstanding, there is still one giant, dark cloud that hovers over this reorganization effort and tends to dilute all the successes the JAF has accomplished with US help over the years: Jordan's inability to sustain on its own its overall readiness, personnel, training, and combat operations due to its still very weak institutional capacity and its lack of national funds for defense spending.

It is primarily the Americans who every year have to contribute time, effort, and billions of dollars to help the JAF meet this readiness goal. The painful reality remains that should Washington terminate or even reduce its aid to Jordan, the entire military assistance program likely would fall apart.

Some of this is self-caused. In an overall population of nearly 7.5 million, over 2 percent—so roughly 160,000—serve in the military, greatly outsizing the country's ability to support it. If it were not for US funding, Jordan would not have been able to pay the salaries and pensions of its soldiers.

The Jordanians have made other poor choices that have complicated or delayed the goal of sustainment. Despite the massive financial investment they've made in their F-16 program—which in itself is questionable because it consumes the crushing majority of their FMF money—they have not strongly committed to English language proficiency, which is critical for flight training and all other mission areas. The outcome is that they do not have enough officer students to go through such training.

The same problem arises with border security. Training of JAF infantry battalions for border duty is conducted almost entirely by the US military. Some Jordanian soldiers do serve as trainers, but in the absence of American guardsmen, the training program's effectiveness would dramatically decrease.

One senior US officer with extensive experience in the Middle East and a recent three-year-long deployment in Jordan grimly summarized the shared US-Jordanian predicament: "We're lying to members of Congress every time we tell them the Jordanians can graduate from US assistance or rely less on us. They can't. I know it because I've lived it firsthand. Because even in [the JAF's] pockets of excellence we still have to have close and continuous contact with them, and I don't know how much longer we can sustain this level of support and engagement given our new global priorities."[48]

## Notes

1. Taylor Luck, "U.S., Jordan Stepping Up Training of Syrian Opposition," *Washington Post*, April 2, 2013.

2. Ibrahim Alharahsheh, "Jordanian Contributions to Afghanistan," *UNIPATH*, February 20, 2015; *Jordan Times*, "Military's Afghanistan Mission Completed," January 5, 2015.

3. "Royal Jordanian Air Force at 60," 4Aviation, December 2015, https://www.4aviation.nl/nl/reports/article-royal-jordanian-air-force-at-60/.

4. Agence France-Presse, "Jordan Publicizes Defense Deal That Allows US Forces Free Entry into Kingdom," March 21, 2021.

5. Jeremy M. Sharp, "Jordan: Background and U.S. Relations," Congressional Research Service, June 18, 2020.

6. US Department of State, "U.S. Security Cooperation with Jordan, Fact Sheet," Bureau of Political-Military Affairs, January 20, 2021, https://www.state.gov/u-s-security-cooperation-with-jordan/.

7. Ibid.

8. Human Rights Watch, *Stateless Again: Palestinian-Origin Jordanians Deprived of Their Nationality*, New York, February 1, 2010.

9. Sharp, "Jordan: Background and U.S. Relations."

10. Shaiyla Hakeem, "Jordan, America Launch New Training Cycle," US Central Command, July 26, 2019.

11. Bryan Elliott and Ernest Wang, "U.S. Army and Jordan Armed Forces Continue Partnership Mission Despite COVID-19 Challenges," US Central Command, May 26, 2020.

12. Jumana Kawar, "Jordan: US Security Assistance and Border Defense Capacity Building," Middle East Institute, October 6, 2020; Barbara Opall-Rome, "Raytheon: Arab-Operated Patriots Intercepted over 100 Tactical Ballistic Missiles Since 2015." *Defense News*, November 14, 2017.

13. *UNIPATH*, "Fostering Special Forces: Col. Sufyan Subhi Al Sulaihat Exemplifies Jordan's Commitment to Partnerships and Peacekeeping," October 25, 2019.

14. *Business Insider*, "The World's Special Forces Train at This Base in Jordan," March 31, 2018.

15. Hardin Lang, William Wechsler, and Alia Awadallah, *The Future of U.S.-Jordanian Counterterrorism Cooperation* (Washington, DC: Center for American Progress, November 2017), 15.

16. Defense Security Cooperation Agency, "Jordan—F-16 Air Combat Training Center," Transmittal no. 20-50, February 11, 2021.

17. Marc V. Schanz, "Eager Lion," *Air Force Magazine* (September 2013): 56–64.

18. Author's interview via online communications technology on April 2, 2021.

19. Ibid.

20. Cassandra Vinograd, "Burned Alive: ISIS Video Purports to Show Murder of Jordanian Pilot," *NBC News*, February 3, 2015.

21. Schanz, "Eager Lion," 64.

22. Lucy Fisher, "British Officer Sent Home for Being 'Too Close to King,'" *The Times*, November 11, 2019.

23. Author's interview with an American service member based in Jordan, April 2, 2021. The source spoke on the condition of anonymity due to the sensitive nature of the topic.

24. Joseph Rank and Bill Saba, "Building Partnership Capacity 201: The New Jordan Armed Forces Noncommissioned Officer Corps," *Military Review* (September–October 2014): 24–35.

25. Ibid.

26. Ibid.

27. Samuel J. Philips, "Jordanian NCOs Learn to Be Warrior Leaders," *NCO Journal* 20, no. 6 (June 2011): 35–37.

28. Alan Belser, "Jordanian NCOs Partner with U.S. Instructors," US Central Command, December 20, 2016.

29. Ty McNeeley, "Jordanian, U.S. Partnership Revamps Noncomissioned Officer Training," US Army Central, November 5, 2017.

30. Thomas Crough, "Jordan Implements New NCO Training Program," US Central Command, March 30, 2018.

31. Ibid.

32. Zach Sheeley, "Fortifying the Backbone," Colorado National Guard, August 29, 2018, https://co.ng.mil/News/Archives/Article/1632500/fortifying-the-backbone/.

33. Veronica McNabb, "NCO Exchange Between U.S. Army and Jordan Armed Forces," US Army Central, April 18, 2019.

34. Matthew McGovern, "SNCO Academy Brings First-Ever PME Course to Jordan," US Air Forces Central, July 1, 2019.

35. NATO, "JFC Naples JMTT Conducts Training in Jordan," September 2016, https://jfcnaples.nato.int/newsroom/news/2016/jfc-naples-jmtt-conducts-training-in-jordan/.

36. Oskar Aanmoen, "King Abdullah Opens New Military University College," *Royal Central*, February 3, 2021.

37. Reuters, "Jordan: Royal Military Academy—the Basis of Jordan's Army," October 15, 1971.

38. Author's interview with a Jordanian pilot, April 3, 2021. The source spoke on the condition of anonymity due to the sensitive nature of the conversation.

39. For more on the revolt of the military veterans in Jordan, see Tariq Tell, *Early Spring in Jordan: The Revolt of the Military Veterans* (Beirut: Carnegie Middle East Center, November 4, 2015).

40. Daoud Kuttab, "Jordan Orders Army Conscription for 25–29-year-olds to Help Tackle Unemployment," *Arab News*, September 9, 2020.

41. Ibid.

42. Author's interview with an American service member based in Jordan, April 7, 2021. The source spoke on the condition of anonymity due to the sensitive nature of the topic.

43. Charles Faddis, "Bin Ladin's Location Reveals Limits of Liaison Intelligence Relationships," *CTC Sentinel*, Special Issue (May 2011): 15–16.

44. Mark Huber, "ISG Wins SECDEF Award for Excellence in Maintenance Training, Advice, and Assistance of Foreign Security Forces—Ministerial Category," Institute for Security Governance, November 3, 2020, https://institutefor securitygovernance.org/-/isg-wins-secdef/.

45. Jaccob Hearn, "1st TSC, Jordan Armed Forces Strengthen Partnership Through Logistics Training," US Army, September 25, 2017, https://www.army.mil /article/194343/1st_tsc_jordan_armed_forces_strengthen_partnership_through_logistics _training/.

46. Christopher Bigelow, "Security Enterprise Shares Logistics with Jordan," US Army, March 27, 2017.

47. Author's interview with a US service member based in Jordan who spoke off-the-record, April 1, 2021.

48. Author's interview was conducted off-the-record via online communications technology, April 7, 2021.

# 5

# Lebanon: Working Against All Odds

been among the weakest militaries in the region mainly because the Lebanese have hardly ever wanted a strong army. Societal attitudes have shifted a bit in recent years partly because of the rise of al-Qaeda and the Islamic State in the north,[1] but certainly not enough to seriously challenge the foundations of the country's confessional political makeup, where the deepest loyalties are to the sect rather than to the state. It is these very sectarian passions that traditionally have led the Lebanese to take up arms and have kept them from building either a stable governing structure or a competent army.

That Lebanon has been a deeply penetrated state since its independence from French mandate in 1943 has made the pursuit of military development even more elusive. In the last forty years alone, Syria and Iran have done everything in their power to keep the LAF impotent, subservient to their interests, and unable to shield the country from internal and external threats.

First it was the Syrians' turn, which started when 4,000 of their troops and 250 of their tanks entered Lebanon in 1976 to prevent the spillover of the Lebanese civil war (1975–1990) into Syrian territory, but also to turn their small and beleaguered neighbor into a satellite state.[2] That same year, the LAF disintegrated along sectarian lines, which it would do again in 1984, two years after the Americans began to rebuild it. It would take the Syrian army more than thirteen years to stop most of the bloodshed in Lebanon and force the local antagonists to reach a deal. The 1989 Taif Agreement produced or perhaps imposed a political settlement, but it did not immediately end the civil war. (The Syrian army still had to fight the forces of Lebanese prime minister Gen. Michel Aoun until he fled the country and landed in France in October 1990.) Nor did it address the fundamental flaws of Lebanese power sharing.

Per Taif, the Syrians were supposed to withdraw their troops from Lebanon within two years. However, they stayed for another decade and a half, during which they ran the show in Beirut and effectively co-opted the LAF, turning it into an ally or surrogate mainly responsible for spying on Lebanese society and suppressing any form of domestic opposition to their hegemony. Damascus grossly mistreated the LAF. It forbade it from planning, training, and even socializing with its Arab peers. It also prevented it from playing any meaningful military role during Israel's occupation of southern Lebanon in 1982–2000. Instead, in partnership with the Iranians, the Syrians helped create the Lebanese Shiite group Hezbollah, a parallel military structure they could trust and control, and enabled it to lead a campaign of armed resistance against the Israelis.

Five years after the Israelis withdrew, the Syrians were forced to leave. The assassination of former Lebanese prime minister Rafik Hariri in February 2005, most likely at the hands of the Syria-Iran-Hezbollah axis, created such intense international and domestic pressure against the Syrian regime that it could no longer keep its troops in the country.

For the LAF, freedom from Syrian diktat was a turning point in its history. And while the problem of Hezbollah and Iran's influence remain to this day, challenging the LAF's authority and the Lebanese state's monopoly over the use of force, the departure of the Syrians created an opening for the United States to rekindle its relationship with the LAF after its brief and ineffective involvement in the early to mid-1980s.

Unlike other Arab partners, the LAF has not sent peacekeeping or combat troops in support of US-led missions in the Middle East. It hasn't made economic contributions to US-led operations in the region. And it hasn't trained friendly forces on its territory to combat jihadists. But it has leveraged the $2.2 billion of military assistance it has received from Washington since 2006 by pursuing three goals: modernizing through training of more than 35,000 soldiers and integration of US equipment; countering Sunni jihadists and narco-terrorists on Lebanese soil and protecting the northern borders; and engaging in a credible process of defense reform.

## Goals of US Military Assistance

Washington uses its military assistance program in Lebanon neither to politically support the country's ruler(s), like it does in Amman, for example, nor to secure access, basing, and overflight, like it does in many other Arab countries (although CENTCOM does seek access to some units in the LAF including the SOF). Instead, the overall object of US assistance in Lebanon is to help create over the long run a Lebanese military strong enough to be able to play the role of protector of all Lebanese. Of course, there is a ceiling to such assistance. Washington will never equip the LAF with more powerful conventional weapons in the absence of a peace deal between Lebanon and Israel (a point Hezbollah's leadership frequently uses to disqualify US assistance). Until that changes, the US focus is limited to bolstering the LAF's ability to maintain civil peace and counter the threat posed by al-Qaeda and the Islamic State in the country's northern region.

Although there's nothing unusual or controversial about Washington aiming to strengthen the counterterrorism capabilities of the LAF (this is after all the predominant emphasis of US military assistance to partners across the region), there is something about the Lebanese case that makes it truly unique: America's partnership with the LAF (forged in 1982–1984 and then resumed in 2006) is, at the end of the day, an act of US *deliberate political subversion* largely meant to weaken the influence and authority of US adversaries in Lebanon—the Syrians until 2005, and Hezbollah and Iran since.

Indeed, even though Lebanon has to deal with Sunni jihadists every now and then, the principal security threats about which the United States is concerned are Hezbollah and Iran and to a lesser extent now Syria given its dramatically reduced military capacities. Although the threat of Sunni militancy no doubt is real, the Americans arguably use it as an excuse to stay engaged with the LAF in hope that US military assistance will enable the latter to overtly or covertly address the primary security threats and help Lebanon regain its sovereignty. Any other assessment of US motivations in Lebanon would be naive or, worse, dishonest.

This is not to suggest that US military assistance to Lebanon seeks to empower the LAF to take on Hezbollah militarily. That would be ridiculous and self-defeating. It would be like the United States deciding to build up the regular Iraqi army of the 1990s so that one day it could defeat Saddam's elite Republican Guard. Rather, the United States is modestly and patiently arming and training the LAF because if the issue of Hezbollah's weapons ever were to be settled, through international diplomacy or regional war, the LAF would be ready to assume its national defense responsibilities across the country.

More broadly speaking, Washington supports the LAF because it is the only reliable tool to preserve US influence in Lebanon. If the LAF collapses, the country as a whole most likely will slip under Hezbollah and Iran's grasp altogether, which could trigger another war with Israel. The LAF's fall also allows al-Qaeda and the Islamic State to return and use the country as a base to regroup across the region. And finally, an LAF abandoned by Washington gives the Russians an opportunity to pounce and expand their influence in the Levant and on the shores of the natural gas–rich Eastern Mediterranean.

None of these outcomes is in the interest of the United States.[3] A partnership with the LAF surely will not solve all those problems, but it can avert the worst and help plan for the future, which is the most the United States can hope for.

So if Lebanon's case is so different from what the United States normally does with other Arab partner militaries, why then look at US military assistance in that country when the structural obstacles are so significant, the political environment is so uninviting, the foreign and domestic spoilers are powerful and numerous, and the odds are stacked so high against success? Indeed, why even bother to examine such an extreme case that doesn't really apply to any other US military assistance context in the Arab world? The answer is that it is *precisely because* the Lebanese case is extreme that it is so important for US officials and interesting for military studies scholars. The assumption is that if certain aspects of US military cooperation worked in Lebanon—and some did, as I will show here—then they should have a very good chance of working almost *anywhere*.

## Train and Equip

Compared to the Egyptians, the Jordanians, and even the Bahrainis, the amount of tactical/operational training and equipment the Lebanese have received from the United States over the years is rather insignificant. It is hard to work and do anything meaningful with a partner military when the host nation, as described previously, has this many structural problems and this many nefarious actors.

But the United States, perhaps credulously, gave it a shot in 1982–1984. US officials in the Reagan administration were encouraged by the effectiveness of US military intervention in Lebanon in 1958, which managed at the time to pacify the country and help elect a new Lebanese president. The Americans thought they could repeat their previous success, but perhaps what they failed to realize was that 1982 Lebanon was drastically different from 1958 Lebanon. In 1982, sectarian killing was rampant across the country. Israeli tanks had reached Beirut and besieged the fighters of Palestinian leader Yasser Arafat. The Syrians had boots on the ground. And the Iranians were training terrorists in the Bekaa Valley and getting ready to unleash Hezbollah. Lebanon had lost any semblance of sovereignty or order.[4]

Caught up in this giant mess, the US effort to help rebuild the LAF, analyzed brilliantly by Mara Karlin, was doomed to fail.[5] "We didn't have any choice," said Leslie Brown, then a State Department official, to the *New York Times* in 1984. "The concept was that the success of the whole Lebanese operation was dependent on the successful reconstruction of the Lebanese Army."[6] That the US mission transitioned from peacekeeping to active participation in the civil war on the side of rightist Lebanese factions friendly to Israel ultimately torpedoed everything the Americans were trying to do in the country.

The same forces Washington was bombing from the sea with the help of the battleship *New Jersey* blew up the US embassy in April 1983 and the Marine barracks six months later, killing hundreds of Americans and forcing President Reagan to withdraw US troops from Lebanon in February 1984. (Hezbollah would strike the US embassy again in September of that year and murder twenty-three people.)

In that very short window, Washington sought the impossible: to rebuild the LAF under conditions of total chaos in Lebanon. Funded with US grants and loans worth a little less than $200 million, the Lebanese Army Modernization Program (LAMP) was run from an office in the Lebanese Ministry of Defense and LAF HQ in Yarze by Brig. Gen. Marty Fintel of the US Army.

The LAMP fulfilled some tactical purposes that included the creation of five LAF intervention regiments and a heavy infantry brigade structure.[7] This was not bad given that a Pentagon team that had visited Lebanon in November 1982 had recommended creating seven brigades (ironically, the same suggestion reached by another US survey team that had visited the country in 1978 when Washington first developed an interest in the LAF).[8] But it couldn't go any further and had to be terminated four months after the deadly Marine barracks attack.

The United States wouldn't provide military assistance to the LAF until a quarter of a century later. During those years, the LAF essentially was co-opted by the Syrians. It was a miserable and dilapidated force, with no real mandate other than to follow Syrian orders, which sought to legitimize and codify Syrian domination over Lebanon.

For more than fifteen years, the LAF was massively underfunded. It could not properly train, modernize, or do anything other normal militaries do. Lebanese infantry soldiers fired an abysmal average of ten rounds per year. They had very little fuel and ammunition, few if any spare parts, and no professional training facilities. Most of the LAF's equipment was old and barely usable. It had no modern ISR, no protected mobility, no personal protective gear, and no useful air defense (which it still does not have).

The LAF's air force consisted of a single rotary-wing, US-made UH-1 squadron and a training squadron with commercial helicopters. In other words, the LAF had no functional fighter planes. The LAF's navy looked and functioned more like a coast guard, and a tiny and underdeveloped one no less. Equipped with simple patrol boats that could barely deal with terrorist and criminal threats, its main duties were and still are coastal security and maritime search and rescue.

The LAF's logistics system was a total disaster, severely hampered by bureaucratic stovepiping and the lack of automated supply, accountability procedures, operational budget, inventory control, stockage levels, and transportation capabilities. The LAF also had no intermediate or regional level of logistic support for training and combat operations.

Human capital was another major weakness. With its top-heavy rank structure, the LAF had more brigadier generals, colonels, and senior lieutenant colonels than it needed, and it had no clue how to maintain its strength and deployments. Its ability to manage the administrative affairs of the defense ministry and the basic needs of the Lebanese soldier was dreadful.

All these problems and many more were on full display in 2007 when the LAF, a force of some 45,000 at the time, was asked to evict hundreds of radical Islamic militants from the Nahr al-Bared Palestinian refugee camp in the north. The LAF entered the conflict with little ability to plan, train, shoot, and move, let alone maneuver, see, and communicate. Its structure, built mostly by the Americans in the 1980s and tailored for a heavier force, was not conducive to special operations and counterinsurgency warfare. Its command-and-control capabilities were completely inadequate, as Yarze directly controlled tactical units without any intermediate headquarters to reduce the span of control. And finally, its tactical units' communications systems were not secure or compatible with those of other agencies in the Lebanese government.

Unable to quickly root out the insurgents, the conflict in Nahr al-Bared turned into a war of attrition, which the Lebanese could not afford. The LAF depleted almost half of its total ammunition stocks barely a week into the fifteen-week battle. International friends including the United States had to provide plane-loads of ammunition, night-vision goggles, and antitank missiles to help the LAF sustain its operations. In the end, the LAF prevailed, but not without suffering considerable losses—174 Lebanese soldiers killed—and only after almost totally destroying the camp.

When the United States decided to return to Lebanon and resume ties with the LAF soon after the departure of the Syrians in 2005, it knew it had a ton of holes to plug. It needed to provide the LAF with a considerable infusion of funds, expertise, manpower, and equipment over at least three five-year cycles so it could function as a modern and capable military.

To get this all going, US officials established a Joint Military Commission (JMC) in 2008. Typically led by the assistant secretary of defense for international security affairs on the American side and the minister of defense (or the LAF commander) on the Lebanese side, the JMC—the first then in what would be an annual series of meetings that continues to this day—was the main vehicle through which the defense relationship between the two countries was restored.

The 2008 JMC focused on all-inclusive training with the LAF, US weapons releases, interoperability, and US funding. During the meeting in Beirut, then-LAF commander Jean Kahwagi bluntly told the US delegation something US officials hardly ever hear from other Arab partners: "I don't want to ask you for lists of equipment. Our main mission is to fight terrorism, defend the borders, and help the people of Lebanon. It is for these reasons that I need to modernize and transform the army to accomplish these tasks."[9] This inclination to temper expectations and eschew prestigious military hardware and unsustainable paths to military modernization would continue to serve the LAF well and guide its approach.

Since 2008, and especially since the 2014 rise of the Islamic State in the region, the United States has sought to develop the capabilities of the LAF in three main areas: land and maritime border security, counterterrorism and counternarcotics, and combined arms. The primary goal behind the border security program is to enable the LAF to effectively deploy land border regiments (LBRs) along the Syrian border and secure the country's territorial waters and exclusive economic zone. The US focus with respect to LAF counterterrorism and counternarcotics is to help turn Lebanese SOF into an elite unit capable of rapidly responding to security threats and detaining weapons and drug smugglers supporting Sunni terrorists. As for combined arms, which is a capability that serves all of these missions, the desired outcome is a Lebanese military able to integrate at least some of its ground and air assets and use them simultaneously and proficiently in combat operations.

To help meet these objectives, since 2006 the United States has shipped various weapons to the LAF—worth more than $1.5 billion— and helped Lebanese soldiers train on those weapons both in Lebanon and in the United States. In addition, the US military has worked with the LAF to enhance interoperability among its various branches and shared best practices on effective kinetic and information operations.

For example, in recent years, US military transfers to Lebanon have included 3 Huey II multimission helicopters valued at $32 million (making it a LAF fleet of 15); command, control, communications, computers, intelligence, surveillance, and reconnaissance (C4ISR) tools for the establishment of a national C4ISR node and a national training and operations center; 50 armored high-mobility multipurpose vehicles (also called Humvees); 40 M198 howitzers; Cessna aircraft armed with Hellfire missiles; 55 mortar systems; 50 automatic grenade launchers; 1,100 machine guns, including 800 50-caliber machine guns; 4,000 M4 rifles; over 0.5 million rounds of ammunition; 320 night-vision devices and thermal sights; and 360 secure communication radios.[10]

Of all the American equipment provided to the LAF, the MD 530G light attack helicopters, the A-29 Super Tucano strike aircraft, and the Bradley infantry fighting vehicles are the most expensive, the most sophisticated, and the most powerful, which means they will require the greatest amount of training and will be the most difficult to sustain. The Bradleys in particular will constitute the biggest burden for the LAF in the coming years. This machine is a versatile and highly maneuverable weapon that is suitable for counterinsurgency operations. Yet despite its advantages, the Bradley is a sophisticated combat system that costs a lot to sustain, which is money heavily indebted Lebanon simply does not have.[11] The LAF never wanted these complex and expensive vehicles—but got them anyway because that's what the Americans thought the Lebanese needed or because the US Army had an excess of those vehicles in its inventory—but now it has thirty-two of them and needs a ton of help from the United States to effectively train for, logistically support, and maintain them.

The MD 530G helicopter is planned to replace the Gazelle and will be used by the Lebanese air force; various LAF SOF, land border, and intervention regiments; infantry brigades; and the navy. Although it is a relatively smaller chopper than, say, a Black Hawk, it has cutting-edge technology that uses advanced communications and delivers impressive maneuverability along with precise firepower—tools or assets with which the LAF does not have much familiarity and experience.

Whenever the six new helicopters are delivered[12] (six others are expected to follow in a few years, making it a fleet of twelve),[13] they will cause anxiety and heartburn in LAF HQ given the huge amount of work that will be required across the DOTMLPF-P to absorb them. This work includes the creation of new TTPs and a life-cycle sustainment assessment for the helicopters' advanced capabilities, which include night-vision devices, video downlink, and communications devices.[14]

A slightly more manageable but still challenging new platform is the Super Tucano plane, of which the LAF now has six (though it has yet to use in real-life combat operations). Like the MD 530G, these strike aircraft are ideal for counterinsurgency operations—and thus are a perfect fit for the LAF—because of their speed, versatility, and ability to employ precision weapons. But they also have hefty training and combat requirements for fuel and ammunition, which the United States is helping the LAF meet.

Some of the more complex training exercises between Lebanese and American soldiers have taken place in the United States. For example, in March 2021, Lebanese pilots completed the first of three training classes on the MD 530 helicopters in Mesa, Arizona, to learn how to fly and maintain these aircraft.[15]

In Lebanon and other countries in the region, NAVCENT and the LAF Navy have conducted an annual, bilateral exercise called Resolute Response since 2016. The drill is meant to enhance the navy's capabilities in explosive ordnance disposal, diving exercises, and maritime vessel visit, board, search, and seizure procedures.

For years, US Marines have shared specialized knowledge with the LAF on urban terrain tactics gained from experiences in Iraq and Afghanistan.[16] US SOF units deployed in Lebanon as part of Special Operations Command Central (SOCCENT) have conducted a program of instruction with their Lebanese counterparts based on the US Army John F. Kennedy Special Warfare Center and School's Instructor Training Course.[17] And US service personnel recently helped the LAF come up with a new Army Operating Concept that codifies the LAF's army, navy, air force, and SOF missions.

## Institutional Capacity Building

Although the 2008 JMC focused on tactical and operational matters, it had an element of defense institution building that addressed the LAF's absorptive capacity and ability to plan and effectively execute its modernization.[18] This US commitment to institutional capacity building with the LAF would mature over the years, focusing since 2014 on strategic planning; acquisition and budget; human capital development; assessment, monitoring, and evaluation; force posture planning and development; and logistics.

### Strategic Planning

It's hard for the LAF to conduct strategic planning when Lebanon as a whole does not have a national security or defense strategy. Since Syria's military withdrawal in 2005, Lebanese politicians have broached the idea of formulating a national defense strategy, but they have failed to make any progress on this issue.

Hezbollah, for one, has no interest in this conversation. For the Shiite group, there is only one national defense formula that it finds acceptable— one that retains its military autonomy and supports a trilateral structure composed of the "resistance" (in other words, Hezbollah itself), the Lebanese people, and the Lebanese army. Of course, this construct flies in the face of state sovereignty and unity of command because it endorses the coexistence of two parallel military forces in Lebanon, one (the LAF) overseen by and accountable to elected national representatives and another (Hezbollah) answering to no one but Iran. The LAF has had to work around the contentious issue of Hezbollah's arms for years and do what it can to execute its own planning and reform processes with no guidance from a divided Lebanese political class and minimal support from an economically bankrupt Lebanese state.

To overcome the absence of a national defense strategy, the LAF's G5 planning unit has sought with the benefit of US advice to map out a reverse process for strategic planning that defines the LAF's national military strategy from bottom to top. Such planning describes the LAF's objectives and assigns resources (budget, human resources, equipment, facilities, technology, etc.) based on the Lebanese army commander's vision and the defense tasks prescribed by the Lebanese Supreme Defense Council.

American advisers have helped the LAF come up with an official document that lays out a comprehensive, five-year plan for capability development (to be revised or updated after each cycle). The current 2018–2022 LAF Capability Development Plan (CDP)[19] describes the key threats to Lebanon's security, identifies the primary missions to address the threats, and prioritizes the necessary capabilities to fulfill those missions.

Endorsed by Lebanon's prime minister and prepared by the LAF deputy chief of staff for planning, the CDP informs the LAF's modernization on the basis of actual needs rather than preferences. To execute this plan, the LAF established with the help of American advisers a joint capability review process, which is a systematic approach to identify priorities and apply national and donor resources and, consequently, use US assistance effectively to build its military capabilities.[20]

A vital corresponding effort, also benefiting from US guidance, is a strategic planning process that allows the LAF to look at potential futures, likely responses to those futures, and operational challenges that may result from those responses.[21] This is an ongoing investment that is continuously refined.

### Acquisition and Budget

Since 2008, the United States has worked with the LAF on improving its budgeting abilities. The LAF now populates a database that seeks to collect costs for various capabilities and for employment of such capabilities (for example, the costs per flying hour for the Cessna Armed Caravan fixed-wing aircraft).[22] These cost data can be helpful for budgeting for future capabilities.

US assistance also has enabled the LAF's reforms of its acquisition, procurement, contracting, and budgeting processes.[23] This has required the formation of an acquisition committee, led by an LAF brigadier general, to oversee the implementation of important goals, including increasing delegation, using automation, developing and referring to metrics, speeding up the processing of letters of request, and improving time management and decision processes of the LAF deputy chief of staff for equipment (G4 unit).[24]

US guidance has taught the LAF how to be smart with its acquisitions, economize where possible, prioritize maintenance, plan for sustainment, and undergo a full-cycle capability development process (except for the Bradley infantry fighting vehicle, which has been forced on the Lebanese despite knowing the major sustainment challenges this capability would bring to an already under-resourced LAF).

### Human Capital Development

The LAF has made substantial improvements in HRM (G5 planning unit) over the years. Thanks to US technical help, it now has proper job description and qualification documents for LAF personnel, which has helped it place the most qualified, available personnel in relevant positions and establish an understanding of expectations between leaders and subordinates.[25]

LAF policies of HRM are mostly based on the tenure of soldiers and civilian employees in service, exam and course results, seniority, discipline, physical fitness test results, medals, decorations, congratulations and commendations, and commanding officer evaluation and assessment. With the help of US advisers, G5 has sought to reorganize its Planning for Personnel Directorate to restructure the existing HRM system and policies in the LAF and to ensure that they are consistently applied on the basis of specific and strict merit criteria. LAF G5 also has worked on developing strategies for talent management and career development in recruitment, promotion, rewards, motivation, and performance management to make sure soldiers and civilian employees with the proper qualifications and experiences are assigned to the appropriate position and are rewarded according to their performance.

US specialists have assisted in the development of educational documents and courses for the LAF Fouad Chehab Academy for Command and General Staff so Lebanese officers can increase their knowledge in strategic, operational, and technical fields.[26] In addition to the Chehab Academy, the LAF has a Military Academy for the Army; two specialized schools, one for the air force and one for the navy; an NCO School; and an NCO Training Institute. These entities, initially modeled after the French system but increasingly US-shaped with American methods of training, offer courses including NCO basic course, officers' basic course, company commander course, battalion commander course, staff course, pilot officer course, and surface warfare officer course.

Lebanon's military schools are acceptable compared to their Arab peers. Lebanese cadets and officers with more junior grades (O-1 through O-3) don't necessarily have to attend Arab or Western military schools to receive their education. Field grade officers (O-4 through O-6) seek higher level training in the United States.

Indeed, the LAF relies on the United States for much of its personnel's specialized training, career development, and professional military education. It sends around 1,000 students each year to participate in US school and training programs. Those who participate in courses in the United States fill roles as instructors for LAF courses when they return to Lebanon, thus proliferating US concepts, principles, and practices.[27]

The Lebanese air force, in particular, has had all of its senior personnel and officers attend US military schools. The impact of the LAF participating in the State Department's IMET program is evident as LAF force development and employment approaches are modeled after US doctrine.[28] With regard to NCO leadership training, Lebanese NCOs have attended various US Army–organized symposiums in the United States and in the region to learn about the roles and responsibilities of NCOs in the military.[29]

### Assessment, Monitoring, and Evaluation

The LAF has benefited for years from US input on how to better track and report unit readiness. Military operational requirements necessitate that the LAF track its readiness, gauge shortfalls, and assess the associated risks. The LAF is now able to pursue these activities more efficiently and send its reports daily through the chain of command.

These reports include assessments of personnel, training, and equipment, which are tracked by the LAF G1, G3, and G4 units, respectively. The G5 planning unit assesses and analyzes those reports, identifies the gaps, and formulates the necessary plans in order to implement critical resourcing decisions and acquire what is needed in accordance with the LAF's vision and doctrine.

Moreover, the LAF can now implement a yearly evaluation process of its operational units through evaluation committees. These committees apply objective and centralized means and standards for tracking, assessing, and evaluating units' operational performance and readiness.

The LAF also has been able to leverage US education and develop technical specifications for patrol carriers and main battle tanks. In addition, it has made progress toward identifying activities across the range of DOTMLPF-P that are essential for the proper integration of new equipment.[30]

### Force Posture Planning and Development

Informed by US doctrine and conducted by the LAF's G3 operations unit, Lebanese force posture planning has effectively incorporated American advice and designed a posture that can evolve to meet the changing operational requirements over the long run but also adapt to meet the urgent demands of current crises and contingencies. In recent years, the security requirements in Lebanon have become more functionally and geographically dispersed. At one end of the spectrum, the LAF is expected to preserve internal security and maintain civil peace, while at the other it is responsible for guarding the Lebanese borders. One of the products of the LAF's reformed force posture planning is the creation of four new LBRs in 2009 with the help of the United States and the UK.

## Logistics

LAF logistics has witnessed modest improvement over the years thanks to recent US attempts to upgrade the system. In the past, LAF logistics processes were almost all paper-based and poorly documented. This made effective equipment management and efficient inventory distribution elusive.

Most of the LAF's military facilities are outdated and inadequately sized to the force, with some established in the 1940s and 1950s. The newly built ones better meet the force's requirements, but they remain too few. The goal now and into the foreseeable future is to ensure better quality spare parts, a better workforce in the LAF Logistics Brigade, more training opportunities, and better repair equipment, all of which will require time, commitment, and persistent funding.[31]

LAF leadership recognizes that its logistics system requires a total rethink and redesign. Through a recently formed logistics committee, American as well as Canadian advisers have helped the LAF Logistics Brigade and Records Directorate assess, analyze, and plan for present and future needs (the planning part has been most challenging because no one has ever engaged in logistics planning in the history of the LAF).[32]

Last but not least is LAF ammunition management, which is a major liability for the LAF. The LAF struggles in estimating annual ammunition needs to support training and operations. Its current estimates appear too large, which is causing the LAF to acquire more ammunition than it requires. The LAF very much could use a supply chain management of the ammunition system, and along with US advisers, it is looking at European Union models that might be relevant.[33]

## Outcomes

Given America's catastrophic legacy in Lebanon in the 1980s and the tiny Levantine nation's chronic, systemic chaos, what the United States has been able to accomplish with the LAF of late is nothing short of miraculous. Within a decade, the United States essentially was able to transform the LAF from a decrepit force mocked by all its regional peers to a professional military that has earned the respect of CENTCOM's leadership. In the annals of US military assistance around the world, the Lebanese case should be recorded as a clear win.

Years of LAF partnership with the US military have generated tangible returns. For example, the LAF has been able since 2018 to exercise greater control over its border with Syria and deploy along the Hezbollah-dominated southern frontier, in support of UN Security

Council Resolution 1701. This is a first in Lebanon's history. Likewise, the LAF has made much progress in limiting the large and international drug trade in the north, with its SOF elements conducting like never before complex raids in recent years against high-value narco-terrorists operating in the Bekaa Valley.

But there's no question that the most remarkable fruit of the US train-and-equip program in Lebanon over the past decade is the LAF's 2017 Fajr al-Jouroud operation against the Islamic State. Of course, it would be incorrect to attribute all the LAF's tactical and operational success in Fajr al-Jouroud to US military aid. But it also would be foolish and dishonest not to view such assistance as a major factor in the LAF's impressive military performance.

In 2013, the Islamic State started to establish an insurgent presence along Lebanon's northeastern frontier. By the summer of 2014, it had increased its foothold and taken over Arsal, a border town that sheltered several thousands of Syrian refugees and rebels. From there, it waged attacks against Lebanese army positions, kidnapping and killing dozens of soldiers. For the next three years, the terrorist army would become a more serious threat to Lebanon's northern region.

On August 17, 2017, Operation Fajr al-Jouroud was born (although technically only the final phase of the battle was given that name). Unlike in Nahr al-Bared, this time the LAF was much better prepared on all three levels of war—strategic, operational, and tactical—in large part thanks to US training, guidance, and advice.

Washington had learned from the mistakes of its past experience in the country. CENTCOM totally changed the structure of the LAF, transforming it from a heavy force that was not cut out for a counterinsurgency mission to a lighter, faster, and more special forces–centric army. This time, the LAF had serious teeth and specifically air power, courtesy of the United States. This time, it would take the Lebanese a little more than a week to defeat their opponent, and they would do it with minimal casualties and in a way that impressed their senior American partners. Although Lebanese troops did all the fighting, the Americans were with them every step of the way, planning, brainstorming, and rehearsing together before the start of combat operations, and providing various forms of nonkinetic support during battle.

The LAF's initial idea was to begin operations in the summer of 2018. But that date had to be moved back by a year due to an unannounced, joint Hezbollah-Syrian army operation against al-Qaeda-affiliated fighters operating east of the Lebanese town of Arsal. This planning hiccup notwithstanding, the LAF was still able to rehearse

aggressively for its offensive for more than twenty days in mountainous and rugged terrain to mimic to the extent possible the movements
necessary on the battlefield.

A couple of weeks into August, the LAF's planning, informed by US
military advice, was complete for an operation of five phases, each of
which would be preceded by heavy preparatory fires targeting enemy
positions. The LAF established three separate tactical operations centers,
each commanded by a designated task force commander. The operations
task force comprised the Air Assault Regiment, the First Intervention
Regiment, and the Sixth Brigade, all equipped with US weapons.

If LAF artillery was king in Nahr al-Bared, US-enabled air power,
along with SOF, was dominant in Fajr al-Jouroud. Indeed, it would have
been virtually impossible for the LAF to destroy the Islamic State's
hardened positions and heavy weapons depots without having the ability to apply substantial and laser-guided firepower from the air, especially in the final phase of the campaign. In preparation for battle, the
Lebanese air force, whose pilots had been training in the United States,
flew 12,000 flight hours over a period of two years to gather high-qual-
ity intelligence on enemy locations, capabilities, and supply routes. For
more than a week, the LAF used both its fixed-wing and its rotary-wing
aircraft—141 flight hours to be precise—to pound the enemy. The
LAF's Cessna planes were equipped with precision-guided Hellfire missiles, which the United States made sure to augment in the months leading up to the operation. The Puma and Gazelle helicopters were
assigned with the task of amplifying close air support.

Yet of all the weapons employed by the LAF in Fajr al-Jouroud, the
laser-guided Copperhead artillery shells were most lethal and effective.
Delivered by the LAF's howitzers and Cessnas, the US-supplied bombs
did a number on the insurgents, destroying both moving and stationary
targets. (The LAF learned how to use the bombs through six months of
training with the US military prior to the operation.)

Fires coordination was key. Synchronized joint fire support was
established by assigning separate shooting tasks to forces operating
from the air and on the ground. Direct fire support, featuring artillery
and mortars, was provided by Battalion 65 companies, while general
fire support, which is of a longer-range nature, was led by Battalion 95
companies, along with some from the First and Second Field Artillery
Regiments and Second Intervention Regiment. Such coordination and
integration of fires worked reasonably well and helped prevent fratri-
cide (the accidental killing of Lebanese soldiers) and economize ammunition, in part thanks to proficient tactical command and control.

ISR capabilities, almost entirely built with US assistance and Scan Eagle equipment, allowed for accurate enemy target identification and poststrike battle damage assessments. The enemy had no place to hide and was constantly on the run, which severely hampered its movement, planning, and operations. Comprehensive and 24/7 visibility, aided by night-vision technology, allowed the LAF to counter nighttime infiltrations by the insurgents of military bases and positions, especially in the region of Dhour al-Khanzir. Multiple ISR feeds were broadcast through full-motion-video screens to the Lebanese Ministry of Defense and forward operations centers, which allowed for effective tactical command and control.

Logistics was a considerable improvement as well, the planning for which started jointly with the US military weeks prior to the beginning of the operation. The LAF's Logistics Brigade was regularly moving ammunition and maintaining equipment, providing the troops with fuel, food, and water and identifying medical evacuation routes. They also ensured relatively adequate weapons storage.[34]

According to LAF estimates, the battle started with a 95 percent military readiness level of the armored vehicles and the logistics units. Medical support throughout the battle was proficient. Forward-deployed medical teams assisted wounded soldiers and when necessary transported them to operational hospitals in Ras Baalbek, Al Qaa, and Arsal. Medical support was based in Wadi Humayyid, which was only three miles away from the fighting, and as the battle moved so did the medical team.

In terms of information operations, unlike in Nahr al-Bared, the LAF performed a lot better in the area of messaging. Following US nudging and advice, they proactively reached out to the local media and engaged the Lebanese population through daily press conferences. As they cleared areas from Islamic State control, Lebanese soldiers simultaneously provided humanitarian assistance for the villages of Arsal, Laboueh, and Al Qaa, and the LAF Orientation Directorate effectively communicated their activities on the ground to domestic audiences to maintain local, village support, which remained strong throughout the battle.

Lastly, communications in Fajr al-Jouroud were heaps and bounds better than in Nahr al-Bared. The LAF came up with a plan weeks prior to the onset of fighting that included the installment of fixed base stations at higher altitudes in the mountains as well as the employment of US-provided frequency-hopping technology that transmits radio signals quickly and securely.

As impressive as the LAF's accomplishments in Fajr al-Jouroud are, they should not obscure the fact that there was limited direct and sustained fire engagement with the enemy (the first direct contact took place during preparatory fires on August 15 as the First Intervention Regiment was moving northeast to destroy Islamic State positions). This was due to two things. First, the LAF had powerful standoff capabilities (air-to-surface and surface-to-surface fires and snipers) that prevented the insurgents from standing their ground. Second, the modus operandi of the enemy centered on hit-and-run tactics and suicide operations.

After nine days of deliberate maneuver, the LAF was prepared for a final assault into the last Islamic State–held position, to begin the morning of August 27.[35] However, the Lebanese government instructed the LAF to execute a cease-fire to allow for an information exchange with the enemy regarding the fate of ten missing Lebanese soldiers. During that cease-fire, the Islamic State was able to negotiate a separate deal with Hezbollah and the Syrian army that provided the surviving insurgents and their families safe passage via a bus to Deir Ezzor in Syria. This escape robbed the LAF of a decisive victory, which was arguably Hezbollah's preference all along.

The LAF's strategic achievement against the Islamic State in 2017 profoundly undermined the predominant narrative among many Lebanese of the Lebanese army being too weak and unable to assume its national defense duties. For the Americans and especially Congress who authorizes funding for foreign partner militaries, Fajr al-Jouroud underscored the importance and fruits of Lebanon's security partnership with the United States.

While nothing speaks success like battlefield prowess, a giant feat of Washington's military assistance program in Lebanon, though hard to measure, is the drastic change of culture in the LAF.[36] American trainers and advisers have taught the LAF how to think more strategically, collaborate more freely, and share information more effectively. Unlike in the past, there is an increased sense of togetherness in the LAF, as evidenced by the proliferation of committees, cells, and workshops, some joint, working on solving *collective* problems.

This new open and cooperative culture has developed organically. In other words, it has not been imposed by LAF Commander Gen. Joseph Aoun or any of his predecessors. LAF leadership has encouraged delegation and decentralization (especially in the area of logistics decision-making), which is typically uncommon among the rigidly hierarchical Arab militaries.[37]

What explains this relative success? There isn't a silver bullet, but several factors have played important roles. First, the LAF has had the right *attitude* toward learning and getting better. It has been an eager listener, willing to absorb US information and advice like a sponge, adopt an open-book policy, share sensitive information, and engage in honest discussions about difficult tactical, operational, and political issues. Not many Arab partners are as candid and trustworthy as the LAF.

To be sure, it hasn't been flawless. One issue, possibly rooted in culture, is the general inability of LAF personnel to recognize problems that are generating costs. The Americans often have to point them out for them. The LAF's passivity and satisfaction with oftentimes a sub-optimal status quo has stood in the way of more deliberate and aggressive reform. Its leadership is open to constructive criticism and receptive to change, but it isn't proactive.

Second, the LAF appreciates its limitations and sets realistic goals. Unlike other Arab partners, it has not been drawn into acquiring the large, sophisticated, and expensive US equipment. It has emphasized military hardware it can more easily use and sustain. Successive LAF commanders since 2005 have been explicit in their desire to keep the force relatively small and SOF-oriented to avoid unmanageable growth.

Perhaps if the LAF had serious money, its own or Washington's, it would have behaved like the Saudis or the Jordanians and splurged. But none of this is relevant because the bottom line is that it does not, and likely never will, have sufficient financial resources. This kind of realism and humility of the LAF is a breath of fresh air for the United States, who often has a hard time dealing with needy and impractical Arab partners when it comes to acquisition.

Third, the LAF has managed to distance itself to some degree from the country's toxic politics. This is huge not only for the LAF but also for Washington. It means that both sides have some flexibility to make important decisions and pursue a military restructuring process without being at the mercy of corrupt, inexperienced, and interfering politicians.

It's not like the LAF is an island, unaffected by the country's systemic challenges, but the fact that it has been able, thanks to continuous US material and political sponsorship, to create some level of autonomy and somewhat shield itself from the constant factionalism and paralysis in Beirut is enormously helpful for Washington. This at least gives the US-LAF partnership *a chance* to succeed. On the other hand, there are costs to this relative freedom from the Lebanese political process, as the LAF is denied any meaningful financial support or strategic guidance from civilian leadership, but such is the environment in which the LAF has had to operate for many years and to which it has gotten accustomed.

This acute dependency of the LAF on Washington naturally presents a challenge, just like it does with the Jordanian military. More than 85 percent of external grants and loans for the LAF come from the United States. Whether the same levels of US support to the LAF can be sustained in the future is unclear, given the unpredictable fiscal realities in Washington and the shifting US strategic environment, which has deemphasized US military investments in the Middle East. So, as fruitful and promising as Washington's partnership with the LAF has been, it is very unlikely that the latter can survive should the former terminate or drastically reduce its military assistance.

## Notes

1. Florence Dixon, "'We Are All Lebanese': Emotional Soldiers Break into Tears After Being Told to Confront Protesters," *New Arab*, October 23, 2019.

2. David Ignatius, "How to Rebuild Lebanon," *Foreign Affairs* 61, no. 5 (Summer 1983): 146.

3. Bilal Y. Saab, "Washington Should Back, Not Punish, the Lebanese Military," *Foreign Policy*, November 5, 2019.

4. Bilal Y. Saab, "The Lebanese Army Needs Cash," *Foreign Policy*, June 18, 2021.

5. Mara E. Karlin, *Building Militaries in Fragile States: Challenges for the United* States (Philadelphia: University of Pennsylvania Press, 2019).

6. Joel Brinkley, "The Collapse of Lebanon's Army: U.S. Aid to Ignore Factionalism," *New York Times*, March 11, 1984.

7. Beirut Embassy, "Lebanon: Inaugural Joint Military Commission," Cable 08BEIRUT1497_a, WikiLeaks, October 20, 2008, https://wikileaks.org/plusd/cables/08BEIRUT1497_a.html.

8. Brinkley, "Collapse of Lebanon's Army."

9. Beirut Embassy, "Lebanon: Inaugural Joint Military Commission."

10. Fergus Kelly, "Lebanon Army Receives 8 Bradley Fighting Vehicles from the US," *Defense Post*, August 4, 2018.

11. Sebastien Roblin, "The Army Decided to Replace Bradley Fighting Vehicles 17 Years and $22b Ago. They Still Don't Have a Prototype," *NBC News*, February 13, 2020.

12. Chyrine Mezher, "Lebanon: Donated Helicopters Highlight Close, Continuing US Ties," *Breaking Defense*, March 18, 2021.

13. Agnes Helou, "Lebanese Air Force Commander on Expanding the Light-Attack Fleet," *Defense News*, July 3, 2019.

14. Author's interview with a CENTCOM staff member, August 7, 2019, Tampa, Florida. The source spoke on the condition of anonymity due to the sensitive nature of the topic.

15. *Frag Out! Magazine*, "Lebanese Air Force Completes First MD 530F Helicopters Training Class," March 17, 2021.

16. Michael Stevens, "FAST Marines Train with Lebanese Armed Forces," US Central Command, May 6, 2010.

17. Michael Foote, "Operationalizing Strategic Policy in Lebanon," *Special Warfare* 25, no. 2 (April–June 2012): 31–34.

18. Ibid.; WikiLeaks Cable, "Lebanon: Scene Setter for CENTCOM Commander General David Petraeus," November 28, 2008.

19. Author's interview with an American adviser involved in the US military assistance program in Lebanon, August 27, 2020, Washington, DC. The source spoke on the condition of anonymity due to the sensitive nature of the topic.

20. Author's interview with a staff member in the State Department, August 12, 2020, Washington, DC. The source spoke on the condition of anonymity due to the sensitive nature of the topic.

21. Author's interview with an American adviser involved in the US military assistance program in Lebanon, August 27, 2020, Washington, DC. The source spoke on the condition of anonymity due to the sensitive nature of the topic.

22. Ibid.

23. Ibid.

24. Ibid.

25. Ibid.

26. Ibid.

27. Author's interview with an analyst in the State Department, August 27, 2020, Washington, DC. The source spoke on the condition of anonymity due to the sensitive nature of the topic.

28. Author's interview with an LAF officer, July 3, 2019, Yarze, Lebanon. The source spoke on the condition of anonymity due to the sensitive nature of the topic.

29. Benjamin Gable, "Senior NCOs from CENTCOM Nations Meet," US Army, August 9, 2010; Leon Cook, "Enlisted Leaders from CENTCOM Region Countries Discuss Role of NCO in Today's Military," US Central Command, June 8, 2015.

30. Author's interview with an American adviser involved in the US military assistance program in Lebanon, June 22, 2020, Washington, DC. The source spoke on the condition of anonymity due to the sensitive nature of the topic.

31. Ibid.

32. Ibid.

33. Ibid.

34. Overall, the LAF's logistics and supply chain management still had gaps and suffered from inefficiencies. At various stages in Fajr al-Jouroud, the LAF appeared to rely on donations of food and fuel from the local population to sustain the fighting. LAF logistics required significant administrative support from the Lebanese Ministry of Defense, which was in short supply.

35. Author's interview with an American adviser involved in the US military assistance program in Lebanon, August 12, 2020, Washington, DC. The source spoke on the condition of anonymity due to the sensitive nature of the topic.

36. Author's interview with an American adviser involved in the US military assistance program in Lebanon, August 27, 2020, Washington, DC. The source spoke on the condition of anonymity due to the sensitive nature of the topic.

37. Ibid.

# 6

# The United Arab Emirates: Breaking New Ground

THE UAE ARMED FORCES ARE CONSIDERED THE ARAB WORLD'S most competent, with only Israel and possibly Turkey ahead of them in the entire Middle East.[1] Some of the more elite units of the Emirati military may even be superior to those of Ankara and several mid-sized NATO countries.

How this tiny nation of roughly one million Emirati nationals, which achieved its independence from Britain only five decades ago and formed a unified army as recently as the late 1990s, has been able to fast-track its military modernization and to a large extent elude the trend of Arab military ineffectiveness continues to both excite and befuddle many in Washington.[2] The UAE's relatively rapid and outstanding military ascension raises a few important US policy questions that could impact how Washington views and handles its military assistance in the region.

First, why have the Emiratis been able to leverage US military assistance better than any other Arab partner? Are there any US lessons that can be gleaned from the UAE example and potentially applied in other US military assistance cases in the Arab world?

Second, how were the Emiratis able to fight so proficiently in Yemen, and *for several years*, despite suffering from considerable defense institutional capacity deficits? Is good defense governance overrated, after all?

## Goals of US Military Assistance

US military assistance in the UAE serves four main US goals: (1) maintain a close relationship with the UAE leadership and influence their decisionmaking in ways that contribute to US interests; (2) ensure some level of military access in a country whose vast oil and gas reserves and whose expeditionary military capabilities allow it to punch well above its weight and play an influential role in the region and beyond; (3) support the US economy through sizable weapons sales to Abu Dhabi; and (4) enable the UAE military to counter transnational terrorism, deter Iranian conventional aggression, and operate in coalition with the United States.

## Train and Equip

Washington has been equipping the UAE with some of the most powerful weapons in the US arsenal for more than two decades. (Although the status of the sale of Reaper drones and F-35 fifth-generation stealth fighters is unclear at the time of writing due to Emirati concerns over US-imposed operational restrictions, the United States confirmed in December 2021 that it was ready to proceed with the transfer process.)[3] The F-16 Block 60 platform, purchased by the Emiratis in the late 1990s, even has features more advanced than those on similar planes flown by American pilots.

It is not just sophisticated hardware that Washington provides to the UAE. The armed forces of both countries train routinely and conduct some of the most credible joint exercises on land, in the air, and at sea to ensure interoperability, enhance preparedness, and build trust. In addition, American and Emirati soldiers fought together in Afghanistan, Somalia, Bosnia-Kosovo, Libya, Syria, and Iraq.

It is remarkable how US-UAE military cooperation has been so effective despite the fact that, compared to other Arab partners, the UAE is not the most generous or flexible when it comes to granting access to the US military. The United States has 3,500–5,000 troops deployed in the UAE, yet it does not have military organizations permanently stationed in the country and devoted to engaging directly and consistently with Emirati political and military personnel, like USMTM, OPM-SANG, and MOI-MAG do in Saudi Arabia, for example.

Also, unlike with Jordan and Lebanon, Washington does not have comprehensive capability development programs with the UAE military. Nor does it have American advisers embedded in Abu Dhabi's national security bureaucracy, like it has in Riyadh, for example.

The United States does not have those official mechanisms of military cooperation with the UAE because this is how the Emiratis prefer things to be, for now at least. As close as the US-UAE security partnership is, and as determined as the Emiratis are to further develop defense ties with Washington, this Arab partner guards its secrets, sovereignty, and autonomy more jealously than most others (the Egyptians being notorious in that department).

This partly explains why there is no long-term basing agreement between the United States and the UAE, and why the Emirati leadership imposes restrictions and limitations on US troops operating on their country's soil. (There is also a legal and practical challenge: each emirate in the UAE federal state has different laws and processes, which makes rules regarding US military movements outside of Abu Dhabi less clear or predictable.)

When it comes to US military assistance, the Emiratis insist on shaping it to suit their own interests. And they are quite good at it. They listen to US advice and are eager to learn, but ultimately they pick the weapons they want to buy from Washington, and then they seize every opportunity presented to them to robustly train on those systems with the Americans.

Very much like the Jordanians, the Emiratis have focused on air power and SOF to modernize and build up their force, but unlike most other Arab partners, the Emiratis don't just want to own prestige weapons, they want to be the best at operating them, combining them, and integrating them into their defense and security strategies. Consider their F-16 Block 60 fighters. To fully leverage the awesome power and flexibility of these planes, the Emiratis have been participating in Red Flag in the United States since 2009. As mentioned in the Saudi case study, Red Flag is no ordinary exercise. It is one of the US Air Force's largest and most grueling combat training regimens. It typically involves a wide variety of aircraft and provides realistic, multidomain training in a combined air, ground, space, and electronic threat environment. At Red Flag, the motto is "you train as you fight."[4]

The UAE pilots have survived the rigor and complexity of Red Flag, and unlike many other Arab partner air forces they have not looked for shortcuts or symbolic victories. For example, the Emiratis could have easily opted to conduct *all their training* inside the United States—in other words, they could have brought their jets from Tucson, Arizona, where they were parked, to nearby Nellis Air Force Base to do the exercise. But two years after they first joined Red Flag, they decided to drastically intensify their training by flying a squadron of their F-16 fighters across the Atlantic Ocean to the American desert.[5] No Arab partner has ever done that.

The Emiratis were warned that the 9,000-mile journey from home would be very difficult—and it was, both logistically and diplomatically—but they were adamant about gaining real-world experience and training the way the Americans did. "Our goal is to strengthen our training and partnership with the United States and to build up interoperability with the U.S.," affirmed UAE Lt. Col. Buti Al Neyadi.[6]

The UAE is interested in becoming a regional leader in air power and a hub for aerial training as well. Since 2004, the UAE has hosted biannually a regional, multiple-week version of Red Flag to cement its training with the United States and other international partners. Coordinated with the US Air Warfare Center at Al Dhafra Air Base, the Advanced Tactical Leadership Course focuses on mission and war planning (which must be achieved in less than twenty-four hours) and commander training. It simulates realistic combat scenarios including countering unmanned aerial threats.[7]

In November 2019, more than 400 personnel—including mission commanders, maintenance technicians, communications specialists, ground controllers, and air defense operators—from the United States, the UAE, and other countries took part in the tactical course and flew 672 sorties over a period of four weeks.[8] "All our Arab partners are improving their capabilities, but it must be said that no one has done it better than the Emiratis," commented one former US senior member of the Air Warfare Center.[9]

The Emiratis' attitude toward and commitment to training are truly unique among America's Arab partners. They've carried it into various other joint exercises with the Americans, including Falcon Shield, Native Fury, Iron Union, Falcon Sentry, and Operation Thundercloud.

Supported by the US Integrated Air and Missile Defense Center, Falcon Shield is a multilateral exercise in the region that happens every year for a period of three weeks. It focuses on best methods and practices in air and missile defense integration. In September 2019, UAE pilots transitioned from mere participation to leadership of the exercise with US planning support.[10]

In January 2021, a combined land force of 200 American and Emirati soldiers participated in Iron Union 14 in the desert of Abu Dhabi for nearly eleven days to enhance interoperability.[11] Iron Union, which takes place twice a year, emphasizes troop mobility, logistics, communication, and coordination, and conducts live-fire exercises with US mortars and armored fighting vehicles operating alongside UAE armed reconnaissance units. "This is the foundation for anything we would do, if we were to go into combat together," said US Lt. Col. Jon Stewart.[12]

The larger Native Fury drill, which is held biannually, involves US troops from the army, marines, and navy as well as Emirati forces. It simulates combat in urban environments and conducts live-fire and maneuver training. More specifically, the exercise is designed to train naval units in maritime prepositioning force operations and perform ship-to-shore offloads of personnel, equipment, and humanitarian resources. In March 2020, some 4,000 US and Emirati soldiers took part in the two-week drill and seized a sprawling model Arab city.[13]

In Falcon Sentry, the UAE Joint Aviation Command and US Air Force, SOF, and maritime units conduct integrated air operations in support of maritime surface warfare in the waters of the Persian Gulf. In September 2020, these combined forces completed a three-day exercise that included live-fire air assaults, fire support coordination with indirect fires and close air support, marksmanship, and small-unit training. A little before that drill, the Emiratis effectively used their JTACs to direct live fires at simulated targets, which helped to enhance their strike capabilities against surface targets. UAE pilots also successfully completed deck landing qualifications aboard an expeditionary mobile base vessel.[14]

Operation Thundercloud is a joint artillery exercise often featuring live fire that seeks to increase fire mission interoperability between the US and UAE militaries. In December 2018, the drill rehearsed deliberate and dynamic strike planning in urban and mountainous terrain, and two years later it trained the Emiratis on how to employ their HIMARS most effectively.[15]

To sharpen their skills and test their capabilities, the Emiratis did not limit themselves to training. They have sought opportunities to engage in live combat against real enemies, some in support of US-led coalitions. For example, for almost two decades, Emirati troops were deployed in Afghanistan, training Afghan commandos with US SOF in Helmand and conducting raids against Islamic insurgents. They obtained vital operational experience, especially in Nangarhar Province, some of which they used later in their interventions in Libya and Yemen.

In his memoirs, former US Green Beret Michael Waltz described his experience with the Emirati forces in Afghanistan. It is worth quoting the full passage:

> The Emiratis had consistently told me that their crown prince, Sheikh Mohammed [bin] Zayed, had wanted his men to get into the fight. I intended to help them do just that. Having worked with the Emiratis

for several months in Uruzgan and the Tagab Valley, I was convinced they would have a fantastically positive effect. They were ready to fight when necessary, but they could also approach development and strategic messaging with a level of credibility that we could not match. Plus we desperately needed the help in Helmand. . . . Throughout the spring [of 2006] I had built support in my headquarters for the UAE to move into the volatile northern Helmand region.[16]

## Institutional Capacity Building

Unlike Saudi Arabia, Jordan, and Lebanon, the United States does not have a defense institution building program in Abu Dhabi. This is not for lack of UAE interest in better defense governance. It's just that for now, the Emiratis have chosen to pursue this process on their own and at their own pace, largely for political reasons.

Whether it is in the UAE or elsewhere, defense reform typically entails some reorganization in the distribution of wealth and power. Which clan or family gets what is still very much the organizing principle of politics in the UAE and elsewhere in the Gulf. Tribal equities must be accounted for, most notably in the armed forces, when it comes to social mobility and political empowerment.

The process of defense reform in the UAE is incredibly nascent. As mentioned previously, it was only two decades ago that the country was able to form a military under a single command. Dubai initially wanted to keep its autonomous security force, but pressure to support the goal of a united federation was building. In 1997, the glitzy and independent-minded emirate finally agreed to disband its army and merge it with the other regional commands. Thus was born the UAE General Headquarters.

At first, the UAE Armed Forces were tiny—which is not hard to imagine given that even today it is a military of only some 63,000 active personnel.[17] They had very little equipment and were largely reliant on expatriates for officers and pilots. Ever since MBZ effectively took on the mantle of modernizing the UAE military at the turn of the twenty-first century, it has grown exponentially in capability and become more indigenous. Defense spending under MBZ's watch has tripled and possibly even quadrupled.[18]

Until a couple of years ago, the UAE's military expansion and modernization were not accompanied by investments in defense institutional capacity. For example, the Emiratis entered the conflict in Yemen without having the benefit of a rigorous strategic planning process that would help them prioritize their present and future military actions and identify their key lines of effort. It is believed that today the Emiratis have a national security or national defense strategy, although the document remains informal and has not been made public (which is not uncommon across defense establishments in the Middle East, including in Israel). Leading this formulation process is a relatively new civilian entity in the UAE federal bureaucracy called the National Security Agency.

The UAE National Security Agency is headed by a rising young official in the main ruling family called Shaikh Tahnoun bin Zayed Al Nahyan, the country's national security adviser since 2016 per presidential decree. Tahnoun is the full brother of MBZ and one of the sons of Shaikh Zayed bin Sultan Al Nahyan, the much admired and revered founder of the UAE.

Most strategic processes in the UAE are reverse-engineered in ways that are consistent with the broad intent and direction of MBZ, who as deputy supreme commander of the UAE Armed Forces is the primary source of ideas and guidance on all things national security. Turning these ideas into reality and concrete action plans has been almost exclusively the job of the UAE military, not civilian agencies in the UAE national security bureaucracy such as the MoD.

The domination of the Abu Dhabi–based GHQ has been most evident in national security policy and practice in the UAE. In fact, until very recently the MoD had no role in defense policymaking, with all matters pertaining to defense run by military commanders and officers in GHQ and the Presidential Guard (PG) Command.

The UAE very recently has begun to work on an organized, professionalized, and institutionalized process of long-term capability development for its military. A five-year capability development plan is believed to be the current focus of Abu Dhabi, though it is unclear where the Emiratis are in this process. What the MoD Policy Directorate put together in 2019–2020 and continues to refine is a national defense policy (NDP) from the ground up, which might prove helpful for strategic planning. The fact that the NDP was signed off by MBZ suggests that the document is official, though technically it remains, like all other Emirati strategic planning documents for force development, acquisition, logistics, and other areas, a working paper, amenable to change and certainly in need of a healthy injection of more integrated strategic guidance.

Although as a physical entity the UAE MoD does exist, it is in many ways still "under construction." In 2012, the MoD had to go through a major transition following MBZ's orders to move it from Dubai to Abu Dhabi, where he could personally supervise its reconfiguration. The move carried some political risks since the MoD had been under the control of Dubai ruler and UAE vice president and defense minister

Mohamed bin Rashid Al Maktoum (MBR), one of the sons of Rashid Al Maktoum, who governed Dubai from 1958 to 1990.

Prior to the MoD's relocation, a year-long UAE review of the MoD concluded that the institution was more like an elephant's graveyard—vastly inadequate, dysfunctional, and contributing very little to national security. All the strategic thinking and decisionmaking had been taking place in GHQ and the PG Command in Abu Dhabi. MBZ wanted to change all that. Once the MoD was moved, the question became which form it would take and what functions it would assume. The UAE cabinet made a collective decision to establish an integrated MoD with GHQ, though not right from the start in order to avoid doing too much in one swoop and creating frictions over authorities among staff belonging to the two entities.

An interim solution, endorsed by MBZ, was to maintain a hierarchical structure where GHQ and MoD would be separate. The former would be involved in all matters pertaining to war fighting and military preparedness, while the latter would at least nominally help with policy guidance, force generation and management, procurement, and strategic intelligence, all of which used to be GHQ's responsibility. Today, the Emiratis report they are in the MoD-GHQ postintegration phase, with this milestone occurring in March 2021.

As part of the MoD transition, both higher- and lower-level personnel decisions had to be made. Mohamed bin Ahmad Al Bawardi, a confidante of MBR, was appointed in 2016 as minister of state for defense, and Matar Salem Ali Al Dhaheri was named under secretary of defense. Although MBR would retain his largely symbolic position as minister of defense while sitting in Dubai, Bawardi would run the day-to-day affairs of the ministry in Abu Dhabi.

In addition to the selection of leaders for the MoD, working-level staff with the right credentials had to be recruited for both the ministry and GHQ. This was and continues to be a significant challenge due to capacity issues in a country with a population of a little more than 9 million, of which only 10 percent are Emirati nationals.

To enable effective interaction and collaboration among staff from the two coexisting entities, joint committees were formed. Depending on the focus, either an MoD or a GHQ senior official would chair the committee. For example, for policy and administrative matters, MoD senior personnel would lead; for operational and military considerations, GHQ would.

Yet the model did not work very well in the beginning, primarily because of issues of culture and jurisdiction. GHQ's concern, likely not illegitimate, was that MoD staff had little knowledge of and insufficient experience in military and strategic affairs. Thus, GHQ was less willing to relinquish control over some of those areas to their new civilian colleagues.

This is where MoD's new leadership was and still is key, and the selection of Bawardi quite smart. Although close to MBR, Bawardi also has an old personal relationship with MBZ, and through his calming presence in the ministry he has played an important role in building bridges and instilling a culture of cooperation. Bawardi does not have a military background, but he has been an effective conciliator, able to manage ties between the two organizations and prevent conflict, which was sorely needed in the earlier days of the relationship-building process. Instead of imposing his way and provoking a confrontation with GHQ, he took a step back and let things organically evolve while patiently building and professionalizing his own staff. (Most senior officials in the MoD, for instance, are officers from GHQ and are on the latter's payroll, not the ministry's.)

As interagency workings patiently developed and processes slowly matured over a period of seven years, MBZ decided in mid-2019 to effectively integrate the two entities. It will take some time before real integration is achieved given the lingering disparities in skill set, knowledge, and capacity between GHQ and MoD. But the fact that MBZ issued a formal decree to pursue this objective to some extent indicates that there is no turning back.

In GHQ-MoD committee meetings, Bawardi speaks for the MoD while the chief of staff represents GHQ. The MoD under secretary is expected to *enable* the chief of staff. There is one joint staff that works for both supervisors, each of whom has the ability to influence decision-making on various issues through government boards or committees.

For example, although the under secretary chairs the policy board, the chief of staff sits on that same board and weighs in on various topics that are not typically within his wheelhouse. Likewise, the chief of staff chairs the operational board, but the under secretary is a member too, providing his own input. This approach allows, at least technically, for horizontal coordination and collaboration, with one team and two captains both working for the same minister—a structure that is not that different from many defense managerial or governance systems in the West.

Consistent with the priority of enhancing jointness in the UAE Armed Forces, MBZ in recent years instructed his military commanders to create a new Joint Operations Command, one that would be small, agile, and populated by staffers with the right kind of skill set, education, and expertise. In March 2021, the Command was born. Its mission is to help promote more UAE joint training and exercises, which do not happen as often as they should in part due to politics.

Because the MoD is still getting its feet wet on defense budget planning and force development (still primarily owned by GHQ), weapons
acquisition is not yet the result of an interagency or collaborative
process. The ministry ultimately will conduct analyses on military capability gaps and, on that basis, issue guidance on procurement. But it is
not there yet. The process thus far indicates that MBZ selects the equipment—at least the larger platforms and systems such as fighter aircraft,
battle tanks, and missile defenses—and depending on its nature commu-
nicates his choice to his respective military commanders and instructs
them to provide him with their feedback. It is a top-down acquisitions
process for sure, but it does allow for review and consultation. In other
words, MBZ makes his preferences known but does not impose them on
his commanders. (Of all the UAE's military units, the PG has developed
the most rigorous procurement process.)

The defense industrial community in the UAE also is expected to
weigh in on defense procurement, although when and how is not yet
known. For a small country, the UAE has one of the most vibrant military industrial ecosystems in the world, thanks in large part to MBZ's
vision and leadership. The Emiratis are building this critical space
largely through joint ventures and strategic partnerships with some of
the top US and Western defense giants in the world.[19]

That said, the UAE defense industry is not a major provider to the
country's armed forces. It does produce spare parts and ammunition, and
it designs, manufactures, and modernizes military vehicles, communication and electronic systems, and unmanned systems including drones.
But that is pretty much the extent of it, and it is not likely to go much
further due to capacity issues. There have been several attempts by the
Emiratis over the past few years to better organize and streamline their
defense industrial process. The latest iteration is Edge, an Abu Dhabi–
based and government-owned conglomerate that employs more than
12,000 people and has managed to consolidate twenty-five subsidiaries.[20]

Faysal Al Bannai presides over Edge, and while he does not have a
defense or military background, MBZ picked him to lead the organization given his entrepreneurial experience and track record of successfully building businesses. MBZ wants to involve Edge in the procurement decisionmaking process, but again this remains aspirational and
evolving. Similar to Riyadh's GAMI and SAMI, how things will work
in practice and how they will be coordinated with other stakeholders,
including GHQ and MoD, remain to be seen.

All these previously mentioned processes point to the fact that a
strategic planning process is sorely needed in the UAE, one that clearly
describes the country's present and future threats and identifies the

capabilities that are needed to meet those threats. In the newly integrated MoD-GHQ structure, this kind of strategic planning would be conducted via a joint committee process, which would still consider the wishes of MBZ and oftentimes benefit from his influence and leverage with international partners, including the United States.

One important consequence of this insufficiently organized and formalized procurement process is that the military services in the UAE, very much like those in Jordan and other Arab countries, are not only the fighters but also the force providers. In other words, the same personnel doing the training, acquisition, logistics, and maintenance are the ones fighting the war.

With regard to logistics, the UAE military suffers from an absence of a coherent strategic policy and a formalized planning process. The Emiratis didn't necessarily run into serious logistics problems in Yemen, but the overall system was and still is disjointed. Again, the developing institutional mechanisms of integration mentioned earlier will seek to streamline the logistics management processes and create a strategic logistics directorate to provide overarching policy. But those elements do not exist yet and most likely will take years to form.

Unit readiness in the UAE's military is neither tracked nor reported systematically because the bureaucratic infrastructure necessary for performing such functions is largely nonexistent. The exception, once again, is the PG, which is the best prepared branch in the UAE Armed Forces.

## Human Capital Development

HRM in the UAE military is a work in progress, to put it mildly. For example, officer career management is conducted haphazardly. The process tends to be based on interviews rather than on career annual reporting. Arab culture plays a huge role here, and not necessarily a positive one.[21] Emirati supervisors prefer to see the officers face to face, and the interviews are done at a very senior level by the chief of staff of the Armed Forces. The experience can be overwhelming at times for the Emirati officers, especially the younger ones. If they do not ace the interview, they receive a poor or failing grade. It is a lopsided approach as too much emphasis is placed on the interview and far less on the officers' accomplishments, which throws many of them by the wayside for no legitimate reason. The good news is that an effort to rewrite the annual performance assessment is underway. The bad news is it will take some time to come into fruition because it is likely to encounter resistance from some of the more senior officers.

Promotion in the UAE, be it in the military or other government agencies, is largely based on loyalty and length of service. However, this does not mean that the Emiratis disregard competence. Far from it. In fact, although they're clearly not running meritocracies, they value aptitude more than most other Arab partners. Just like in other Arab contexts, the Emiratis have to preserve the equities of influential tribes and families in the system, which means taking on recruits with inferior skills and oftentimes promoting them when they should be roundly kicked out.

Zoltan Barany nicely documents promotion practices and procedures in the UAE (and elsewhere in the Gulf), and these are not very encouraging. For example, it takes five to six years to be promoted from any rank in the UAE. Barany writes, "The time requirement for colonels to be promoted to brigadiers is almost twice as long in the UAE than it is in the US; on the other hand, the chance of being promoted to such high ranks is better in the Gulf."[22] Like their Saudi counterparts, Emirati senior officers retire late and as they get to higher ranks their productivity progressively declines.

Despite the emphasis the Emirati political leadership places on human capital development, be it in the military or in society writ large, the country's professional military education institutions are not stellar. Until the considerable investments made by MBZ in those schools start to generate returns, most Emiratis will continue to be sent abroad for academic, technical, and physical training, and the more elite (and politically connected) officers, like those in Jordan, Saudi Arabia, Kuwait, Qatar, Oman, and Bahrain, will attend Western academies, including the UK's Sandhurst, America's West Point, and France's Saint Cyr (the unlucky ones get to go to Egypt and Sudan).

Yet even in those situations, it's a mixed bag as it is hard to tell if the Emirati officers are able to effectively leverage their Western education when they return to the UAE due to cultural constraints and/or lack of opportunities at home to thrive—an issue not unique to the Emiratis among Arab partners. Pollack cautions that "there are many stories of Emirati officers attending various US war colleges and getting nothing from them, or at least applying nothing from them when they got home."[23]

The UAE has three military schools, one for the army, one for the navy, and one for the air force, and in some respects they are hybrid. They train enlisted Emirati men and women in combat and teach academics, some more than others. Naturally, the air force and navy academies are more focused on technical degrees—such as engineering and aeronautics—whereas the army's is more centered on humanities and social sciences.

The UAE also has a Joint Command and Staff College, a military college for women called Khawla Bint Al Azwar Military School, a National Defense College, and a semi-independent academy called Rabdan.

Founded in 1992, the Joint Command and Staff College seeks to train Emirati officers to occupy command and staff positions in GHQ and serve in units in the UAE Armed Forces. It offers accredited bachelor's degrees in management and military sciences and master's degrees in HRM and leadership, jointly with the University of Abu Dhabi. The consensus among American military personnel and foreign advisers based in the UAE is that the quality of teaching at the Joint Command and Staff College is bad, though not much worse than other similar institutions in the Arab world. Very little if any critical thinking is preached or practiced at the school. Instead, Emirati students are primarily taught to memorize, which can be helpful to pass a test but useless for the day after graduation.

The National Defense College, a joint UAE-US project, officially opened in 2013 with the goal of offering Emirati military and civilian leaders first-rate graduate education (master's and doctoral degrees) in strategic and security studies. The college is MBZ's baby, and he ultimately supervises it. His idea was to create a premier institution at home that would produce Emirati strategists and defense professionals who could competently staff the MoD and other national security agencies.

However, there's very little that's actually Emirati about the National Defense College, at least so far. This is not by default but by design. A quick look at its faculty shows that all are foreign nationals, and primarily Westerners. This suggests that Emiratis are being taught strictly Western methods of learning and research and mostly in English, which has its advantages and disadvantages. On the one hand, there's tremendous merit in the critical thinking approach of Western societies. It's hard to tell how much Emirati students are actually absorbing or benefiting from this method of learning, but Nathan Toronto offers evidence showing improvement in the participants' analytical capabilities.[24] On the other, Jean-Loup Samaan, who has taught at the college for several years, believes very little in the college's curriculum is effectively tailored to the needs of Emiratis. This means that Emiratis end up learning more about topics such as the Cold War, nuclear weapons, and Western grand strategy than more relevant subjects like regional security or the history of the Arab-Israeli conflict.[25] To be most useful, academic training has to fit in and be responsive to the strategic and political culture of the country.

Perhaps the incorporation of Arabic into the curriculum could help, but it is not a straightforward process. Toronto writes that the creation of a separate Arabic-language War Course for senior UAE officers with poor English skills could present challenges regarding learning patterns and habits that might deviate from the Socratic, critical thinking method.[26]

Although MBZ aspires to turn the National Defense College into a US-accredited, go-to place for training for not only his senior military officers and civil servants but also those from across the region, and he's poured in a considerable amount of resources to achieve that aim, he recognizes that this is a marathon and the college's administrators are only at the very beginning.

Created in September 2014, the Khawla Bint Al Azwar Military School provides training, physical fitness, and leadership development and helps prepare Emirati females for military service (although Emirati women have been among uniformed personnel since the 1980s).[27] In 2019, the school launched a military and peacekeeping program for Emirati women that provides training in military sciences, including infantry, weapons, combat paramedics, internal security, field engineering, and physical fitness.[28]

The UAE has four female fighter pilots, which is unique in the Arab world.[29] According to UAE official and press reports, Maj. Mariam Al Mansouri is the first in the history of the country to become an F-16 pilot. She graduated from Khalifa bin Zayed Air College in 2007. Seven years later, the Emiratis claimed she was bombing Islamic State targets over Syria.[30]

Established in 2013, the Rabdan academy focuses on the subject of national resilience and uses a multidisciplinary approach that aims to train Emiratis in homeland security matters and crisis response contingencies. Rabdan is run by expatriates as well as Emiratis. (The chief executive officer is a British national and the chair of the board is the Australian PG commander, but all the other leadership positions including dean, vice chief executive officer, and senior staff are occupied by Emiratis.) The faculty also is mixed. It combines academic and vocational education and teaches Emiratis at both the undergraduate and graduate levels how to integrate issues and policies from different domains to produce what American officials call a whole-of-government approach. Current students are nominated and sponsored by stakeholder organizations including GHQ, the Abu Dhabi Police, and the Ministry of Interior. Little is known about the quality of academics at Rabdan given its fairly recent creation, but unlike the Joint Command and Staff College, for example, it is a highly regarded institution among locals. Emiratis compete among each other to get into Rabdan because the academy is committed to specialization and technical training, which means it provides better opportunities for employment in the UAE public sector after graduation.

What Emiratis do following graduation is perhaps the biggest challenge facing the country's professional military schooling. For example, when Emirati cadets graduate as young officers, they are less confident about their abilities and unsure about their career paths partly because the academies, according to a UAE military commander, tend to inject academics a bit too much into their training.[31] Many of these graduates, though endowed with stronger intellectual skills, are not groomed to become war fighters and are not learning how to become platoon leaders.

Finally, the Emiratis are in the process of establishing a new Military University based on the Australian Defense Force Academy and other Western joint academies. This new institution might help solve some of the problems that are described above, including the single-service academies. The new Military University will partner with Rabdan and a couple of other local universities and provide academic degrees over three to four years (arts, engineering, science, etc.) for tri-service cadets (army, navy, and air force) who upon completing their degrees will then disperse to their single-service academies for pure military training for the next twelve months before commissioning, thus helping the UAE to produce educated war fighters.

## Outcomes

There is nothing about US military assistance to the UAE per se that fundamentally separates it from that of the rest of the Arab partners. Some might point to the recent US decision to sell F-35 fighter jets to Abu Dhabi to suggest that such assistance is indeed special, but that wouldn't be very convincing because this is not the first time Washington has agreed to transfer to its Arab partners arms that are first-rate and likely unparalleled on the global stage. For example, in the late 1970s, the Carter administration transferred sixty F-15 Eagle fighter aircraft to Saudi Arabia in a deal that was hotly debated in Congress and opposed by Israel. With its superior maneuverability, power, and acceleration, the F-15 indeed was the F-35 of its era. There was nothing like it in the international arms industry, and to this day it still has features that are second to none. Nor is the frequency or scope of US-UAE military training incomparable in the region. As I described in Chapter 2, the United States trains just as much and in some cases just as hard with the Jordanians, the Lebanese, and others as it does with the Emiratis.

The one aspect that *is* distinctive about US military assistance to the UAE ironically has nothing to do with the Americans. It is the fact that the Emiratis have utilized that assistance more effectively than any other Arab partner, and they showed it both in joint training exercises and in live-combat operations in Afghanistan, Libya, Syria, Iraq, and especially in Yemen. In the Arab world, no one has sought opportunities to grow and learn from the Americans more aggressively than the Emiratis. That is a reality that's hard to dispute. Former SOCCENT commander Lt. Gen. Michael Nagata, who worked closely with the

UAE's SOF during his deployment in the Middle East, concurs: "What has made the US military partnership with the Emiratis so effective has far more to do with *their* willingness, *their* leadership, and *their* work ethic than with our desires or ambitions."[32] He added, "The Emiratis are one of the few Middle Eastern SOF commands that are *eager* to actualize the connection between the development of first-rate skill and ability with the fundamental requirements of hard work, risk-tolerance, and relentless leader development."[33]

It's worth highlighting very briefly how the Emiratis effectively leveraged US assistance and, for example, performed in Yemen at a level higher than that of any other Arab army, at least in counterinsurgency environments. The Emiratis shot, moved, and communicated extremely well. They had a well-thought-out operational plan for every major battle they waged, especially for Aden and Mukalla, and they executed those plans to the teeth, sometimes by resorting to combined arms—the ultimate test of any modern military—with the PG and the air, naval, and land forces working collectively in several theaters.

What's remarkable about the UAE's military operations in Yemen is that some of the most complex and effective ones relied on TTPs from exercises they had conducted with the US military in different environments. "They took everything they learned from our joint exercises with them and applied them in Yemen," said one former CENTCOM commander.[34] Added two US Marines, "It's like they knew *precisely* what they wanted out of those drills and where they were going to employ their new capabilities in places where they were deployed."[35]

Aden was the UAE's first major fight in Yemen. Abu Dhabi's goal was to kick the Houthi rebels out of the strategic port city, which they had used as a base to expand their presence in the southern region.[36] Prior to intervening in the summer of 2015, the Saudi and Emirati militaries did everything they could to break the resolve of the Houthis and push them out of Aden. They bombed their military camps, arms depots, air bases, air defenses, and surface-to-surface missiles. They also hit roads and bridges to degrade their adversary's ability to hold territory they had seized and reach Aden in larger numbers. But the Houthis stood their ground and the air campaign didn't achieve its intended objectives.

The Emiratis knew they had to deploy a relatively large ground force (and knew they couldn't rely much on the Saudis due to their less reliable capabilities), and that's precisely what they did, quite effectively, bringing personnel and assets belonging to the PG and Emirati Land Forces by sea to the port to conduct operations. Aden was liberated on July 17, 2015.

While the coalition was pursuing offensive operations against the Houthis and liberating areas in the south, al-Qaeda seemed to be taking advantage of the resulting power vacuum, lawlessness, and growing sectarianism. Its militants had taken over Mukalla after the Yemeni army collapsed in 2014 and used the port as a center of operations and fundraising.[37]

It took the UAE roughly a year to create a Yemeni force of thousands of fighters to enter Mukalla and evict al-Qaeda from the country's third largest port. The UAE relied on local fighters, this time from Hadramawt Province, as well as Yemeni government soldiers that it had trained and equipped. But it also deployed many of its own troops in the fight, using combined air, sea, and land operations with some intelligence and logistical support from the United States.[38]

Al-Qaeda in the Arabian Peninsula (AQAP) retreated following heavy air strikes against military facilities and government buildings where the terrorists had congregated, but not before it was dealt a considerable blow.[39] Some reports suggest that the Emirati military offered many al-Qaeda fighters cash in return for pulling out of the city.[40]

Overall, the Mukalla operation took a few days, and the Emiratis pursued economic rehabilitation and stabilization efforts to help prevent AQAP from returning. Once again, the UAE's operational soundness and tactical proficiency surprised many in Washington.[41] The PG requested non-kinetic support from the amphibious warship USS *Iwo Jima*, which was deployed nearby and undergoing maritime security operations as part of the US Fifth Fleet, but the US response was negative. The Emiratis ended up using their own assets, including their US-made CH-47 Chinook helicopters, which allowed them to land on water.

The Emiratis were well positioned militarily to continue their campaign and cut off the supplies of the Houthis in the port of Hodeida. But they felt snookered by the UN-brokered Stockholm Agreement of December 2018, which they believed failed to hold the Houthis to account and push them to withdraw from Hodeida. (The deal has three components: the first concerns the exchange of up to 16,000 prisoners between the Houthis and the Yemeni government; the second, a ceasefire and demilitarization of Hodeida city and port as well as the two ports of Salif and Ras Issa; and the third is the formation of a committee to work toward de-escalation of fighting in Taiz.)[42]

In addition, a protracted battle in Hodeida most probably would have worsened the humanitarian crisis. (Hodeida is Yemen's largest port. It feeds the city's 700,000 people and imports more than 70 percent of the country's food and fuel.)[43] It also would have resulted in many Emirati casualties, given the Houthis' fortifications in the area, and hurt the UAE's ties with Washington, whose leadership made it very clear to Abu Dhabi it did not support an assault on Hodeida.

Those battlefield achievements were impressive on an operational and tactical level but even more so on a strategic and cultural level. The UAE's military services used to not talk to each other, which is typical among many armies not just in the Middle East but around the world. Yemen changed some of that. The culture of joint operations sometimes trickled down to the officer ranks, too, with soldiers coordinating on their own in theater. The UAE's Red Sea campaign was especially joint, with the navy providing fire support and supplies across Mocha from Assab base in Eritrea, launching three raids behind enemy lines using Rangers to assist the PG in special operations, and the air force using F-16 fighters and other assets to ensure air support.

In Aden, the Emiratis effectively utilized the know-how they had obtained from the Americans on stabilization operations and went in with comprehensive and detailed briefs about the local conditions of the city including the sewer and health-care systems. This made repair tasks after the liberation of Aden a lot faster and more manageable, which was key to the crucial mission of winning hearts and minds. The Emiratis knew what to bring with them on ships, including generators to power the whole area. UAE intelligence in Yemen was particularly good, which helped the planning process tremendously. The Emirati military had fairly large networks of local agents and informants across the country that provided crucial information on the enemy and the conditions of local administration.

In summary, the UAE *itself* is a major factor why US military assistance to the country is more rewarding and mutually beneficial than any other in the Arab world. Indeed, the country's determination to cultivate world-class military leadership and real-world operational experience and to accept the long-term, grueling, and relentless personal and physical commitment this requires is unmatched in the Arab world.

These peculiar Emirati qualities and predispositions suggest that the Americans are less able to replicate what they have with the UAE elsewhere. Each Arab country has different cultural and behavioral customs, practical abilities, and political, financial, and administrative constraints, all of which affect in very distinctive ways how they view and treat US military assistance.

That said, there might be general concepts or principles that the Americans can follow. The UAE experience underscores the merits of the Arab partner interacting consistently not only with US troops but also with its own armed forces in order to better understand their needs, strengths, and limitations, like MBZ does so regularly and capably with his soldiers. US officials might want to at least try to persuade senior Arab leaders of the value of engaging in such processes.

It is hard to overstate the importance of sound political leadership to a country's armed forces. MBZ played a crucial role in Yemen—not for what he did, but largely for what he *didn't do*. Despite his military acumen, training at Sandhurst, and previous experience commanding the UAE Air Force, MBZ did not interfere in tactics and try to play general. Instead, he empowered his commanders, which gave them great confidence. He provided broad but decisive commands of intent. And he did not micromanage the war, like many Arab leaders do, instead leaving it to the military commanders to figure out the planning and execution.

Whenever MBZ intervened it was merely to provide key military assets, which he would acquire rapidly from Western powers given his political influence. Promoted from the top and embraced by most of the generals, the culture in the UAE Armed Forces is such that lower-level personnel including lieutenants and captains are given real responsibilities, held accountable, and groomed to become the next military leaders.

No unit has preached and practiced this custom better than the PG, whose leadership constantly hammered task force commanders in Yemen about letting their battalion and company commanders on the ground take ownership and do their job without much interference from their bosses. Commanded by Australian Maj. Gen. (ret.) Michael Hindmarsh (who acquired UAE citizenship recently), the PG was conceived as a center of excellence. One common misconception is that the PG is purely SOF. It is not. It is a spearhead organization with both conventional and unconventional capabilities. The Emiratis are trying to disseminate its practices and experience to the rest of the military, but they seem to be failing more than they are succeeding. While the UAE is seeking to empower junior officers and decentralize command, it is having a considerable problem getting even the good junior officers to accept decentralizing and acting on their own. That was an issue even with the PG in Yemen.

With the UAE being more effective in its employment of US military assistance than all other Arab partners, one wonders whether institutional capacity building should still be regarded as an indispensable ingredient of US military assistance. Or should the United States relax the priority of defense institution building in US military assistance and focus more on ways to amplify its train-and-equip activities with its partners?

The answer is no for two main reasons. First, as impressive as the UAE's performance in Yemen was, it wasn't without its problems, several of which can be traced back to defense institutional shortcomings. Second, what works in the UAE most probably will not work in other Arab nations because the country has some exceptional attributes.

The Emiratis struggled in Yemen in a number of areas. For example, they did not have a field commander with a joint staff to try to integrate at all times the different components of army, navy, and air force (although it must be said that all militaries face this formidable challenge when they fight their first major war). Force rotation was another issue. Because theirs is a small and unequal force in terms of capability, with pockets of excellence including the PG, the Emiratis felt the need to constantly rotate uniformed personnel in Yemen to the tune of almost every couple of weeks. That could be interpreted as a strength or a weakness. On the one hand, it is wise to keep the troops fresh, but on the other, accountability suffers a bit and the benefits of having all the units fighting together for longer periods are much reduced. In Yemen, it was like having pick-up teams, which ultimately undermined force cohesion.

The Emiratis may have handled logistics in Yemen effectively but certainly not efficiently. When equipment broke down, they could not fix it on the spot or transport it to a nearby maintenance facility, so they had to evacuate everything, which ended up being hugely expensive. The Emiratis' inability to perform maintenance, repair, and overhaul highlights problems on institutional and strategic logistics levels.

Overall, the UAE's maritime capabilities were a relative weakness in Yemen. The UAE Navy did play an important role in providing fire support to various operations, but despite their wealth and access to the top defense firms in the world, the Emiratis did not have effective naval equipment nor did they put in the training for naval operations.

Because of inferior strategic and force posture planning in Abu Dhabi, the UAE Navy is vastly underfunded. This is common among Gulf Arab nations even though this is where they all are most vulnerable due to nefarious Iranian activity, including smuggling and mining. To Abu Dhabi's credit, Emirati sailors patrolled the waters of Yemen for a long time.

If the UAE was able to get away with very limited defense governance support in Yemen, it does not mean it will be able to easily repeat its tactical and operational success in other fights, especially not in ones against more powerful and resourceful foes than the Houthis, like the IRGC, for example. The assumption is that as the duration, scope, and complexity of war increase, so does the importance of institutional capacity to the management and sustainment of the war effort.

What makes the shortage of defense institutional capacity in the UAE less detrimental to its military operations and effectiveness, at least for the time being, is the fact that the country has a tiny military with a very flat command and control chain; a wealth of financial resources; a political leadership—MBZ, more than anybody else—who knows how to manage those resources and lead, inspire, and support the country's armed forces; and a working environment that is not overly bureaucratic.

Those are attributes that do not exist in other Arab countries, at least not all of them at once. The Saudis have deeper pockets than the Emiratis, but they have an army twice as big with a lot more equipment. They also have a less effective leadership and a public administration with a ton of red tape. All of that requires much higher levels of defense institutionalization in Riyadh, for example, than in Abu Dhabi.

Meanwhile, Jordan, Lebanon, and other Arab recipients of US military aid—that is, those who do not have national funds to purchase US arms—do not have the luxury of possibly overlooking or paying less attention to defense institution building. That's because the sustainability of their military modernization and development is very much dependent on their attainment of higher levels of institutional capacity. Also, importantly, they cannot ignore defense governance because it is now a legal condition of US military assistance.

## Notes

1. For an excellent overview of UAE military effectiveness, see Pollack, *Sizing Up Little Sparta.*
2. In 2014, former US Secretary of Defense James Mattis referred to the UAE as "Little Sparta." See Chandrasekaran, "United States Has a Quiet, Potent Ally."
3. Ghaida Ghantous and Humeyra Pamuk, "U.S. Says It Is Ready to Move Forward with Fighter Jet Sale to UAE," Reuters, December 15, 2021.
4. Walter J. Boyne, "Red Flag," *Air Force Magazine*, November 1, 2000.
5. *Air Force Magazine*, "Desert Falcons Travel Afar for Red Flag," February 4, 2011.
6. Benjamin Wilson, "F-16 Fighting Falcon News: U.A.E. Crosses Atlantic for Red Flag," F-16.net, February 3, 2011.
7. Oriana Pawlyk, "US Had Light Footprint in Recent UAE-Led Exercise," Military.com, January 25, 2019.
8. 380th Air Expeditionary Public Affairs, AFCENT AWC/AWD, "Advanced Tactical Leadership Course Graduation," US Air Forces Central, December 5, 2019.
9. Author's interview over the phone on August 13, 2020. The source spoke on the condition of anonymity.
10. Chris Thornbury, "Falcon Shield Strengthens Coalition's Air Defense," 380th Air Expeditionary Wing Public Affairs, US Air Forces Central, October 8, 2019.
11. Ahmed Maher, "UAE and US Forces Commence Iron Union 14 Military Exercise," *The National*, January 30, 2021.
12. Sanderson, "Exclusive: Inside the 'Iron Union.'"
13. Gambrell, "US, UAE Troops Hold Major Exercise."
14. US Central Command, "UAE, U.S. Forces Conduct Aviation Live Fire Exercise in Arabian Gulf," August 17, 2020.
15. US Central Command, "115th Field Artillery Brigade and 4-133rd Field Artillery Regiment Participate in Bilateral Exercises with UAE," April 3, 2020.
16. Michael G. Waltz, *Warrior Diplomat: A Green Beret's Battles from Washington to Afghanistan* (Lincoln, NE: Potomac Books, 2014): 123–125.
17. Dominic Dudley, "The 10 Strongest Military Forces in the Middle East," *Forbes*, February 26, 2018.

18. Taylor Luck, "New Aran Military Force to Reckon with as 'Little Sparta' Rises," *Christian Science Monitor*, February 28, 2019.

19. Bilal Y. Saab, *The Gulf Rising: Defense Industrialization in Saudi Arabia and the UAE* (Washington, DC: Atlantic Council, May 7, 2014).

20. Agnes Helou, "UAE Launches 'Edge' Conglomerate to Address Its 'Antiquated Military Industry,'" *Defense News*, November 6, 2019. For more on EDGE, visit its official website at https://edgegroup.ae/about.

21. See Pollack, *Armies of Sand,* for a careful examination of the role of culture in Arab military effectiveness.

22. Zoltan Barany, *Military Officers in the Gulf: Career Trajectories and Determinants* (Washington, DC: Center for Strategic and International Studies, November 5, 2019): 5.

23. Pollack, *Sizing Up Little Sparta*.

24. Toronto, *How Militaries Learn*, 78.

25. Jean-Loup Samaan, "The Strategy Behind New Gulf War Colleges," *Sada* (Carnegie Endowment for International Peace), March 5, 2019.

26. Toronto, *How Militaries Learn*, 76.

27. Barany, *Military Officers in the Gulf,* 2.

28. *Arab News*, "UN Praises UAE for Arab Women Peacekeeper Training," February 8, 2019.

29. Consulate General of the United Arab Emirates, "Women in the UAE," accessed May 4, 2021, https://boston.uae-embassy.org/about-uae/women-uae.

30. Ishaan Tharoor, "U.A.E.'s First Female Fighter Pilot Dropped Bombs on the Islamic State," *Washington Post*, September 25, 2014.

31. Author's interview via online communications technology, September 12, 2020.

32. Author's interview on May 6, 2021, Arlington, VA.

33. Ibid.

34. Author's interview via web communications technology, July 17, 2020. The source spoke on the condition of anonymity.

35. Author's interview via web communications technology, July 18, 2020. The sources spoke on the condition of anonymity.

36. The Houthis core support base is in the north and especially in their home province of Saada, with a presence dating back to the early twentieth century when they established a Zaydi monarchy in North Yemen with Taiz as its capital.

37. Adam Baron, "The Gulf Country That Will Shape the Future of Yemen," *Atlantic*, September 22, 2018.

38. Phil Stewart and Yara Bayoumy, "In Yemen Conflict, a Window into Deepening U.S.-Gulf Ties," Reuters, April 27, 2017.

39. William Maclean, Noah Browning, and Yara Bayoumy, "Yemen Counterterrorism Mission Shows UAE Military Ambition," Reuters, June 28, 2016.

40. Maggie Michael, "Details of Deals Between US-Backed Coalition, Yemen al-Qaida," Associated Press, August 6, 2018.

41. Michael Morell, "The Giant Al Qaeda Defeat That No One's Talking About," *Politico Magazine*, May 2, 2016.

42. United Nations, "A Year After the Stockholm Agreement: Where Are We Now?" Office of the Special Envoy of the Secretary-General for Yemen, accessed July 21, 2021, https://osesgy.unmissions.org/year-after-stockholm-agreement-where -are-we-now.

43. Mohammed Ghobari, "Yemen's War-Damaged Hodeidah Port Struggles to Bring in Vital Supplies," Reuters, November 24, 2016.

# 7

# Cultural and Structural Challenges

THE US SECURITY COOPERATION REFORMS THAT WERE enacted by Congress in 2017, coupled with the practical incorporation of a measure of defense institution building into US military assistance programs in the region over the past few years, offer hope for the future. If anything, they indicate that the United States and some, but not all, of its Arab partners are now approaching the issue of Arab military capability development with a level of urgency and seriousness unseen before.

That said, both sides still have a huge mountain to climb, and there is no better way to show the incredible amount of work that still needs to be done than by highlighting the Arab partners' military contributions to OIR, the US-led campaign against the Islamic State, which can be described as measly at best. At its height in 2014, the Islamic State ruled over some 10 million people in the region and held about a third of Syria and almost half of Iraq. Yet, despite this terrorist army's methodical and wide-ranging assault on Arab politics, culture, and religion, the Arab states, for all their talk of solidarity and common destiny over the years, failed to effectively mobilize and launch a coordinated campaign to eradicate the threat.

This outcome was most shocking and discouraging to the Americans who were having flashbacks of Desert Storm. Similar to Saddam, the Islamic State was an existential danger, and yet the Arab partners once again could not unite and come together militarily to defeat it.

155

At first, the Obama administration was vastly reluctant to intervene, having removed US troops from Iraq in 2011 and vowed to avoid more American wars in the Middle East. But with the Islamic State's cancer rapidly spreading and threatening to remake the regional order and terrorize the West, US inaction was no longer an option.

Washington's expectation was that after launching a military offensive under its leadership, the Arab partners would join the fight. And to some extent, they did, but certainly not in ways that were decisive or satisfactory to the Americans. The wealthier Arab partners committed billions of dollars to offset US military expenses. They provided economic assistance to struggling neighbors including Iraq, Jordan, and Lebanon, and funneled cash and arms to Syrian rebels. They permitted American and other foreign air forces and navies to use their airfields and ports. Some agreed to host a larger number of US troops to aid Washington's military planning and operations.[1]

Jordan helped train a Syrian opposition force on its soil, and along with Bahrain, Egypt, Qatar, the UAE, and Saudi Arabia it flew an unspecified but relatively small number of sorties to bomb Islamic State targets primarily in Syria (the Saudis and the Emiratis began to reduce their air power contributions after they launched their campaign in Yemen in March 2015).[2] But what the Arab coalition partners could not manage to bring to the table, despite their promises, was ground troops. A collective Arab army could have prevented further death and destruction in the region by rolling back the territorial gains and crushing the caliphate of the Islamic State. Alas, such a joint force never came into being.

Many Arab partners were in no position to contribute ground troops because they were struggling to put out jihadist fires on their own territory. Sending soldiers outside their borders to combat the Islamic State could have led to military overstretch and therefore risked the home front. However, with proper military planning, coordination, and pooling of resources among the Arab partners, the formation of a sizable Arab land force was entirely achievable. After all, despite the size of the Islamic State, the Arab partners had an overwhelming numerical and firepower advantage.

Jordan's King Abdullah II himself stated in 2016 during meetings at the Pentagon with senior US officials that the Islamic State could be defeated "fairly quickly."[3] His plan, though, was to strictly increase the tempo of air strikes without introducing ground troops, which would not have made much of a difference. Air power alone was not going to declaw a well-armed and resourceful terrorist movement with hundreds of thousands of followers.

In OIR, the Arab partners had a political constraint too. Many of them did not have ideal bilateral relations with Iraq, and the Iraqis themselves would not have allowed troops from various Arab countries to operate on their territory due to sectarian and political sensitivities. The Iranians, who wield a good bit of influence in Baghdad, would have played a spoiler role too.

Meanwhile, Syria was an even tougher nut to crack. Because most Arab partners wanted Assad gone, they had no interest, at least initially, in fighting the very actors who were most effective at battling the Syrian regime. This allowed the Islamic State and al-Qaeda to flourish for years, until Washington began to lead a more organized effort to create a secular Syrian rebel force to take on the extremists.

In OIR, the Arab partners' direct military contributions were, not unlike in Desert Storm twenty-three years before, extremely disappointing. They also were not surprising. They were partly the result, despite much progress made in recent years as described in previous chapters, of long-standing problems in US-Arab military cooperation. Let's start with the American side.

## Nation-Building Paranoia

With the benefits of defense institution building in US military assistance programs being as significant as they are, why is the United States currently not doing everything it possibly can to help its Arab partners engage in this crucial process?

First, Washington is increasingly aware, mainly due to its taxing experiments in Iraq and Afghanistan, of how incredibly hard it is to bring about any kind of structural change in the internal affairs of its regional partners. Seeing how hesitant most of its Arab partners are to wholeheartedly embrace comprehensive reform, especially in defense and security matters, Americans are almost self-deterred from doing more and seem much less enthusiastic about the idea altogether.

Look no further than Washington's timid reaction to the Arab popular uprisings of 2011, the single most promising opportunity for lasting change in the Middle East since the emergence of the Arab anticolonial movement in the nineteenth century. Hundreds of thousands of young protesters filled town squares in Arab capitals hoping for Washington to provide them with more than rhetorical support, yet none came (many other protesters, however, merely wanted US officials to step aside and at least stop backing authoritarian governments in the region). Some in the Obama administration at the time wanted to side more robustly with the Arab street, but in the White House the "center of gravity was a don't-rock-the-boat approach" largely because of the fresh and painful memories of the freedom agenda of the Bush 43 administration.[4] Leaning too hard in support of human rights and democracy risked, as US decisionmakers saw it at the time, the collapse of order in some key countries such as Saudi Arabia and the undermining of America's traditional interests, including the stability of the world energy markets, Israel's security, the fight against terrorism, and the containment of Iran.

Second, the United States is much less inclined to push for structural defense reform in the region because it worries about getting into a slippery slope toward nation building, something for which it currently has zero appetite and fewer resources to try to pursue, especially in the aftermath of the Afghanistan debacle. Here, it is less about the challenges of implementation for Washington and more about the concerns regarding the commitment to an open-ended process that might compete with other more pressing priorities. At a time when great power competition is the compass of US foreign policy, anyone suggesting greater and more long-term US involvement in the Middle East is sure to be met with censure and ridicule.

Of course, the idea that all US-supported defense institution building efforts in the region would ultimately turn into full-fledged nation-building exercises is absolutely ridiculous. But US officials and lawmakers cannot help but evince a psychological reaction to the idea due to the traumas of Afghanistan and Iraq.

## Anemic Leadership and Ineffective Organization

Another major reason why the United States has fallen short in pushing its Arab partners to integrate institutional reforms into US military assistance is because American civilian and military decisionmakers have yet to take on the mantle of the enterprise of security cooperation and its associated discipline of defense institution building. The lack of US leadership on security cooperation has manifested itself in a couple of ways. First, top US officials including the secretary of defense have failed to explicitly and robustly endorse the substantial security cooperation reforms that appeared in the FY 2017 NDAA and emphasized the integration of defense institution building into capability development programs in US military assistance.

Second, and as a result of the first factor, these US officials have failed to set up processes and mechanisms to seriously and continuously oversee the execution of those security cooperation reforms to make sure all the relevant stakeholders in the US bureaucracy are doing what they are asked to do and what American taxpayers expect them to do.

The irony or perhaps tragedy of US security cooperation is that the United States has some of the world's finest soldiers, military trainers, and professional educators, all of whom are perfectly capable of forming the strongest security partnerships and closest bonds with their Arab and foreign counterparts. But what the United States does not have is an effective *system* in Washington that can enable and maximize the security cooperation activities of its uniformed personnel out in the field and set them on a more strategic and sustainable course.

Congress's reforms have helped to initiate the bureaucratic setup for the formulation and implementation of security cooperation by creating an Office of the Deputy Assistant Secretary of Defense for Security Cooperation. As mentioned previously, in January 2022 this entity became part of a new office called the Office of the Deputy Assistant Secretary of Defense for Global Partnerships. This latest creation, though, has solved very little. One person, and a small staff, no matter how competent and entrepreneurial, cannot fix the structural woes of US security cooperation on their own and especially without top cover from the Pentagon's most senior policy official. It all starts at the top.

In the Department of Defense, it is very much unclear to what extent institutional capacity building activities with international partners are effectively promoted, monitored, executed, assessed, overseen, and evaluated, despite the fact that now everybody must get on board with the new program per Congress's wishes. New laws, authorities, directives, offices, procedures, and coordinating mechanisms have been set up to fulfill the requirements of defense institution building, but in reality, little has actually been implemented, especially on a systematic basis. Nobody in the Pentagon's senior leadership really takes any of these useful changes seriously.

Partly because of the tensions and overlap in responsibilities between DSCA and this new global partnerships office, the priority of helping weaker partners build stronger defense institutions has yet to truly take off. At its core, there is a difference in culture and a problem of command and control between these two Defense Department entities. Although DSCA says that its mission is, among other things, "to advance U.S. national security and foreign policy interests by building the capacity of foreign security forces to respond to shared challenges," the way it has implemented this mission since the organization's creation in 1998 is by focusing a little too much on the processing of FMS and equipment releases and paying far less attention to defense institution building.[5]

It is true that Arab partners cannot effectively participate in coalition operations and become interoperable with the United States without the military tools and technologies from Washington. And DSCA has played an immensely important role in that regard. However, if there is one argument I've had no problem repeating throughout this book, it's that security cooperation is not just about the supply of hardware to weaker partners; it's also about helping them create the supporting institutional infrastructure to effectively use and sustain that hardware.

DSCA is a military-focused organization that until recently was run for more than two decades by senior military personnel (Heidi Grant, who succeeded Lt. Gen. Charles Hooper as director in July 2020, is the first civilian to run the office, but she stepped down fifteen months after she took on the job[6]). It is not an ideal place for the meaningful promotion and execution of capacity-building activities because its mandate overwhelmingly emphasizes the delivery of tactical and operational equipment. Indeed, this responsibility accounts for more than 90 percent of the hundreds of billions of dollars DSCA manages; accordingly, it consumes an equal amount of attention by the agency's workforce.

To be fair, DSCA does more than manage FMS. As I described at the end of this book's second chapter, the agency has gone through various organizational changes in recent years in response to a growing interest by Congress in generating better returns on US security cooperation investments worldwide. All these changes, including most recently the creation of the Defense Security Cooperation University, were heralded on DSCA's communications platforms, touted by the DSCA public affairs office, and announced with great enthusiasm by DSCA senior personnel.

However, it's not unfair to say that these adjustments are of a cosmetic nature. Changing names and accruing more resources for its bureaucracy has not shifted DSCA's focus—and DSCA should *not* shift its focus. Management guru Stephen Covey is known for saying, "The main thing is to keep the main thing the main thing."[7] For DSCA, that is FMS. That's what it has always done, that's what it does best, and that's what it should keep doing.

It hasn't helped that for years DSCA has run its operations, all of which *directly* impact US foreign and security policy objectives, with little effective oversight by civilian leadership in the Pentagon. This has allowed it to become a virtually autonomous entity, whose size and power have increased over time through no fault or deliberate plan of its own. (Indeed, this isn't a conspiracy!)

To be clear, it is not that DSCA and the Office of the Deputy Assistant Secretary of Defense for Global Partnerships do not agree on the merits and priority of defense institution building as well as on the assessment, monitoring, and evaluation of US security cooperation activities. They do, but their views on how to pursue these legal requirements are markedly different. Whereas the latter pushes for the early integration of capacity building into security cooperation programming, the former incorporates capacity building much later in the process in what often ends up being an ad hoc manner. The latter recommends a patient and holistic security cooperation method that first assesses the partner's willingness and absorptive capacity before providing it with new equipment. DSCA's transactional "trucks-and-guns" approach, on the other hand, is much faster and less appreciative of these basic requirements.

Command and control between these two entities is another complicating factor in their relationship. The head of DSCA used to answer directly to the Pentagon's under secretary of defense for policy, without having to report to the latter's subordinates. Even though this changed very recently, with the DSCA director having to report to the assistant secretary of defense for strategy, plans, and capabilities, it doesn't entirely fix the chain-of-command problem. DSCA still has leverage over the Office of the Deputy Assistant Secretary of Defense for Global Partnerships, which makes it harder for the latter to influence the direction of overall security cooperation planning, budgeting, and programming processes in ways that are more consistent with the content and aims of Congress's reforms.

## The US Military

Out in the field, CENTCOM, through the military departments of the US Armed Forces, is responsible for executing capacity building with Arab partners as part of its train-and-equip initiatives in coordination with US ambassadors and country teams in host nations. These efforts are presumed to be in accordance with strategic guidance from civilian leadership in the Defense Department that is consistent with the priorities of the National Defense Strategy (NDS). That, of course, is all in theory. In practice, CENTCOM and other geographic combatant commands (GCCs) run the show of security cooperation planning and execution and rely on the Joint Staff in the Pentagon to back them up and preserve their habits and equities in the enterprise.

Indeed, the GCCs effectively are the center of gravity of US security cooperation. Their priorities, objectives, concerns, and planning constructs, all of which focus on contingency and warfare planning, often drive the whole process. To a large extent, this sort of ownership by the GCCs makes sense because they have a unique understanding of the nature of the military environment and the requirements of regional security. However, healthy civil-military dynamics require that civilian leadership determine the strategic direction of overall US policy, including security cooperation.

It is not that the GCCs are incapable of thinking and acting strategically—in fact, they have branches and divisions, including J5, that are tasked with thinking more long-term about the best ways to *shape* the security environment during peacetime. Rather, their number-one concern, as their adjective "combatant" clearly indicates, is to prepare for battle and win wars. The tyranny of the immediate operational environment of CENTCOM, for example, which has been operating in an unstable neighborhood for more than two decades, is a very real and near-constant challenge. Asking the GCCs to overhaul their security cooperation approach with partners by integrating institutional capacity building into their plans indeed is a heavy lift, both culturally and practically. CENTCOM has been accustomed to using security cooperation primarily as a tool to gain access, basing, and overflight, and because more and constant access is always better, CENTCOM has sort of resorted to a "peanut butter spread" approach—that is, a little bit of security cooperation with as many Arab partners as possible.

Access, basing, and overflight are critical enablers, especially now in an era of great power competition, but they should be viewed as means rather than ends. Furthermore, security cooperation has its own set of objectives, standards, and metrics of success, some of which have nothing to do with access, basing, and overflight. CENTCOM, in addition to other GCCs, typically is wedded to its own integrated country strategies and theater campaign plan. It has little interest in what the Pentagon has to offer in terms of security cooperation planning guidance.

Also, just like DSCA, not one GCC has ever pursued defense institution building with fervor, strategic purpose, and consistency. Much of this, however, is not their fault. The GCCs do not have the expertise to follow the new guidance of defense institution building, and they are not receiving the proper help from the Defense Department, or anywhere else.

As the lead on security cooperation workforce development, DSCA is responsible for providing capacity-building training to security cooperation officers abroad, but its efforts have yet to meet the huge demand. The GCCs have succeeded in doing things the way they prefer due to the previously discussed lopsided relationship between DSCA and the Office of the Deputy Assistant Secretary of Defense for Global Partnerships.

The GCCs are not blind to the power dynamics between the two entities and sometimes exploit them to pursue their goals.

Because it shares with the GCCs the same military-focused language, DSCA defers a little too much to them, thus failing to play the role of honest broker—a role that is absolutely crucial to the success of security cooperation. The generals cannot afford to ignore the Pentagon's guidance—otherwise funding for their security cooperation plans would be at risk—but they do have considerable leverage, and that leverage is one a deputy assistant secretary of defense cannot match due to relatively weak support from their own senior leadership in the building.

It's not that the GCCs do not appreciate the value of defense institution building—they certainly do, and CENTCOM more than any other is desperate for reliable military partners to share the load of regional security. It's just that, as war-fighting machines, they oftentimes do not have the luxury to pursue defense institution building. It is difficult for CENTCOM, for example, to help an Arab partner build or improve its institutional capacity when existential dangers are lurking, people are dying, and bullets are flying, as sadly is often the case in the Middle East.

## Strategy and Funding

One of the most notable consequences of weak US leadership on security cooperation is the absence of an *official strategy* for security cooperation. The Pentagon has formal strategies for other functional domains such as irregular warfare and cybersecurity, but it does not have one for security cooperation.

This isn't a fatal flaw of the enterprise. After all, there are plenty of documents issued by Pentagon leadership containing directives and guidance that purport to include security cooperation. But the mere fact that no official strategy for security cooperation exists opens the door to substantive confusion, inadequate bureaucratic coordination, and ineffective execution. It also shows where the Defense Department's priorities lie (or don't lie), despite the critical role security cooperation officially plays in the NDS.

It is also hard to pursue a more holistic approach to security cooperation with Arab and international partners when there is not enough US money dedicated to such activities. US funding allocated to capacity-building programs and initiatives constitutes a tiny percentage compared to what is being spent on the mechanisms to provide weapons and equipment to partners. For example, using even the most generous or comprehensive definition of institutional capacity building, in 2019 the United States spent a little less than $5 million to pursue such activities in the entire Middle East, while it allocated hundreds of millions of dollars to FMS cases.[8] Although the funding numbers for training security cooperation personnel are unclear, civilian professionals and CENTCOM staffers have routinely complained about the lack of resources devoted for that objective.

## The State Department

The Defense Department may currently be the biggest player in US security cooperation with partner nations, but it is certainly not the only one. Since 9/11, more US entities, including the Department of Homeland Security and the Department of the Treasury, have taken part in this colossal universe to deal with the various US security challenges emanating from abroad.

None plays a more critical role than the State Department. Through its FMF and IMET programs and others, the State Department every year is able to commit hundreds of millions of dollars *of US taxpayer money* to train, equip, and educate the military forces and security services of various US partners around the world. For those who are more affluent and do not need the security assistance funds from Washington, such as several of the Gulf Arab partners, the State Department plays a huge role in helping to approve the sale of US military equipment through the FMS program. (The secretary of state determines which countries will receive US arms, and the secretary of defense is responsible for executing the program.)

Long before the Pentagon started upping its engagements in train-and-equip activities with global partners, the State Department was leading such efforts (particularly during the Cold War), sometimes in successful collaboration with the Defense Department. However, the prominence of the State Department's role has decreased considerably since 9/11. With transnational terrorism rising and failed states proliferating over the past two decades, US military commanders, empowered by Capitol Hill, began to increasingly encroach upon traditional spheres of influence and legal jurisdictions of US diplomats and development experts by gaining more resources and authority to pursue security cooperation with international partners. This process has led to tensions between the Pentagon and Foggy Bottom. These two very large bureaucracies understandably have different understandings of security cooperation and security assistance, different laws and authorities governing their work, different budgets, and different procedures. For them to effectively coordinate on security sector assistance (a term now more commonly used to include all the security assistance responsibilities, functions, and authorities of the State Department under Title 22 of the US Code of Law and all those of the Defense Department pertaining to security cooperation under Title 10), as the US law specifically instructs them to do, would require both secretaries to make this a priority, which has yet to happen.

This lack of integration of the role and input of the State Department (and those of various other relevant agencies in the US government) into security cooperation represents the enterprise's biggest structural handicap. As cliché as it sounds, defense institution building, given its multisectoral nature, fundamentally requires a whole-of-government approach. Capacity building involves planning, management, human resources, budgeting, human rights training, and the rule of law. Therefore, it is part and parcel of the *development* universe, in which the State Department and the US Agency for International Development (USAID) are naturally better versed than the Defense Department and the US military.

As made clear in the Foreign Assistance Act of 1961, "the Secretary of State is responsible for the continuous supervision and general direction of economic assistance, military assistance, and military education and training, including determining whether there shall be a security assistance program and the value thereof, to the end that such programs are effectively integrated both at home and abroad, and that the foreign policy of the United States is best served thereby."[9] For example, it is one thing to help an Arab country train and equip its coast guard or police force (typically a Department of Defense function), but it is another altogether to help its government create legal systems and authorities that are necessary for that security service's role and jurisdictions (a Department of State responsibility).

The problem is that the Defense Department and the State Department have not worked well together since the end of the Cold War for various reasons that include the absence of top-level stimuli and the existence of turf battles and competition for authority, influence, and resources. As a result, they have not effectively conducted joint planning on institutional capacity building, despite all the congressional laws and executive directives precisely calling for that, and they have not been able to pool their resources, bring their respective expertise to bear, and complement each other's activities.

It is often said that the Department of Defense, with the blessing of Congress, has taken over the capacity-building portfolio of security cooperation over the past two decades, effectively pushing the State Department to the sidelines. That's a misleading interpretation, however. The reality is that the Department of Defense (and congressional leaders) grew impatient with the State Department's post-9/11 struggles in helping partners around the world and specifically in the Middle East develop their counterterrorism capabilities and capacities. So the Pentagon proceeded to implement its own strategy, gave it a label (DIB or ICB), and described it in a way that sought to differentiate it from the State Department's Foreign Assistance responsibilities (in part to avoid legal complications).

Ultimately, the Pentagon got its own set of Title 10 authorities to pursue capacity building, but it was like the dog that caught the car. It was overwhelmed by the new mission and practically unable to do that much better than Foggy Bottom, primarily because the Department of Defense is not a developmental assistance agency. It has a military culture that is naturally hostile to longer-term development timelines and procedures.

## Lack of Political-Military Integration

For the GCCs, this lack of political-military integration at the higher levels of the US government when it comes to security cooperation has been a heavy burden and a liability. Resource planning for all aspects of security cooperation, including defense institution building (i.e., getting the money to pursue a certain capacity-building initiative) has been an intensely time-consuming, labor-intensive, and frustrating exercise for the GCCs because it is akin to "fitting together a puzzle—a puzzle that changes every year as the planned activities and resources change."[10]

The GCCs must not only concern themselves with war and contingency planning—a top priority and an already demanding undertaking, especially in the Middle East—but also master the kaleidoscope of disparate legal authorities and requirements that belong to the Defense Department and State Department, which only a seasoned expert and lawyer can comprehend and navigate.

So what often ends up happening is that the GCCs stick to what they know best and take the path of least resistance in security cooperation, which for them naturally gravitates toward training and equipment. As a result, they either implement capacity building with partners inconclusively or pay lip service to the whole process.

## The Implementation Challenges for GCCs

Even in those rare cases where the GCCs do manage to successfully seize the "right package" from both the Defense Department and the State Department—that is, the right set of legal authorities and enough funds—and develop a stronger interest in pursuing a more holistic approach to a certain security cooperation initiative, the executional challenges are still great. The GCCs for the most part have insufficient expert knowledge to conduct baseline assessments of the partner's institutional capacity and ability to absorb and sustain more military equipment. Some GCCs disagree with this assessment and argue that they do have that knowledge. What they admit they lack is an ability to gather all of that information, integrate it, and employ it to effectively promote real changes in those areas.[11]

What is also missing is thorough and comprehensive *political*-military analysis by country-specific, regional, and functional experts from various parts of the US national security system, including embassies and the intelligence community. Yet the roles and inputs of these actors are not effectively sought after or integrated into this critical, initial assessment process. This often leads to the launch by the GCCs of security cooperation initiatives that do not even pass the sniff test due to major questions about the partner's suspect institutional infrastructure and commitment to human rights and the rule of law. It is not uncommon for the GCCs to submit their proposals for security cooperation initiatives in their respective theaters to the Defense Department for review without identifying the capacity-building objectives or how those might be achieved. What is even worse is that the majority of those security cooperation proposals, particularly in CENTCOM's case, ultimately get approved by the Pentagon's leadership despite all the red flags and concerns over the absence of any plans to help the partner build institutional capacity.

Things most often go CENTCOM's way because few in the Defense Department wish to seriously challenge the CENTCOM commander. That is partly because doing so is rarely a smart career move in the absence of effective civilian oversight and leadership at the top, but also because many senior US defense officials genuinely believe that if they do not respond favorably to the general's requests, "people will die," "the relationship with the partner will fall apart," and/or "the United States will lose influence in a critical part of the world"—scenarios that seem a little too implausible and inflated.[12]

That senior civilian leaders in the Pentagon often come from the US Armed Forces typically, though not always, makes them more receptive to the views and preferences of the generals, with whom they might have close personal ties developed through joint service in previous years. This personal connection with and affinity for the commanders generally makes it more difficult for the Pentagon to institute a more objective, effective, and civilian-led assessment of security cooperation resource planning.

## The US Defense Industry

Arab military efficiency and sustainability, attained partly through rigorous adherence to defense institution building, is not exactly a cause that many US and other international defense companies are excited about, given that their financial security depends to a large extent on reaching more and larger weapons deals with Arab partners. Of course, the new strategic imperative and congressional legal requirement of defense institution building in Washington's security cooperation approach, at least on paper, compels US defense firms to adjust. But the sway the industry has over the US foreign policy process is not small, as President Dwight Eisenhower warned some six decades ago in a famous speech about the formidable and "unwarranted" influence of the US military-industrial complex.[13]

It is not as if those defense companies have had to twist the arms of US officials and lawmakers to secure their permission to export arms to the Middle East and around the world. It's more of a symbiotic relationship. As US senator William Proxmire observed more than fifty years ago, "The movement of high-ranking military officers into jobs with defense contractors and the reverse movement of top executives in major defense contractors into high Pentagon jobs is solid evidence of the military-industrial complex in operation."[14]

Also, many members of Congress represent regions where the defense industry is a major employer.[15] Pushing for a more-restrained arms transfer policy that might reduce US weapons exports to some partners, for example, could lead to fewer jobs in that member of Congress's district, which is akin to political suicide.[16]

## Standards and Certification

How is defense institution building with Arab partners, whenever it happens, assessed and evaluated? How much of it is enough? And how does the Department of Defense certify that this new major legal requirement in security cooperation initiatives with partner nations has actually been met?

On paper, there are ready answers to all these questions, but what matters most is how things are executed, and there, confusion is noticeable. The law says that defense institution building efforts should be "relevant, focused, and scaled," but in reality they rarely are. "Relevant, focused, and scaled" is reasonable guidance for defense institution building *planning* in the Department of Defense, but nowhere near sufficiently specific to enable anyone to "certify" a project for capacity building.

Let's say the United States wishes to help an Arab partner improve its ability to handle a security incident involving weapons of mass destruction, be it along its borders or in its urban centers. This would require very specific, hands-on training. Yet what officers of that partner often get from DSCA is the opportunity to participate in seminars hosted by the George C. Marshall European Center for Security Studies (one of the Department of Defense's Regional Centers for analysis and education) about broad concepts of international security cooperation, which do little to help the partner build capacity. And yet such an educational opportunity or experience is often viewed by DSCA as enough to meet the criteria of "relevant, focused, and scaled" when of course it is not.

Certification also means different things to different actors in the US national security bureaucracy. For Congress, capacity building need only be "complementary," which is a bit ironic and disappointing given the leadership role Congress initially played in creating the security cooperation reforms that turned defense institution building into a core requirement.

This lack of intra- and interagency consensus on the meaning and procedures of capacity-building certification presents challenges for the managers and administrators of defense institution building: Are they certifying for leadership in the Department of Defense or in Congress, and to what standard?

## Lacking Arab Commitment

There's nothing peculiar or exceptional about why Washington's Arab partners have shown little interest in committing to defense institution building. I can think of three possible reasons. First, Arab leaders resist pursuing a holistic approach to military capability development because they are apprehensive about its possible effects on their grip on power. Second, even if on some level they recognize the importance of defense institutional capacity, they just do not see it as a critical priority. Third, they are not interested in adopting foreign concepts and methods that clash with their own habits and culture. Let's briefly take a look at all three of these explanations.

Arab leaders are generally unwilling to invest in defense institution building primarily because they fear losing control, even the smallest fraction, over their armed forces and the political process. The national security club is an exclusive one in the Arab world. It is typically composed of the head of state along with his top military commander, maybe a handful of close relatives, and one or two trusted advisers. By nature, defense institution building is an *inclusive* process as it seeks to create and empower various organizations, communities, centers of influence, and sources of expertise. As a result of institutional capacity building, the determination of national security and defense policy is more of a collective affair, and decisionmaking, now decentralized, rests on and benefits from inter- and intradepartmental coordination and consultation.

Yet even the thought of giving authority, and guns no less, to entities that might one day challenge the rule of and even unseat incumbent leaders is anathema to Arab political behavior and experience.

While we shouldn't fall into the trap of overstating the impact of coup-proofing on overall military development (and I'll come back to this point in a minute),[17] we definitely should acknowledge the role politicization plays, which will vary depending on the local political context. In some Arab quarters, including Oman, Morocco, and Kuwait, such political fears are less pronounced, but still the idea of liberalizing and professionalizing defense ministries and intelligence agencies is unattractive because it might also undermine favorable clientelistic networks run by the Arab leader and his tight entourage.

In the world of defense, there is potentially a lot of money to be made and a lot of influence to be gained. Every year, the United States provides billions of dollars in security assistance and cooperation to many of its less wealthy Arab partners—money that has allowed them to retain power partly by channeling financial resources to pro-regime elites.[18] It is not only knowledge and arms that Arab rulers wish to control, but also economic privileges as those remain a critical means to consolidating power and buying off the silence of societies (or at the very least, the opposition). For defense institution building to generate returns and have positive effects on military development, it has to be merit-based. However, most if not all Arab rulers prioritize political loyalty above all else, be it in the armed forces or in the bureaucracy.

As the previous case studies show, it's not that Arab leaders do not engage in institutional capacity building at all. Even the most authoritarian political systems have to invest in some form of conventional military power to fend against various national security threats from within and abroad. This inevitably requires a degree of defense organization at the ministerial level and within the armed forces that is less hierarchical and politicized and more open and professional. So, Arab leaders have to balance between the priority of political control and the necessity of military power. They have pursued a measure of defense management because they recognize it is important to national security and thus to political survival, but they have done that in a limited fashion and on their own terms—indeed, the bare minimum to make sure their armies and national security bureaucracies do not completely fall apart.

It's one thing to engage in defense institution building to meet very narrow objectives that center on regime survival; it's another altogether to leverage that process and unleash its potential to create credible and sustainable military power. The Arabs have done the former. They have hardly ever appreciated the value of a sound and properly functioning bureaucratic apparatus of national defense. They have hardly ever come to grips with the reality that effective defense governance is a cornerstone of military power.

As always, there's a cultural element at play here as well. The Arab partners have stuck to their ways and resisted borrowing defense institution building concepts from Western powers because those concepts are, quite naturally, based on Western values and norms that aren't consistent with Arab culture.

Much of this is perfectly understandable and eminently defensible. It makes no sense, and in fact is counterproductive, for the Arab partners to impose foreign customs, be they political, economic, or security in nature, on their armies and defense establishments. Each defense governing structure should be a reflection of the sociopolitical culture and environment in which it operates. That said, just like there are universal values and norms in politics that cannot be refuted or challenged given their proven and measurable impact on political and societal development—such as legitimacy, inclusiveness, representation, free elections, the rule of law, the separation of church and state, and an independent judiciary—there are principles in defense that are indispensable for military development—such as the delegation of authority, the empowerment and promotion of lower ranks in the military, decentralization, teamwork, and inter- and intradepartmental cooperation and coordination.

All of those concepts and practices are not Western per se; they are cross-cultural. In the Arab world, however, they are not preached and practiced, at least consistently and all together, because they're mostly incompatible with Arab political culture, which emphasizes hierarchy, seniority, loyalty, patriarchy, and clientelism. This helps explain why most Arab armies were and to a large extent still are more comfortable with Soviet military and organizational principles and practices—favoring quantity over quality, having an ambiguous attitude toward military professionalism, elevating hierarchy over egalitarianism, prioritizing political reliability over military skill, establishing dual command as opposed to single command, and so on[19]—because to some degree they resemble those of the Arabs.[20]

To be sure, political culture constantly changes, and this is especially true in the Arab world in the aftermath of the Arab Spring. Avoiding assumptions that feed the orientalist notion of "Arab exceptionalism" and that are often based on simplistic and anachronistic dichotomies—autocracy versus democracy and sectarianism versus secularism—is more than prudent and necessary.[21] That said, it is impossible to deny the very real persistence of political authoritarianism in the Arab world, and it is foolish to downplay the role Arab culture has played in sustaining this authoritarianism for so many decades.

## The Arab Bureaucracy

Regardless of the level of interest some Arab partners recently might have developed in defense institution building, alone or thanks to US nudging, *all of them* face considerable implementation challenges due to their weak administrative capacities and badly functioning bureaucratic apparatuses. The brilliant and ever more relevant Arab Human Development Report of 2002 correctly noted that "reforming public administration is . . . a central and urgent task for [Arab] countries; it lies at the core of the wider agenda of institutional reform."[22] The following Arab Human Development Report of 2004 doubled down on the issue of institutional reform and affirmed that the "principles of rational public administration" ought to be observed as a prerequisite for not only good governance but also, more fundamentally, the very cause of freedom.[23]

Existing flaws in Arab defense organizational capacity have roots in postcolonial pathologies in Arab public sector planning and administration that have yet to be effectively rectified. Late to the process of industrialization and having just gained their political independence from their French and British masters, countries in the Arab world of all types and sizes—big republics and small monarchies alike—saw public sector expansion as a promising vehicle for state building and modernization.

Rapid and aggressive bureaucratic growth served its purposes for a while as it led to the employment of large amounts of people; allowed for wide nationalizations of industry, trade, and finance; provided law and order; and delivered critical social goods and welfare services, including subsidized food and medicine as well as free education. This process seemed rational, given the historical weakness of the private sector, and it was necessary for the management of demographic growth and societal complexity. But the Arab bureaucracy grew so much and so fast from the early 1950s to the late 1980s that expansion almost became an end in itself with very little consideration for performance.

With such an unbridled enlargement, problems such as red tape, overstaffing, rent-seeking, poor salaries and conditions, low morale, lack of creativity and initiative, and most of all corruption emerged. Arab rulers had neither the desire nor the ability to slow down the bureaucratic Frankenstein they had created.

A bloated bureaucracy, despite its many imperfections, was a critical instrument for the promotion of rentier and patronage systems, and it served the critical function of control. Indeed, no Arab ruler wanted to shed the huge number of public sector workers because it was too politically risky and inconsistent with their populist policies.

Naturally, some Arab countries handled this process better than others. For example, despite the enduring problem of corruption in its public administration, Morocco has to some extent managed to escape the bureaucratic inflation trap.[24]

In his classic work *Political Order in Changing Societies*, Samuel Huntington analyzed the level of institutionalization of any political system by looking at the adaptability, complexity, autonomy, and coherence of its organizations and procedures.[25] All Arab government institutions score fairly low on most if not all of these indicators. That's not to say that there has not been improvement over the years, or that administrative performance does not vary across the region. There has, and it does. As Nazih Ayubi rightly emphasizes, "cases of managerial, organizational and developmental success *do* occur in the Arab world. . . . In Egypt, the same bureaucracy that failed in promoting the agrarian reform is the one that succeeded in managing the Suez Canal and in building the Aswan High Dam. The same Egyptian people had managed . . . to plan and implement the impressive crossing of the Suez Canal in the October War of 1973, and managed . . . to keep the war a total surprise."[26] More recently, corporate entities that are owned by the ruling families in the UAE such as Abu Dhabi National Oil Company and Dubai Ports World have yielded better economic and governance outputs over the past two decades due to their strong management profiles. Jamil Jreisat argues that the Jordanian bureaucracy has performed more ably than in the past in part because of the government's efforts to establish new central and local-level public administration bodies to better utilize scarce resources.[27]

The Saudi bureaucracy is by no means a paragon of effectiveness and efficiency—certainly not in the health and education sectors—but reasonable minds can agree that the kingdom's national oil company Aramco, a large bureaucracy, is run even more competently than many of its major international competitors. That is why the Saudi authorities often ask Aramco, aptly described by the *Economist* as an "overburdened champion," to carry out development projects unrelated to oil production.[28]

In Bahrain, the Labor Market Regulatory Authority is a high-performing government body whose mission is to regulate and control work permits for expatriate employees and self-employed individuals. Established by King Hamad bin Isa Al Khalifa in 2006, this organization has been recognized by the Department of State and awarded by several international institutions for its executive excellence. For three years in a row since 2018, it has been classified as Tier 1 in the Department of State's Trafficking in Persons Report for fully meeting its obligations toward the elimination of trafficking.

In Morocco, efforts by the monarchy in recent years to decentralize, modernize, increase transparency, streamline the management of human resources, and simplify administrative procedures have contributed to job creation and overall better public governance, according to a 2013 study on administrative reform by Khalid Ben Osmane.[29]

Tunisia's decent institutional infrastructure allowed it to deal with the initial wave of the Covid-19 pandemic better than most others in the broader region, argue Yasmina Abouzzohour and Nejla Ben Mimoune.[30] For example, its National Observatory of New and Emerging Diseases, which operates under the Ministry of Health, coordinated effectively with the government-created National Coronavirus Response Authority and implemented a range of health-care measures.

These encouraging cases and promising bureaucratic enhancements across the region notwithstanding, Arab public sector organizations, generally speaking, have struggled greatly to adjust to emerging challenges and opportunities in the globalized world of the twenty-first century partly because their functions, values, norms, and processes have barely changed. Even the Moroccan government, which tends to be ahead of the rest in the Arab world when it comes to public management and institution building, still has a long way to go when it comes to further decentralization of economic growth and more efficient use of public resources.[31] Khalid El Massnaoui and Mhamed Biygautine document that Morocco's overly regulated and fiscally constraining tenure system still favors seniority over performance, and its compensation framework is neither professional nor predictable.[32]

Despite Tunisia's relatively strong response to the first wave of the Covid-19 pandemic, it struggled quite a bit later on because of structural economic problems, including inequality, poverty, poor public management of state resources, and high unemployment. Administrative hurdles and deficiencies have made it more difficult for the Tunisian authorities to effectively implement their own economic recovery plan.[33]

Abd El-Mahdi Massadeh posits that the establishment of public administration agencies in Jordan is based neither on state needs nor on work requirements. "Nor is there any proof," he says, "to the effect that some of them tackle their business in a way dissimilar from their predecessors' procedures, techniques, and processes to justify their establishment."[34] He adds, "the same criticism applies also to state ministries. Their number exceeds work needs and requirements. Duplication in the work of many ministries is due to this fact."[35]

In a 2015 investigation of public service in Egypt, Dina Wafa describes the rigid and resilient nature of the Egyptian civil service, which hasn't changed since the era of Nasser in the 1950s and 1960s. Guaranteed employment, seniority-based advancement, and excessive regulation have contributed to administrative overinflation and decreased talent, leading to below-average work performance.[36] In her interviews and surveys of managerial-level government officials and public sector employees, Wafa reports that only half the participants felt that the right people were selected for their jobs, and only half claimed they were able to apply what they learned from the training they received most of the time.[37]

The World Bank assesses that a key reason why Egypt's growth in the past three decades was "neither sustained nor inclusive" is because of weak public governance, including a public sector that is not transparent or accountable.[38] The International Monetary Fund reached similar conclusions, suggesting in 2018 that the lack of good public and corporate governance, transparency, and accountability has denied Egypt the opportunity to unlock the potential of necessary fiscal and monetary reforms.[39]

In their analysis of the state of Saudi Arabia's health-care system and its role in Saudi Vision 2030, Redwanur Rahman and Ameerah Qattan find the Saudi bureaucracy to be "unduly complex due to overcentralization, nepotism, limited accountability, undue formality and intransigence, and heavy workloads. These issues are compounded by the overlap of functions, bureaucratic corruption, the ubiquity of rules and procedures, fragile implementation and monitoring capacity, the inefficient flow of information, and lack of information to make decisions."[40]

What explains this pattern of poor public governance across the Arab world? Ayubi argues, and he is right on some level, that "Arab rulers appear to prefer a system of administrative authority in which all power emanates from a single political leader, and where the influence of others is derivative in rough proportion to their perceived access to him or their share in his largesse."[41] This assessment, to which should be added the role of Arab culture, helps explain why most technical initiatives, funded and/or supported by Western governments, to even modestly reform various defense and security ministries in the Arab world have amounted to little because none has effectively addressed—or frankly is able to address—the structural issue of control by the Arab ruler and the pattern of behavior that is consistent with Arab culture.

However, politicization, as a theory that purports to explain why Arab bureaucracies are thoroughly ineffective and inefficient, is incomplete and perhaps even misleading. Consider this: no Arab autocrat is worried that his Ministry of Agriculture, Tourism, Labor, or Sports is going to overthrow him or undermine his political position, so these organizations tend to be given more room to function independently and without the Arab ruler breathing down their necks. Yet, they *all* show very similar problems and operate in almost exactly the same fashion as defense and interior ministries. There is no shortage of detailed and comprehensive accounts written by Arab authors, analysts, and political scientists such as Samer Shehata, Hisham Sharabi, Abbas Ali, Ali Al-Kubaisi, Abd El-Mahdi Massadeh, and M. K. Badawi describing the multitude of ailments that have plagued the Arab bureaucracy for so long.[42] These public sector management specialists and many others remarkably end up with similar conclusions regarding the functioning of Arab public sector organizations even though they analyze different countries, different administrative bodies, and different societal contexts.

Of their findings, three deserve emphasis. First, lower- and- mid-level staff in Arab government ministries hardly ever produce, innovate, initiate, or act with drive, determination, and independence. Second, problems in Arab public sector organizations, from the simplest to the more complicated, are rarely solved or effectively managed because very few wish to take responsibility or risks; the exchange of information, laterally and vertically, is atrocious; and the level of cooperation and coordination is woeful. This is as true for Cairo as it is for Muscat.

Third, efforts on the part of the very few well-intentioned Arab political leaders to reform the bureaucracy often are obstructed or resisted by dominant conservative forces in society.

This all should lead us to suspect that the problem is not necessarily politicization or coup-proofing as conventional wisdom suggests but is more generally tied to Arab cultural factors. In fact, autocrats like Nasser and even Saddam repeatedly tried to get their bureaucracies to be more assertive, creative, and independent. Their thinking, and that of other autocrats, was that a better-functioning state and economy, enabled by better public governance, would improve the lot of average citizens and in turn increase these rulers' political power and legitimacy.

The coup-proofing literature predicts that the defense and interior ministries of authoritarian states should be the worst because of the ruler's establishment of rigid hierarchy and exercise of strict control. And yet, they hardly ever are. At worst, these national security ministries are as bad as most—but never as bad as ministries of planning or agriculture, for example—and typically, they are much less incompetent, although none of them are ever high-performing.

In fact, most civilian ministries or bureaucracies in the Arab world make defense and interior ministries look like Amazon or Google. One is better off dealing with Egypt's Ministry of Defense than with its Ministry of Labor, for example; or with Iraq's Ministry of Interior than with its Ministry of Water Resources; or with Saudi Arabia's Ministry of Defense and Ministry of Interior (especially when Mohamed bin Nayef and his team ran the latter) than with its Ministry of Economy and Planning.

Having said all that, the Arab bureaucracy has not always failed and is not doomed to fail. The examples of relative administrative success that are mentioned above and several others help demonstrate that there is nothing deterministic about the behavior and productivity of the Arab bureaucracy. It depends to a large extent on the sociopolitical and economic conditions under which the bureaucracy is operating and the set of incentives and disincentives that are presented to it.

This brief assessment of Arab administrative capacity makes clear that Washington's efforts to help build military capability in the Arab world through US assistance programs are going to be *really* hard because it means nudging Arab partners to organize and operate in ways totally different from how they do everything—ways, again, they will resist because they see them as "Western" (although the UAE has been more accepting of Western norms and approaches than most others in the region).

## Notes

1. Lead Inspector General Report to the United States Congress, *Operation Inherent Resolve, April 1, 2019–June 30, 2019,* August 2, 2019, 37; Steven Lee Myers, "U.S. Joins Effort to Equip and Pay Rebels in Syria," *New York Times,* April 1, 2012; C. J. Chivers and Eric Schmitt, "Saudis Step Up Help for Rebels in Syria with Croatian Arms," *New York Times,* February 25, 2013.

2. Kathleen J. McInnis, *Coalition Contributions to Countering the Islamic State* (Washington, DC: Congressional Research Service, August 24, 2016); Helene Cooper and Eric Schmitt, "Airstrikes by U.S. and Allies Hit ISIS Targets in Syria," *New York Times,* September 22, 2014; Becca Wasser et al., *The Air War Against the Islamic State: The Role of Airpower in Operation Inherent Resolve* (Santa Monica, CA: RAND, 2021), 34.

3. Kevin Liptak, "King of Jordan Says ISIS Could Be Defeated 'Fairly Quickly,'" CNN, January 13, 2016.

4. Bob Dreyfuss, "Washington's Weak Response to the Arab Awakening," *The Nation,* August 24, 2011.

5. Defense Security Cooperation Agency, "Mission, Vision, and Values," accessed May 17, 2021, https://www.dsca.mil/mission-vision-and-values.

6. Marcus Weisgerber, "Head of Pentagon Foreign Arms Sales Division Stepping Down After 15 Months on the Job," *Defense One,* October 13, 2021.

7. Stephen R. Covey, A. Roger Merrill, and Rebecca R. Merrill, *First Things First* (New York: Simon and Schuster, 1996), 75.

8. Author's interview with a Pentagon staffer with responsibilities for the Middle East, October 22, 2019.

9. Foreign Assistance Act of 1961, Section 622(c), Public Law no. 87-194, 75 Stat. 424 (1961).

10. Aaron C. Taliaferro, *A Framework for Security Cooperation Planning* (Alexandria, VA: Institute for Defense Analyses, August 2018), 18.

11. This is based on email correspondence with military analyst Kenneth Pollack, March 12, 2021.

12. These are expressions the author often used to hear during his service in the Pentagon from 2018 to 2019.

13. NPR, "Ike's Warning of Military Expansion, 50 Years Later," January 17, 2011.

14. William D. Hartung, "Defense Contractors Are Tightening Their Grip on Our Government," *The Nation,* July 16, 2019.

15. Andrew Exum, "What Progressives Miss About Arms Sales," *Atlantic,* May 23, 2017.

16. Saab, "Broken Partnerships," 86.

17. For one perspective on the likely role of coup-proofing and politicization, see Pollack, *Armies of Sand,* 107–205.

18. For more on this topic, see Shana R. Marshall, "The New Politics of Patronage: The Arms Trade and Clientelism in the Arab World" (PhD diss., University of Maryland, 2012).

19. Reina Pennington, "Military Culture, Military Efficiency, and the Red Army, 1917–1945," in *The Culture of Military Organizations,* ed. Peter R. Mansoor and Williamson Murray (Cambridge: Cambridge University Press, 2019), 226–246.

20. See Michael Eisenstadt and Kenneth M. Pollack, "Armies of Snow and Armies of Sand: The Impact of Soviet Military Doctrine on Arab Militaries," *Middle East Journal* 55, no. 4 (2001): 549–578.

21. Lina Khatib, *Political Culture in the Arab World: Assumptions and Complexities*, Med Dialogue Series no. 34 (Berlin: Konrad Adenauer Stiftung, January 2021).

22. United Nations Development Programme, *Arab Human Development Report 2002: Creating Opportunities for Future Generations* (New York: UNDP, February 13, 2003), 116.

23. United Nations Development Programme, *Arab Human Development Report 2004: Towards Freedom in the Arab World* (New York: UNDP, April 15, 2005), 172.

24. Nazih N. Ayubi, *Over-stating the Arab State: Politics and Society in the Middle East* (London: I. B. Tauris, 1995), 310.

25. Samuel P. Huntington, *Political Order in Changing Societies* (New Haven, CT: Yale University Press, 1968), 12–24.

26. Nazih N. Ayubi, "Bureaucratization as Development: Administrative Development and Development Administration in the Arab World," *International Review of Administrative Sciences* 52, no. 2 (June 1986): 215.

27. Jamil E. Jreisat, "Managing National Development in the Arab States," *Arab Studies Quarterly* 14, no. 2/3 (Spring/Summer 1992): 12.

28. *Economist*, "Saudi Aramco: An Overburdened Champion," February 19, 2015.

29. Aziza Zemrani, "Teaching Public Administration: The Case of Morocco," *Journal of Public Affairs Education* 20, no. 4 (Fall 2014): 521.

30. Yasmina Abouzzohour and Nejla Ben Mimoune, *Policy and Institutional Responses to COVID-19 in the Middle East and North Africa: Tunisia* (Washington, DC: Brookings, December 15, 2020).

31. Jean R. AbiNader, "Facing High Public Employment, Morocco Continues to Build Support for Small and Medium Enterprises," Morocco on the Move, February 10, 2020, https://moroccoonthemove.com/2020/02/10/facing-high-public-employment -morocco-continues-to-build-support-for-small-and-medium-enterprises-jean-r -abinader/.

32. Khalid El Massnaoui and Mhamed Biygautine, *Downsizing Morocco's Public Sector: Lessons from the Voluntary Retirement Program,* Case Studies in Governance and Public Management in the Middle East and North Africa, no. 2 (Dubai: World Bank and Dubai School of Government, November 2011).

33. Abouzzohour and Mimoune, *Policy and Institutional Responses to COVID-19*.

34. Abd El-Mahdi Massadeh, "The Structure of Public Administration in Jordan: A Constitutional and Administrative Law Perspective," *Arab Law Quarterly* 14, no. 2 (1999): 108.

35. Ibid.

36. Dina Wafa, "Capacity-Building for the Transformation of Public Service: A Case of Managerial-Level Public Servants in Egypt," *Teaching Public Administration* 33, no. 2 (2015): 117.

37. Ibid., 122–125.

38. World Bank, "CLR Review, Arab Republic of Egypt," Independent Evaluation Group, December 9, 2015.

39. International Monetary Fund (IMF), "Arab Republic of Egypt," IMF Country Report No. 18/14 (Washington, DC: IMF, January 2018).

40. Redwanur Rahman and Ameerah Qattan, "Vision 2030 and Sustainable Development: State Capacity to Revitalize the Healthcare System in Saudi Arabia," *Journal of Health Care* 58 (January–December 2021): 7.

41. Ayubi, *Over-stating the Arab State*, 321.

42. Samer Shehata, *Shop Floor Culture and Politics in Egypt* (Albany, NY: SUNY Press, 2009); Abbas Ali, "Decision-Making Style, Individualism, and Attitudes Toward Risk of Arab Executives," *International Studies of Management and Organization* 23, no. 3 (1993): 53–73; Ali Al-Kubaisi, "A Model in the Administrative Development of Arab Gulf Countries," *The Arab Gulf 17*, no. 2 (1985): 29–48; Massadeh, "Structure of Public Administration in Jordan"; M. K. Badawi, "Styles of Middle Eastern Managers," *California Management Review* 22, no. 2 (Spring 1980).

# 8

## Achieving Security Cooperation

I HAVE MADE A DELIBERATE DECISION TO START THE BOOK
with what the United States has to do to enhance the effectiveness of its
military assistance programs with its Arab partners. To summarize,
these programs are above all a *US investment*. Indeed, this isn't charity.
And like any other investment, only its author can protect it and do
everything in their power to enable it to generate better returns.

As the senior partner with immense knowledge and experience in
national security policy and planning, the United States is best positioned to offer advice to its junior Arab partners on how to build military capability the right way. Also, the United States is the main supplier of arms to its Arab friends, and it has a vital interest in helping
them better employ and sustain this equipment (along with a moral obligation to do those things). Saudi Arabia's Yemen war and the Arab partners' insufficient military contributions to various coalition campaigns
across the region, including OIR most recently, are examples of the
obvious, negative consequences.

The US military presence in the Middle East can be both an enabler
of and an inhibitor to more effective US-Arab security cooperation.
Depending on how the United States decides to posture itself in the
region moving forward—keeping a large footprint that tries but fails to
do it all or switching to a trimmed one that focuses on training, advising,
and equipping partners and making the "by, with, and through" approach
of CENTCOM actually work—the Arab states might either feel incentivized or disincentivized to implement much-needed defense reforms.

In the previous chapters, I identified leadership and organization as two critical variables that have been in short supply when it comes to US security cooperation. Therefore, it seems only reasonable that I base my thoughts about how to fix some of US security cooperation's larger problems on those two fundamental ailments of the enterprise.

## A US Global Security Cooperation Command

To properly elevate institutional capacity building in the ecosystem of US security cooperation, structural surgery is required. The first of such major readjustments is the formation of a global US security cooperation command that can integrate the American security cooperation community on a global level, centrally manage and coordinate its activities, and emphasize defense institution building with foreign partners.

It is tempting to limit the security cooperation fix to the Middle East region and create a security cooperation command just for CENTCOM, instead of having to reform the enterprise worldwide, but this is not feasible. Nor is it advisable. Here's why.

From a US bureaucratic and budgetary standpoint, there is one *global* pot of security cooperation money. It is one consolidated security cooperation budget, per Section 381 of Title 10's Chapter 16, that gets to be distributed to six GCCs (the new US Space Command has yet to receive security cooperation funds). Things are constructed as such for at least three good reasons.

First, CENTCOM's security cooperation problems are not unique to CENTCOM. They are shared by all the other GCCs. Therefore, this has to be addressed on a *global* level. Keeping things the way they are now, where each GCC conducts its own security cooperation activities with no effective communication and integration among all the GCCs, is detrimental to US partner capability development goals worldwide. Resourcing decisions and personnel development and employment in particular benefit from a global rather than a regional perspective.

Second, the GCCs do not "own" their security cooperation personnel (outside of a few staff officers at the headquarters); rather, the US military services do—that is, the army, marine corps, navy, air force, and coast guard. (Again, it's unclear how much the new space force is involved in security cooperation.)

This creates tension in that the GCCs are the customer for security cooperation in their respective areas (through the theater security cooperation plan) and therefore want to influence that process, but the forces being used for security cooperation are not normally assigned to them in the way that combatant forces are. The GCCs don't necessarily get a vote in security cooperation outside of spending their own Title 10 money (i.e., for military exercises).

Third, training for security cooperation is a huge issue because no one wants to pay for it and there is relatively little specific resourcing for it. A global command, on the other hand, is not only easier to resource but comes with the added benefit of a unified approach to security cooperation planning and employment.

That's all on the administrative side of things. Politically speaking, it is highly doubtful that senior American officials would make a decision to fix security cooperation in the Middle East while ignoring other geographical areas. This is even less likely to happen now at a time when Washington is trying to de-emphasize the Middle East and prioritize the Indo-Pacific and Europe.

The example of SOCOM, while not a perfect one, offers clues as to why a global command for security cooperation is not just desirable but probably necessary. On April 24, 1980, US SOF were sent by President Carter to a desolate staging area in Iran, designated "Desert One," to rescue fifty-three Americans held captive by the Iranian regime at the US embassy in Tehran. Operation Eagle Claw, as it was code-named, failed miserably. The US aviation assets flown to the area faced significant mechanical problems, and only six of the eight arrived at the location. The mission had to be aborted. As the withdrawal of US forces proceeded, however, a helicopter crashed into a C-130 military transport plane carrying fuel and American servicemen. The collision killed eight of them.

The Desert One debacle was followed three years later by another tactical failure of US SOF in Grenada. In Operation Urgent Fury, US forces managed to effortlessly invade the tiny island nation, rescue Americans, and roll back communist influence in the Caribbean. But the way the mission was executed brought back painful memories of Desert One. The US Marine Corps and the US Army led totally separate operations in Grenada and could not even communicate with each other because their radios were not technically compatible.[1] Flaws in joint command structures hampered the operation's overall effectiveness.

Despite the strong objections of the Pentagon and tepid endorsement (if not downright objection) of the Reagan administration, SOCOM was established in 1987 by way of the bipartisan Nunn-Cohen amendment. In line with the recommendations of several retired and active-duty generals and admirals, Congress made SOCOM a four-star command to afford it the gravitas required to secure adequate funding, appropriations, and authorities, and to interact on an equal footing with other military commands. By combining the skill sets of special operators from distinct elements in the US military and developing a joint culture that stressed cooperation, SOCOM turned its most stubborn doubters into its most ardent believers.[2]

A global security cooperation command would essentially seek to solve similar problems to those that afflicted the special operations community in the past: competition and lack of effective communication and integration among the GCCs on security cooperation. Such a command would have budget authority and organize, employ, train, equip, and sustain a joint security cooperation force. It would provide a coherent global framework for action and synthesize the perspectives and inputs of the GCCs into a single comprehensive assessment of the Pentagon's security cooperation efforts worldwide. It would help adjudicate security cooperation prioritization and resourcing, which every fiscal year turns into an unproductive food fight among the GCCs that ends up getting resolved in rather haphazard and less-than-strategic ways by the Office of the Under Secretary of Defense for Policy. It would introduce the same kind of discipline into the security cooperation system that SOCOM did into special operations. And like SOCOM, it would be a functional command, and thus a force provider.

Like special operators, security cooperation officers are not general-purpose forces. They are low-density, high-demand personnel, and they ought to be treated as such. Given that these officers would still come from the individual US armed services, ensuring their proper training in the integration of institutional capacity building into security cooperation planning would be key.

As things currently stand, security cooperation is not an important part of the services' core mission. The services primarily rely on foreign area officer (FAO) programs to "develop" security cooperation officers. The US Army has a large FAO program compared to the other services, but not many candidates are trained to become and *remain* security cooperation specialists. FAOs are simply not the answer because they are not defense management experts.

One model that could serve the goal of training personnel who would make up this new security cooperation command is that of theater special operations commands (TSOCs). TSOCs are sub-unified commands under their respective GCCs.

What these TSOCs do is provide the planning, preparation, and command and control of SOF from across the US military. Each is ultimately responsible to its geographic combatant commander for integrating and employing SOF in theater plans and ensuring that fully trained staff participate in theater mission planning.

Some of this bureaucratic engineering might be overkill, and perhaps the better examples to look at for a security cooperation command are US Cyber Command, US Space Command, and US Transportation Command. Frankly, it matters less which model is more relevant so long as the goal of effective planning, prioritization, and resource allocation on a global basis is achieved. An independent security cooperation command that can work together with the Office of the Secretary of Defense to set global priorities and then manage the crucial program to build partner capacity is what is most crucial.

What would be different about a security cooperation command, and arguably less challenging in terms of its creation, is that it would not need to procure peculiar equipment and supplies from the individual armed services to fulfill its mission.[3] Indeed, its capabilities, whether it is combat tanks, a surface action group, or a squadron of fighters, would not have to be built from scratch and instead come straight from the services.

Overall, a security cooperation command's mission would be less kinetic or lethal and more comprehensive than that of SOCOM, for example. And ideally, it would be less bureaucratic than what SOCOM has become, although that might be less likely since integration would naturally require and lead to a higher level of administration. Lastly, a security cooperation command would not necessarily have to be huge and could operate with only a fraction of the budget of SOCOM, which in 2020 was a whopping $14 billion.[4]

One significant practical challenge that is likely to undermine the effectiveness of a security cooperation command, and security cooperation in its current structure more broadly, is the issue of acquisition. Even if such a command were to be granted budget authority like SOCOM, the defense acquisition system in the US government is heavily biased for larger platforms and almost rigged against smaller weapons systems when it comes to transfers to allies and partners.

It is a service-centric acquisition process, which is perfectly understandable because it is supposed to respond to the needs of the services. In other words, the US defense industry builds weapons that the services require to fulfill their respective missions, but sometimes what an Arab partner truly needs in order to build a capability does not cost hundreds of thousands or millions of dollars and may not even be US-produced.

To enable security cooperation to operate at a higher level, American security cooperation personnel should be granted a bit more budget flexibility and limited contracting authority (which of course would not be divorced from broader planning) to allow them to procure equipment from either the local economy or other allies that could help build the capability of the partner.

This would present challenges to both US policy and process, but they are not insurmountable. With regard to the latter, the US acquisition system is not agile enough to procure non-US equipment for partners and engage in what can be termed as *microfinance*. If the weapons system is not a "program of record" (i.e., not part of the normal planning, programming, and budgeting process), it is extremely difficult to procure. (However, it has been done repeatedly in Afghanistan in the mid- to late 2000s, for example, when the United States provided its Afghan partners nonstandard equipment following special congressional authorization.)[5]

In terms of policy, there is an ongoing intense competition in the international arms trade between the United States and its key adversaries (and even its closest allies). So going to the Russians, or even the French or the British, to procure arms for a partner will be difficult to digest by many senior US officials and lawmakers.

Those two big barriers notwithstanding, the items under consideration would be small-scale and high-impact and thus should not affect the already dominant position of the United States in global weapons sales. If there's a will, Washington is perfectly capable of finding a balance between preserving its equities in the arms trade and generating greater returns on its security cooperation investments.

In addition to these considerations, there are various other psychological, political, and budgetary roadblocks that would have to be overcome in order to create a security cooperation command. It took a tragedy—Desert One—for Washington to rethink how it did special operations. Recall also that major reforms in the US intelligence community were instituted only after terrorists struck New York City and the Pentagon on September 11, 2001.

It is hard to foresee any misfortune as visible and catastrophic as Desert One or 9/11 occurring in the realm of security cooperation that could prompt an overhaul of the enterprise. Although deeply troubling, the possibility that American weapons could occasionally end up in the hands of terrorists or be misused by Arab partners is not likely to be a major catalyst (although that possibility did lead to the formulation of historic security cooperation reforms). In fact, US-supplied weapons have found their way to the Islamic State and other anti-American jihadist groups, and Saudi Arabia has devastated the civilian population of Yemen substantially using American weapons and intelligence assistance, to little effect on thinking in Washington.

Bureaucratic inertia is a significant impediment. Active resistance to standing up a security cooperation command is likely to arise from various stakeholders largely because the new command would inevitably rearrange the rice bowls (military slang for jealously guarded resources). In other words, like SOCOM did, a security cooperation command would require dedicated money, authorities, and access to US political and military leadership that have traditionally been the prerogatives of the individual armed services. The same, of course, was true of SOCOM.

One source of opposition is likely to be DSCA, which not only executes and administers all security cooperation programs and activities for the Defense Department but also helps conduct planning and set priorities. DSCA would be forced to surrender those security cooperation prerogatives. Next in line is the Office of the Under Secretary of Defense for Policy because it seems to be happy with the current state of play, having failed to provide effective policy oversight and guidance for resource allocation for security cooperation.

If history is any guide, the service chiefs and the joint staff would vehemently oppose a new security cooperation command as a dilution of their resources and supervisory power. In turn, the secretary of defense is not likely to be very sympathetic to the idea either, precisely because of the headache it would cause him or her vis-à-vis the service chiefs and the joint staff.

The secretary of state, on the other hand, might be agnostic or even supportive, since a security cooperation command would theoretically yield better global strategic planning, which would provide a stronger basis for foreign military sales, over which the State Department has statutory authority. A stronger rationale for FMS, one that is undergirded by more coherent planning, is in the interest of the State Department.

The GCCs probably would not contest the formation of a security cooperation command as long as it did not take away from them what they care about the most: funds to secure and maintain access, basing, and overflight in the partner nations.

The executive body that would have the most credibility, clout, and positioning to push effectively for the establishment of a security cooperation command is the National Security Council Principals Committee, which is the preeminent interagency forum for consideration of policy issues affecting US national security. Whether the current array of senior officials would be able to reach consensus on such a major defense reform is an open question.

In any case, Congress would ultimately play the most important and decisive role in the potential creation of a security cooperation command. The history of SOCOM shows that were it not for far-sighted leaders on Capitol Hill—in particular, senators Sam Nunn and William Cohen—the executive branch never would have agreed to establish SOCOM.[6]

Should power politics and turf battles be managed for the sake of the US national interest (this wouldn't be inconceivable because it has happened before in similar contexts) and a security cooperation command were to be formed, it does not mean that it would be smooth sailing afterwards. For example, when the Pentagon lost the fight of SOCOM to senators Nunn and Cohen, its leadership found more subtle ways to delay or obstruct execution. Through classic bureaucratic warfare, US defense officials induced enough friction in the system to make the senators almost regret their legislative success. There is no reason to expect anything different with security cooperation. The service chiefs and senior defense officials probably will employ similar tactics.

## Effective Civilian Oversight

If a security cooperation command were to be established, it would be headed by a four-star general or admiral, subject to oversight by senior civilian leaders in the Pentagon. I support the creation of a new position of an under secretary of defense for security cooperation to ensure the most effective civilian oversight. Some might view this as unnecessary or overkill given that the current chain of command provides the under secretary of defense for policy the authority to oversee security cooperation and make sure its output is in line with the priorities of the NDS. However, because the Pentagon's top policy official has several other priorities and a saturated agenda, that responsibility tends to fall by the wayside. The under secretary of defense for policy does have two deputies, one at the assistant secretary level and one at the deputy assistant secretary level, helping him or her fulfill oversight duty, but neither official has the bureaucratic heft to instruct four-stars to pursue courses of action that they might otherwise perceive as contradictory to their commands' missions and priorities.

Just as a four-star commander of security cooperation would immediately send a strong signal to the *military* community of the increased strategic significance of the enterprise, an under secretary would swiftly elevate it within the *civilian* community in ways a deputy assistant secretary or an assistant secretary could not. The United States has an under secretary of defense for intelligence and security, for example, and another one for personnel and readiness. And although I'm by no means downplaying the role intelligence plays in national security, for example, I'm also not entirely certain that security cooperation is any less strategic, especially when it is now officially described as an essential component of the NDS.

For those less convinced, recall that security cooperation costs the United States *billions of taxpayer money every single year*. It directly shapes events on the ground and impacts US security interests on a daily basis in a way that very few US foreign policy tools do.

Again, the case of SOCOM is instructive. Per the Nunn-Cohen amendment, an assistant secretary of defense for special operations/low-intensity conflict (SO/LIC) is responsible for providing oversight over all SOF. However, that official has generally been unable to effectively perform their statutory duties because of two reasons: (1) their interlocutor in SOCOM, a four-star general, clearly outranks them, thus complicating the chain of command picture, and (2) the special operations community has become so large and prestigious since 9/11 that an assistant secretary of defense is less capable of managing it on their own.

This oversight construct was an evident mistake by Congress from the outset, but it has yet to be rectified. If security cooperation is to be put on the same strategic level as special operations—which I'm arguing it should—then it definitely deserves more senior civilian oversight than is presently the case. The security cooperation process that currently exists in which DSCA plays an oversized role and overemphasizes equipment transfers, and a deputy assistant secretary of defense fails to have their voice heard, is deeply flawed. For security cooperation to be taken seriously, it needs a more senior official dedicated full-time to managing the enterprise, making tough decisions and tradeoffs, generating products, and sharing those products with the community. More broadly, security cooperation needs a more senior official to gradually change the culture of the security cooperation community and push for some difficult and necessary reforms that, among other goals, seek to effectively integrate institutional capacity building into security cooperation planning.

Although comprehensive legislation has been enacted by Congress to steer security cooperation in a more strategic direction, the reforms of the FY 2017 NDAA require a policy champion to oversee their implementation. An under secretary of defense would emphasize to all civilian and military stakeholders that pursuing defense institution building in conjunction with train-and-equip programs is neither a charity nor a luxury—it is a necessity, one that benefits first the security interests of the United States, and second those of the partner.

Let me offer one final important point on the issue of civilian oversight. Underscoring the importance of civilian and policy oversight over security cooperation does not mean that such oversight should be uncompromising or overwhelming; it just has to be effective and conducive to some kind of balance in civil-military dynamics and interactions.

After all, during the Eisenhower administration, the Mutual Security Program, which created a network of defensive forces that amplified US deterrence in the Asia-Pacific, was personally overseen by the president and run by a strong civilian Foreign Operations Administration. But the program was ineffective and could not survive US domestic politics as the Kennedy administration sharply cut its funding and divided its management between the Defense and State Departments.[7]

## If the Status Quo Prevails

As crucial as these proposed structural reforms to security cooperation are, it is entirely possible that they may not be endorsed and implemented due to their transformative and politically contentious nature. But that does not mean that the status quo, where DSCA maintains its planning, budget, coordination, and management roles in security cooperation, ought to remain untouched.

Some steps could be taken to ameliorate the existing process. First, the under secretary of defense for policy would have to rearrange their priorities to exercise more effective oversight over DSCA's security cooperation portfolio. This is critical because DSCA's work impacts, oftentimes directly, core defense *policy* matters, which are and should always remain the prerogative of civilian leadership in the Pentagon.

In 2008, DSCA reported to Assistant Secretary of Defense for Global Security Affairs Joseph Benkert, and in 2009–2012, it reported to Peter Verga, the chief of staff to Under Secretary of Defense for Policy Michèle Flournoy. The latest measure that requires the DSCA director to report to the assistant secretary of defense for strategy, plans, and capabilities is a step in the right direction, but as stated earlier, it doesn't effectively limit DSCA's oversized influence over security cooperation policy.

In the absence of any structural reforms to security cooperation, it is worth considering reinstating either one of these command and oversight models because experience shows that it worked with both.

Second, the functions of planning and budgeting should be taken away from DSCA and transferred to civilian leadership in the Pentagon. Walls have to be created between budgeting and oversight, planning, and execution, all of which now reside in DSCA. DSCA is like the fox guarding the security cooperation henhouse, which needless to say is thoroughly misguided. To put it in even starker terms, DSCA cannot be allowed to grade its own homework.[8]

Third, DSCA would have to conceptualize and approach defense institution building differently. Its total package approach to an arms sale, while supremely valuable, should not be equated with institutional capacity building. The former focuses on how to help the partner better operate and tactically maintain the equipment, whereas the latter is more comprehensive and addresses the critical issues of sustainment and governance. First comes the advice and training of the partner on what weapons systems to invest in, *then* the procurement. But DSCA does it in reverse, with the equipping part preceding the training part. Defense institution building is only impactful if it's integrated *in advance* into the capability development plan in consultation with the partner, and not treated as a supplementary item after the acquisition is made.

As mentioned earlier, institutional capacity building will never be a priority of DSCA because the organization will continue to be judged—and it's definitely not its fault but rather that of senior civilian policy officials—on how many weapons it sells, not how it helped a partner establish stronger defense governance mechanisms and military capability.

Fourth, DSCA and the Office of the Deputy Assistant Secretary of Defense for Global Partnerships must speak the same language and truly marry their planning processes. Otherwise, confusion in the GCCs will prevail, giving them an excuse to continue to rely on their own planning processes and constructs, which tend to be more tactical and operational and less strategic.

Fifth, the strategic guidance that the Office of the Deputy Assistant Secretary of Defense for Global Partnerships issues to the GCCs has to be more logically compelling, and equally important, it should come out promptly to inform the planning of the GCCs. Otherwise, once again, the GCCs will fall back to what they are most familiar and comfortable with.

Sixth, DSCA needs to devote greater resources to training the security cooperation officers in the GCCs on how to do better planning, and how to more effectively assess the partner's goals, political and security context, and capacity to absorb and sustain new equipment.

Seventh, it would be most advisable to create greater synergies between the global partnerships office and the regional policy offices of the Pentagon (so in the case of the Middle East, it would be the Office of the Deputy Assistant Secretary of Defense for Middle East Policy).

These offices have unique regional and country-specific expertise, yet they lack a thorough understanding of how US security cooperation legally and procedurally works. By joining staff from security cooperation and the regionals, the ability to help achieve US strategic objectives improves.

The risk is that the regional offices, like the GCCs, prioritize the preservation of bilateral ties with the partner and thus are less likely to push it to pursue defense reforms if they feel this would risk the relationship. But with defense institution building now being required by US law and with the under secretary of defense for policy ideally emphasizing this requirement moving forward, there is hope that security cooperation can be better utilized by the regional offices. If such a bureaucratic integration were to take place, it would free up the Pentagon's global partnerships office to focus on the already enormous job of assessment, monitoring, and evaluation of the enterprise.

## Congressional Authorization, Oversight, and Accountability

For a security cooperation command to be instituted, Congress first has to pass legislation like it boldly did in 1986 when Cohen-Nunn established SOCOM. In partnership with Lt. Gen. Samuel V. Wilson, who "planted the seed [of SOCOM] and nurtured it along the way," Senators Nunn and Cohen pushed the envelope and took the legislative process to the finish line.[9] Like Nunn and Cohen, McCain was a visionary and the main author of security cooperation's monumental reforms, but with him recently gone, it is hard to see new congressional leaders in this especially polarized political environment in Washington emerging, commanding the respect of both political parties, and not being afraid to shake things up and push for reforms that might be unpopular and politically costly.

Congress is to be commended for exercising leadership and proposing the far-reaching security cooperation reforms in the FY2017 NDAA, but that is not enough. US lawmakers should perform consistent oversight and insist on accountability by more frequently holding public and closed hearings on security cooperation.

They need to ask the commanders, the civilian leaders, and the DSCA director the hard questions, such as what is the desired, specific end state of security cooperation with the partner, and when can it realistically be achieved? Is the partner able to absorb, sustain, and integrate US equipment into its force structure in order to develop the desired military capability? And if it is unable to do that, or unwilling to address US concerns, what are the risks to ending or conditioning US support?

Should there be no attempt to answer these questions in good faith, and if security cooperation reforms do not proceed at a faster pace, Congress should consider punitive measures, including cutting budgets. None of this will come easily for a couple of reasons. First, senior staffers and sometimes even senators are awed by the power of the generals and predisposed to giving them everything they need with few strings attached out of a commendable, albeit misguided, sense of patriotism. There are not enough strong personalities in Congress, like the late Senator McCain, who have the knowledge and confidence to smartly challenge US personnel in uniform and are willing to take political risks.

Second, as mentioned previously, security cooperation does not typically sell in Congress because it does not have a constituency. Arms sales lead to American jobs—a major concern for members of Congress.

## Bring Back the State Department

Security cooperation is less likely to help the United States achieve its strategic objectives around the world absent deeper involvement by the State Department. More specifically, this will require a more serious process of joint planning for security cooperation and security assistance between the Defense Department and the State Department.

This might be a pipe dream, given how far apart the two departments are in terms of how they run their operations and how they plan (State does not do much strategic planning for security assistance, which is a big part of the problem). But this reality does not make this old objective any less critical. Only a combined approach, enabled by both secretaries, will work, one that leverages each department's unique skill set—diplomatic engagement and development assistance in the case of Foggy Bottom, and military cooperation in the case of the Pentagon—and creates a joint-planning roadmap for the Pentagon's Section 333 and Foggy Bottom's FMF that helps to prioritize and guide what each department would request for capacity-building resources.[10]

Despite claims of the "militarization of US foreign policy," it is worth noting that the State Department's financial equities in international security engagement (a large umbrella term) are larger than those of the Defense Department. And yet, there is little visibility into what goes into FMF, for example, let alone USAID's budget, which is a black hole.

As keen as Congress is to inspect the Pentagon's security cooperation activities, it should keep an even closer eye on the State Department's foreign aid. Formulating a set of reforms of Foggy Bottom's security assistance that parallel the scope and breadth of those of the FY 2017 NDAA is a good idea too.

## The Arab Partners' End of the Bargain

The United States can take all the right steps to get its security cooperation house in order, and it can provide the best gear and advice to its Arab friends, but if these partners are unable or unwilling to absorb the counseling, seriously chip in, and commit to better defense governance practices themselves, this collaborative effort will never reach its potential. As with any other element of structural reform, defense institution building in the Arab world is not likely to go very far absent a measure of government openness. Indeed, for the process to yield tangible results, it has to allow for a degree of empowerment of people and decentralization of decisionmaking structures, about which Arab autocrats are always particularly sensitive.

If the Arab leader himself is unconvinced of the merits of defense institution building, does not think it is a priority, or believes that the aggressive and unconditional pursuit of such a process could take him out of power or reduce his privileges, he is not likely to authorize it, and neither the United States nor any other foreign power can force him to do it.

That said, it is possible to temper such resistance through the issuance of negative and positive incentives by US officials. In some situations, such as Egypt, where the authorities' commitment to improved defense governance is suspect at best, Washington should consider applying conditionality to US security assistance and cooperation. Yes, it is an old idea that might induce some yawning because it does not have a good track record, but that doesn't mean it cannot be more effectively implemented through the US adherence to clearer standards.

On many occasions, Washington did freeze assistance or stop a weapons sale to several countries including Bahrain and Saudi Arabia for suspected violations of human rights. There is no reason why it cannot do the same if it sees no progress on institutional capacity building.

In fact, the two disciplines are interrelated. Better defense governance makes partners not only more capable but ideally also more responsible, accountable, and respectful of US and international law.

What's the point of having core US legislation in the FY 2017 NDAA committing American officials to assess, monitor, and evaluate security cooperation if partners receiving US funds never face consequences for cheating or underachieving? US assistance to any Arab partner, whether it comes from the Defense Department or the State Department, should never be treated as an entitlement program. Those who show greater commitment to defense governance among other US requirements will be rewarded, whereas those who dismiss or delay it ought to have their assistance frozen or cut.

Naturally, Arab partners who do not receive security cooperation and assistance grants from Washington and use their own national funds to buy US military equipment—Saudi Arabia, the UAE, and Qatar—are in a better position to politely (and sometimes not so politely) snub US advice on defense institution building if they want to. That is perfectly their sovereign right. But those who are recipients of billions of dollars under the FMF program, including Egypt, Jordan, Iraq, Morocco, Bahrain, Tunisia, Lebanon, and Oman, must be subjected to much greater scrutiny. After all, it is America's *own money*. These funds do help combat terrorism; provide access, overflight, and basing rights to the US military; honor strategic agreements; and solidify political ties. Yet, that does not mean that these countries should be offered a blank check.

Furthermore, as mentioned previously, the significance of many of these interests has changed due to a shifting strategic environment and new fiscal realities in Washington. It is now in the United States' interest to counsel all Arab partners to invest in defense institution building. This should not be viewed or presented to the partner as a nice thing to have or as icing on the cake of US assistance. It should be a core requirement.

With regard to positive US incentives, French emperor Napoleon Bonaparte's words might be instructive: "Success is the most convincing talker in the world," he said.[11] By sharing the insights and lessons from positive experiences of defense institution building that they have had with other international partners, US officials can get their Arab counterparts to at least listen and possibly show interest in the process.

Not all of Washington's security cooperation experiences with developing partner nations have been failures. Outside the Middle East, Colombia, the Philippines, the Republic of Georgia, and a few others have been relatively successful cases in part because—in response to partner request—the United States has provided long-term and comprehensive assistance in defense institution building with those countries. Washington has helped the Colombian, Philippine, and Georgian armed forces in recent years not only address security threats more effectively but also plan, manage, recruit, budget, and solve logistics more effectively. Again, it all starts with the partner. Every one of these countries recognized the need for defense transformation or improved defense governance, reached out to the United States for help, identified shared goals, and committed to execution. These partners drove the process, not the United States.

Progress in defense reform in the Colombian, Georgian, and Philippine cases was made not because US defense and societal culture was a better match for the Colombians, the Filipinos, or the Georgians. Rather, it was because those partners were able to make those US norms *their own* and tailor them to their needs. That is where the Arabs have struggled a great deal.

The Colombian government leveraged US foreign aid to upgrade and redesign the country's armed forces throughout the 2000s. This process, which escalated in early 2008, has sought to enable the Colombian defense and security sector to more effectively address evolving threats in the twenty-first century beyond narco-terrorism through a set of reforms in defense management including capability-based force planning, budget planning, and HRM.

Defense transformation in Bogotá led to serious inroads in the war against narco-terrorism, pushing the Revolutionary Armed Forces of Colombia, after suffering significant military losses, to reach a historic agreement with the government in 2016 through which the former promised to declare all its assets and hand them over to the Colombian authorities. US support of Colombia's defense restructuring officially started in January 2010 and has continued since. At the institutional level, US administrators of the DIRI program have worked very closely with the Colombian Ministry of Defense, as well as its police and armed forces, to develop a Capability Planning and Development Model. This construct lays out the requirements for the Ministry of Defense and the Colombian army, navy, air force, and national police to connect their budget submissions to their national security objectives and then monitor and evaluate progress toward their overall strategic objectives.

Despite the relative weakness of state capacity in Colombia throughout its modern history, the US effort to help Colombia revamp its Ministry of Defense and strengthen its law-enforcement capabilities has been particularly effective, generating outcomes that have proven to be long-lasting. These include better civilian oversight of the armed forces, more coherent defense policy guidance, institutionalization of various planning and budgetary processes, and cultural changes within the Ministry of Defense that now emphasize sustainment and intra- and interdepartmental coordination.

In a thorough analysis of the US-Colombia defense partnership, Michael Miklaucic and Juan Carlos Pinzón attribute success to "a common perception of the shared burdens, mutual respect, trust in each other, reciprocal commitment, and frequent, if not constant, consultation."[12] Lina Gonzalez, Aaron Taliaferro, and Wade Hinkle, who were assigned to lead several parts of the US defense reform program in Bogotá for many years, concur on the huge importance of shared security interests between the United States and Colombia. Two other enabling factors, they argue, are a relatively stable and consistent leadership in the Colombian Ministry of Defense and the Colombians' eagerness to research best practices, seek advice from international partners, and build their own intellectual capital in defense reform.[13] More broadly, that the Colombians had undergone profound political change and very much enhanced the functioning of their national bureaucracy since the 1991 Constitution, partly through the decentralization of some public services, aided the defense reform process considerably.

Over the past three decades, the Colombian state has pursued a robust governance-reform agenda. It has instituted important fiscal adjustments. It has promoted inclusive participation and access to information. It has made major efforts to fight corruption. And it has acquired better regulatory capacity in issues like justice administration and the protection of property rights.[14]

Of course, there's a ton of room for institutional improvement still, especially in the areas of public transparency and balanced, sustainable development. Deepening the modernization of administrative structures and decisionmaking capacities and enhancing coordination among different levels of government continue to be critical in addressing poverty and reducing regional disparities. But by the time the Colombians launched their defense restructuring effort, their overall institutional baseline in the public administration wasn't terrible, and the legacy of reform was real, which made implementation of the defense restructuring plan a lot more manageable.

Like Colombia, Georgia has mutual foreign policy and security interests with the United States, which is always a good foundation for stronger defense ties. The country is a close partner of Washington in the fight against Russian revanchism in Eastern Europe and Western

Asia. And despite its small size, it was an important contributor to NATO-led operations in Afghanistan from 2004 to 2021 and a leading recipient of US foreign and military aid in Europe and Eurasia especially since the 2000s, benefiting from billions of US dollars.[15]

One critical lesson the Georgians learned from the 2008 confrontation with Russia, aside from not underestimating the Russians' interests in South Ossetia and Abkhazia, was that an arms buildup does not equate with real combat power (a piece of advice the Arabs very much should heed given their emphasis on equipment rather than full-spectrum capability).

For years, the Georgians kept growing their military, though with little strategic logic or planning, despite NATO's counsel to trim and sustain the force and pay close attention to interoperability with Western partners.[16] The humbling outcome of the 2008 war began to change the Georgians' attitude toward military development, with Tbilisi seeking to reorganize its armed forces and drastically reform its defense enterprise with the full-fledged support of the United States and NATO.

In June 2016, NATO established a Defence Institution Building School in Georgia. The initiative is part of the Substantial NATO-Georgia Package, and it consists of a set of thirteen capacity-building measures that seek to strengthen Georgia's defense capabilities by focusing on "professional development and information exchange and collaboration in the areas of security and defense policy and management."[17]

In February 2017, the Georgia Defense Readiness Program (GDRP) was officially born. A bilateral security cooperation framework on which the United States embarked *at the invitation of the Georgian government*, the GDRP has sought over the past few years to support the Georgian Ministry of Defense and train all of Georgia's nine light infantry battalions on national defense missions through live-fire exercises.[18] In that respect, the program has two main components: one for tactical and operational training and one for institutional development.

Before the GDRP began in earnest, the Georgians had met certain prerequisites to demonstrate their seriousness with respect to embracing defense reforms, including completing a Strategic Defense Review, making a budgetary plan to implement it, and reallocating funds to support unit readiness requirements. The Georgians also committed to cutting back on funding for legacy programs and systems that were diverting resources from readiness objectives.

Although key challenges remain in terms of planning, resourcing, and budgeting for training and sustaining the readiness of their military, the Georgians, with US and international support, have made key strides with their Ministry of Defense and General Staff in rationalizing the organization of their forces, inculcating command responsibility for readiness standards, streamlining their HRM system, and optimizing their acquisition and procurement processes to preserve resources for their readiness goals.

The US military assistance program in Georgia has produced positive and perhaps enduring outcomes because, first and foremost, the Georgians recognized that the way they were pursuing military development, focusing a little too much on hardware and neglecting sustainment, was misguided.[19]

Georgia's administrative capacity has undergone a remarkable evolution, much like the country's politics. The official transition from Soviet rule to independence in April 1991 was celebratory but also very rough for the Georgians. They emerged as a fractured nation, with secessionist movements in Abkhazia and South Ossetia challenging state control, and with physical capital destroyed due to instability. Successive governments slogged through the political fragility and economic hardship, barely able or even willing to reform. For years, government ministries were disorganized, with overlapping responsibilities and little accountability.

Things took a dramatic turn for the better in January 2004 when President Mikheil Saakashvili was elected following the so-called Rose Revolution in November 2003. The new government immediately committed to bold and holistic governance reform in order to make a total switch from socialism to a market economy and a better functioning bureaucracy.

The results were brilliant and recognized by numerous international organizations such as the UN, the European Bank for Reconstruction and Development, and the World Bank. New laws were issued, corruption was controlled, institutions were built, transparency and accountability improved, more effective HRM systems were introduced, and liberalization and deregulation were promoted, all of which increased confidence in the Georgian economy and brought back international investors.[20]

These impressive gains notwithstanding, the Georgians no doubt are still in the midst of transition and not out of the woods yet. The "size of Georgia's state bureaucracy and the resources required to keep it running significantly exceed [the country's] economic capabilities and require further optimization," cautioned one international study of the Georgian public sector.[21]

Although significant efforts have been made to combat corruption, public service in Georgia is very much under the influence of nepotism and cronyism. In addition, wasteful spending by the Georgian authorities is rampant due to a lack of effective planning, regulation, and monitoring. These problems and many others will continue to affect the pace and effectiveness of governance as well as defense reform.

The United States is well-positioned for long-term success in Georgia in large part because top leadership in the US government for many years have considered the relationship with Tbilisi as a foreign policy priority in the region and a key asset, especially now in an era of increased strategic competition with Russia. The significance of consistent, high-level US political support when it comes to building stronger strategic and military ties with any foreign partner is absolutely huge. More practically, the fact that the GDRP's two parts— the tactical/operational and the institutional—worked hand in hand was invaluable. This helped the Georgians, whose institutional capacity was quite weak prior to US and NATO involvement, better absorb US equipment and resources.

Last but not least, the US deployment of security force assistance brigades to Georgia, instead of regular military training teams, proved to be beneficial. Although those brigades are by no means specialists in defense management and governance, a dedicated team of advisers on these issues is often assigned to them. As a result, these brigades, which resemble SOF from a conceptual standpoint,[22] tend to have better cohesiveness, cultural awareness, and language and foreign weapons training, all of which are good assets to have when engaging in at least some aspects of institutional capacity building, including logistics and doctrinal development.[23]

As far as the US-Philippines partnership is concerned, news in recent years of the Philippine leadership threatening to terminate a defense pact with Washington—a threat they ultimately reconsidered— and complaining about the allegedly low amount of US assistance they receive compared to other international partners should not obscure the long legacy of security cooperation between the two nations.[24] The Philippines is more than a partner of the United States; it is a two-decade-old *treaty ally*, which means that Washington is legally committed to its defense like it is to all NATO members. At the invitation of the Philippine government, the United States has provided advice and mentorship on defense restructuring to its ally since the late 1990s.

From 2003 to 2016, the Philippine government, with the technical and financial support of the United States, prioritized the implementation of deep institutional reforms that centered on strategic planning, operational and training capacity, logistics, HRM, acquisition, civil-military operations, and budget management.[25] This required not just reform but a total transformation of the defense and security sector, and the Filipinos in charge understood and internalized it as such in their new strategic documents. They agreed to reengineer all their systems of planning, programming, budgeting, logistics, procurement, and management, and retool their personnel architecture by professionalizing the workforce, all of which required legislation and various other government procedures that sought to replace the old with the new and make sure the old did not creep back into the system.

Over the years, the Filipinos have improved the most in the areas of strategic planning and resource management. But human capital development remains a big challenge, mainly because, as in the case of the Arab partners, culture has been an inhibiting factor. The process of developing and empowering Philippine NCOs has had to face "significant cultural hurdles" due to the patriarchal nature of Philippine society, a trait shared by Arab societies.[26]

The Americans did a few other things right, and the Filipinos too. According to a team of US defense management specialists assigned to the transformation project, US strategic communications with all levels of the Philippine Armed Forces was comprehensive. The Philippine authorities provided solid access to the American advisers at both lower and higher levels, and both sides coordinated closely and often and worked hard toward the institutionalization of reform measures to ensure their longevity.[27]

## US Lessons Learned

The Arab partners have much in common in terms of history, politics, and culture. However, each has a distinctive political system, legal framework, institutional infrastructure, leadership style and qualities, and level of economic development. So, as always, the local context matters a great deal when discussing and implementing defense or any other kind of structural reform.

The following seven general lessons, which are drawn from the cases of Colombia, Georgia, and the Philippines, could serve as useful guidance for both the United States and its Arab partners.

First, the larger and more comprehensive the defense institution building project is, the more difficult it will be to implement it simply because the challenges that would have to be overcome, be they cultural, political, or otherwise, would be greater. The United States understands by now that it cannot transform its Arab partners' larger conventional forces for all the reasons I laid out before. But what it can do, and arguably has done with some success in Jordan, Iraq, Lebanon, and the UAE, is focus on supporting the creation of smaller and more elite combat units—the QRF in the case of Jordan, the PG in the UAE, the CTS in Iraq, and SOF in Lebanon—that are capable of engaging in combined arms and contributing effectively to coalition operations.

Second, no defense governance reform effort is likely to succeed if it starts by trying to fix operational or tactical problems and *then* by looking to address institutional capacity issues. Rather, the program first should uncover the root causes of operational and tactical deficiencies and then assess the capacity of the institution that's being reformed to tackle those root causes.

This has to happen before either party spends money, time, and effort on operational and tactical improvements. Trying to redesign the institution on the basis of an operational and tactical enhancement effort is akin to reverse engineering, which in this context at least is a very bad idea. If Washington helps the Arab partner pursue institutional capacity building first, it can help the partner decide what it truly needs, not what US officials want it to have. The partner will value and take ownership of its decisions and preferences and as such will plan to try to sustain the equipment on its own.

Third, as emphatic as I have been about the importance of being able to conduct combined arms, this may not be the most urgent or critical goal when it comes to US military assistance to Arab partners. The Jordanians, the Egyptians, the Omanis, the Saudis, the Lebanese, the Bahrainis, and many others surely need to do a ton to achieve greater levels of military jointness, but there are dozens of *other* areas they need to improve upon first before even thinking about jointness. Because it is too hard for Americans to make real changes in Arab human capital development areas, however, they focus on jointness, which is something they understand better and are able to more easily fix. Is it important for modern warfare? Absolutely. Is it the partner's greatest need? Absolutely not. For all of America's Arab partners, it is HRM that requires the greatest attention because this is where the political, economic, and cultural issues all come down hardest.

Fourth, should the Arab partner commit to a defense reform program and express a desire to work with Washington, both parties should establish a permanent US security cooperation office within the Ministry of Defense or some other national security institution of the partner. This would strongly communicate US commitment and help underscore US credibility.[28] That is the model the Colombians pursued and the Saudis adopted recently (the Afghans had a version of that model too until everything collapsed in 2021).

Fifth, the United States should always remember that its advisers are there to advise and exchange ideas, not dictate, prescribe, or impose US preferences and approaches. They should neither do the work for the Arab partner's staff nor write policy guidance and instructions for them. They should remain agnostic and limit their activities to observing, gaining understanding, asking questions, and explaining without judgment.

Ideally, US advisers would pair with the Arab partner's staff and embed in its national security ministries—through MODA programs, among other mechanisms—to teach and help them both implement their own initiatives and improve to the point of reaching the goal of sustainment. At its core, this effort is about transferring a particular set of skills to the Arab partner rather than trying to solve its problems.

In the operational realm, US military members have been able to a large extent to embrace the advisory role and refrain from controlling the activities of Arab partners. A case in point is the US advise-and-assist effort with the Iraqis during the fight against the Islamic State. US Col. J. Patrick Work, commander of the Second Brigade Combat Team, 82nd Airborne Division in Iraq, wrote in 2018 that US military commanders appreciated the processes of preparation, decisionmaking, and operational execution of their Iraqi partners and did not seek to control them.[29] The Iraqis came first, and the Americans largely enabled. There is no reason why the United States can't adopt a similar mindset and approach to partnership in the domain of institutional capacity building.

Sixth, defense institution building, though geared toward generating combat power, should be the concern of Arab civilian leadership as well. While civil-military relations in the Arab world differ from one case to another, there are not many cases where those relations are healthy or balanced. Generally speaking, it is either the civilians dominating the process, like in the Gulf Arab region, or the generals, like in Egypt. Rarely is it a partnership where civilians oversee and provide guidance and the military executes.

Should Washington be invited by an Arab partner to get involved in a defense reform initiative, it should always emphasize effective dialogue and interaction between the civilian and military leaderships of the partner. Of course, having relatively stable and consistent leadership at the Arab partner's ministerial and military levels is always advantageous. This does not mean that having *the same* leaders throughout the reform effort is obligatory, but that the role of political leadership, whether it's new or the same, in championing and enabling defense reform matters a great deal. The defense reform program should be able to survive a change in political and/or military leadership.

Seventh, just like it would be highly preferable to have continuity in terms of US advisory presence, having low turnover of civilian and military staff on the Arab partner's side would help. Consider this as a relationship: the longer the parties interact with and learn from each other, the more productive the exchanges and the better the outcomes. This is not something Washington can control, but it can always remind its Arab partner of the benefits of lower-level staff continuity.

These lessons and principles require a high level of patience and an ability to shape expectations—things at which Washington typically is not very good. With these time-consuming and politically sensitive defense reform initiatives, it is almost always better to go slow and steady than fast and reckless—a piece of advice that applies to both Washington and the Arab partner. Progress must be observable and recognized, however, otherwise the motivations of the partner are likely to fade.

## From Dominance to Partnership

I titled this book *Rebuilding Arab Defense* fully recognizing that Washington is *not* the one doing or leading this rebuilding. The Arab partners are. They are the ones who have to rethink how to create dependable military power and how to better defend themselves against internal and external threats.

However, I also want to emphasize one last time that the United States is not a distant observer or an innocent bystander in this process. With its provision of countless arms and billions of dollars every year to its Arab partners and its pursuit of minimal accountability with them along the way, Washington has enabled some bad customs and behavior in the region for many decades, which has come back to bite it.

The United States cannot impose defense institution building on its Arab partners. Americans can't want it more than the Arabs do and make it happen. But Washington must push for this goal in ways more determined and diligent than ever because, first and foremost, it is in the US interest to do so. Americans also have a moral obligation to more effectively support their Arab partners, many of whom, despite all their imperfections, have made important contributions to America's safety and economic well-being for decades. Those partners cannot do it alone, at least not the right way, even if they wanted to.

The United States is in an ideal position to help because it has remarkable expertise in defense institution building and a unique knowledge of its Arab partners' military secrets, strengths, and vulnerabilities. Washington remains the main source of equipment, training, and advice to the Arab states, despite all the talk lately of them seeking to diversify their security portfolios and buy more arms from countries like Russia and China.

This shared US-Arab experience spanning many decades suggests that the Arab partners should not be solely blamed for failing to build dependable military capability. Washington has been so invested and involved in their most intricate security details for such a long time that any notion of absolving it of responsibility for their relative military inferiority would be both ludicrous and disingenuous. Indeed, America's efforts to help its Arab partners boost their military power have had a distinctly miserable record because *both sides* were disinterested for a long time, *both sides* have encountered challenges, and *both sides* have made bad choices.

The United States is trying to change its approach because that is what its new global priorities demand. But it's safe to say that Washington is only at the very beginning, and if the United States does not make a concerted effort to view and treat military assistance to its Arab partners in a fundamentally different way, it will remain at the very beginning, and the Middle East will go on serving as a stubborn barrier to its shift in foreign policy. Washington does not have to reinvent the wheel of security cooperation; all that is needed is to attach the four perfectly good wheels it has to a cart and then add on a determined operator, a steering mechanism, and an engine to have a perfectly good vehicle. This is largely about leadership, organization, prioritization, and integration; *not* about inventing the parts.

I'm under no illusion that the Arab partners' pursuit of defense institution building, alone or even in full-fledged partnership with Washington, is going to be an easy or short-term affair. Even if the drive and determination are strong, the money is available, and the politics are right, this is a generational endeavor.

Look no further than America's experience in defense reform, which started back in 1903 with the Militia Act (also known as the Dick Act, named after one of its champions, Congressman Charles Dick), which together with his 1908 amendment created a reserve guard and a national guard, giving the president of the United States the power to call the latter into federal service. Eight years later, Congress asserted federal control over state military forces and strengthened the national guard, thus allowing it to fulfill its role as a strategic reserve.[30]

The United States did not really get serious again about defense reform until after it fought two world wars. On July 26, 1947, President Harry Truman signed the National Security Act of 1947, which fundamentally reorganized and modernized the nation's armed forces along with its foreign policy and intelligence architecture. In terms of defense reengineering, the War and Navy departments, separate until the passing of this landmark legislation, were combined, and the air force gained its autonomy from the army. Fast-forward to the last few years of the Cold War when Washington came up with the most consequential and perhaps controversial pieces of legislation on defense reform—the 1986 Goldwater-Nichols Defense Reform Act, which imposed strategic and operational-level jointness on the US military for the first time in its history.

Thanks to Goldwater-Nichols, the chain of command for more effective US joint operations and the provision of military advice by the chairman of the Joint Chiefs of Staff to the civilian leadership became clearer and more streamlined. The role and influence of the service chiefs were reduced, and the defense acquisition and personnel management systems, both emphasizing jointness, became a lot more effective and efficient.

This much abbreviated history of key defense reforms in the United States (which did not stop with Goldwater-Nichols but certainly slowed down) shows that even for the most powerful and resourceful nation on earth, achieving higher levels of defense organization took some eighty-plus years.

The Arab partners have neither huge militaries that require enormous bureaucracies to manage nor global interests and responsibilities like the United States. Their defense reforms, which will vary from one country to another depending on their initial institutional baseline, economic development, and political context, need not require this much time or effort. However, no credible attempt at reorganizing defense establishments and building more competent militaries is likely to succeed within a handful of years. This is a process of at least two or three decades, especially in the case of Saudi Arabia, which is a total redo.

Yet reaping at least some of the fruits of reform does not have to wait until the entire initiative is finished (although it arguably never "finishes," but just slows down depending on progress). This must be an *incremental* approach. National security cannot wait and does not take breaks. It is a constant concern and responsibility, especially in the perennially unstable Middle East. That's precisely why the installment of and rigorous adherence to policies, processes, and procedures that have immediate impacts on security but also seek to gradually build for the future are so paramount.

Some might claim that it is too hard and unrealistic for Washington to commit to the systematic integration of defense institution building into US military assistance programs in the Middle East given the fact that America's Arab partners are overwhelmingly autocratic and not the most receptive to various concepts and practices of defense governance. A transactional approach, as employed by the United States over the better part of the past four decades, is more attainable and not as bad as it seems so long as it ensures some key US strategic interests including US military access, basing, and overflight.

I probably would have been more sympathetic to this proposition had the United States not been in a period of strategic transition in the Middle East and around the world. But the reality is that US global strategy *is* making a steady shift away from the region and toward the Far East. This means that the old way of doing things, where Washington was overcommitted to and overinvested in the Middle East and where the Arab partners were unwilling and unable to do their fair share, is no longer viable.

If US decisionmakers determine that it is truly access, basing, and overflight they value above all else and that US military assistance programs should prioritize those deliverables, then there are other far cheaper and more sustainable ways to acquire those enablers, including side payments. I strongly agree with retired US Marine Corps officer Peter Munson, who opined that "if policymakers want a quid pro quo, they need to admit as much and use much more precisely targeted incentives: paying a fee for access or head-of-the-line transit privileges for example."[31]

What Washington has done all these years is say all the right things about helping Arab partners build their military capabilities and optimizing US-Arab security cooperation, but it has hardly ever committed to doing any of those things. The US approach to military assistance in the Arab world has been only partly effective, profoundly inefficient, and grossly hypocritical because Americans keep making promises they know they will not fulfill.

It's encouraging that US law is now forcing the Pentagon to overhaul the way the United States does security cooperation and incorporate institutional capacity building. Congress's security cooperation reforms cannot be easily ignored or wished away by the executive branch.

But just like the Arab partners need a culture change with regard to defense organization, so does Washington in its gargantuan US security cooperation bureaucracy. Culture changes, especially within the Department of Defense, do not happen overnight. "We are perfectly capable of working more effectively with our Arab partners," said a veteran American specialist in defense management with many years of experience in the Middle East. "But what we don't know how to do is cooperate amongst ourselves as Americans."[32]

How far can the Arab partners go with defense institution building without democratizing? A comprehensive answer to this policy-relevant question is beyond the scope of this book. History shows that a democratic government is not a precondition for generating combat power and fighting effectively.[33] Many examples throughout history, including Sparta, Germany in both world wars, Japan in World War II, Soviet Russia, and contemporary China, support this statement. In the Arab world, the UAE has shown that it can display military effectiveness despite its authoritarian governing structure. Egypt, a military-led autocracy, did so too in the 1973 October War.

There is no question that the more open the governing structure, the less challenging it is to decentralize military power and decision-making and thus form more effective defense institutions. Even so, there's a ton the Arab partners can do still in the areas of policymaking, strategizing, planning, budgeting, management, and logistics that could have very positive effects on their military power without having to politically convert or drastically alter their politics—which, let's face it, they will not do.

In an ideal world, Washington would have both democratic and militarily effective Arab partners, but this is the Middle East, and the more realistic choice is between an authoritarian Arab partner that can't fight and can't contribute to common security causes with the United States and an authoritarian Arab partner that can hopefully do both. It is obvious that the latter option is better for US strategic interests.

The United States cannot and should not push for better political governance in the Middle East through the security cooperation back door or other shortcuts. If this were truly Washington's intent, then leave it to US foreign policy writ large, not US military assistance, to help achieve it. Security cooperation is meant to achieve *security cooperation*, not engage in some political reengineering in the Arab partner, which will almost always fail or, worse, backfire.

One likely point of contention in Washington about building up the capabilities of Arab partners is the extent to which this strategic goal would be pursued. I made the point that US decisionmakers are now more serious than ever about that objective. But how much more Arab military capability does the United States want to create and against whom would such improved capabilities be used?

This issue merits a frank and serious policy debate. It is relatively easy for the United States and its Arab partners to agree on combating violent extremists and on checking Iranian aggression in the region, but it is a lot harder and maybe impossible to see eye to eye on the threats posed by a range of other actors. These include peaceful political Islamists and activists whom Americans do not consider as illegitimate but several of their Arab friends, including the Egyptians, the Emiratis, and the Saudis, view as terrorists.

Washington and its Arab partners will never share the same assessments on all aspects of national security. That is normal. The threat landscape in the Middle East will always look different from Washington than it does in various Arab capitals. Even within the region, not all Arab partners perceive and prioritize threats similarly. For example, how Saudi Arabia, the UAE, and Bahrain view and deal with the challenge of Iran is not the same as how Oman, Kuwait, and Qatar do. Also, Doha and Abu Dhabi's approaches to political Islam are polar opposites. The Qataris have provided various forms of support to political Islamists in the region, while the Emiratis have essentially been at war with those actors wherever they have operated.

Those serious discrepancies notwithstanding, the United States has more than enough in common with its Arab partners in terms of shared challenges and collective security interests to justify developing their military capabilities. The real and imaginary risks of stronger Arab partners must be weighed against the increasingly costly alternative of Arab military incompetence. Washington has seen the effects of the latter on US interests and national security for many years, and they are detrimental.

Being crystal clear on *why* the United States commits billions of dollars every year to help its Arab partners build military capability is paramount. Helping Arab partners become more militarily independent sounds like the right thing to say and do, but the truth is that Washington has little interest in such a partnership model. That's because an independent Arab partner, though presumably better able to pursue its own goals and fight its own real and imaginary battles, has no actual obligation to strategically coordinate with the United States or consider its preferences and interests (think Saudi Arabia's intervention in Yemen or that of the UAE in Libya as two examples).

The United States wants its Arab partners to be both interdependent and interoperable with it—that is, it wants them to be closely tied to it on multiple levels, both willing and able to contribute to common causes and shared interests. It is not enough that they have weapons systems that technically match with those of the United States. Washington benefits a lot more when its Arab partners are *strategically* interoperable with it, which can only be achieved if both sides commit to real partnership.

If that ideal model is not attainable, however, and US tradeoffs must be made, then Washington is better off having an interdependent partner who is less interoperable over one who is more independent and interoperable. The key characteristic or asset here for the United States is *strategic and policy interdependence* with the Arab partner, which should take precedence over military ability and compatibility.

No matter what type of Arab partner the United States is seeking to help develop, a physical US military presence in the region is necessary to actively and consistently mentor, advise, and train Arab friendly forces and to assess, monitor, and evaluate US security cooperation efforts, as instructed by Congress. If the United States withdraws, like it did recently in Afghanistan, it will not even have a chance to engage in any of these invaluable pursuits, at least not effectively. Not only that, but it will probably lose a few key Arab partners along the way too. The US presence in the region represents the barometer of the US commitment to the security of those partners. Their hearts pound and anxiety levels rise every time there is the slightest movement of US military personnel and equipment in and out of the Middle East. Certainly, the United States should not be hostage to its Arab partners' psychologies, but it should admit that it played a role in feeding their fears by oftentimes being unreliable.

If the United States leaves, it will have a much harder time encouraging and helping its Arab partners to invest in comprehensive defense reform. This effort requires consistent personal engagement on the US part. Americans just cannot pursue defense institution building with their Arab partners from Washington or anywhere outside the region.

There's no point in trying to identify what precise US troop levels in the region would be required to meet the above-mentioned US objectives. What is far more important and what should precede this exercise is the formulation of a new US *strategy* for the Middle East in an era of great power competition. Strategy informs or guides posture, not the other way around.

The United States doesn't have that new strategy yet. What may be clearer now in the minds of US decisionmakers is that US regional dominance is no longer sustainable or desirable. But what's still vastly uncertain is how to transition to a new strategy, one that is based on more effective partnership with our regional friends. If partnership is to replace supremacy in US Middle East strategy, then security cooperation, with all its rules, tools, and principles, has to play a much more prominent role. It also has to be totally revamped by Washington.

Transferring more arms to US Arab partners, as Americans have always done, will not magically turn them into more effective and responsible fighters. Helping them create and invest in defense norms, processes, and institutions—which are all part of the indispensable universe of defense governance and management—certainly can, and it offers a more sustainable course for the United States in the Middle East.

## Notes

1. John J. Hamre, *Reflections: Looking Back at the Need for Goldwater-Nichols* (Washington, DC: Center for Strategic and International Studies, January 27, 2016).

2. Alex Hollings, "The Birth of SOCOM: How America's Special Operations Command Was Born of Tragedy," SOFREP, March 7, 2019, https://sofrep.com/specialoperations/the-birth-of-socom-how-americas-special-operations-command-was-born-of-tragedy/.

3. For a view of how SOCOM had to adjust its acquisition approach to become more efficient and fiscally disciplined, see Jonathan M. Duncan, *The Dilemma for USSOCOM: Transitioning SOF-Peculiar to Service-Common* (Maxwell, Air Force Base, AL: Air War College, Air University, February 15, 2012).

4. Congressional Research Service, *U.S. Special Operations Forces (SOF): Background and Issues for Congress* (Washington, DC: CRS, updated March 22, 2019).

5. C. J. Chivers, "Supplier Under Scrutiny on Arms for Afghans," *New York Times*, March 27, 2008.

6. See Susan L. Marquis, *Unconventional Warfare: Rebuilding U.S. Special Operations Forces* (Washington, DC: Brookings Institution Press, 1997).

7. Setzekorn, "Eisenhower's Mutual Security Program."

8. A point also made by Thomas-Durell Young, although he didn't single out DSCA. See Thomas-Durell Young, "Experimentation Can Help Build Better Security Partners," War on the Rocks, August 30, 2019, https://warontherocks.com/2019/08/experimentation-can-help-build-better-security-partners/.

9. William G. Boykin, *The Origins of the United States Special Operations Command* (MacDill Air Force Base, FL: US Special Operations Command, April 24, 1980).

10. Max Bergman and Alexandra Schmitt believe that the Pentagon's Section 333 should be transferred entirely to the State Department because it considerably overlaps with FMF. See Max Bergman and Alexandra Schmitt, *A Plan to Reform U.S. Security Assistance* (Washington, DC: Center for American Progress, March 9, 2021).

11. Jules Bertaut, *Napoleon: In His Own Words* (Chicago: A. C. McClurg & Co., 1916), 2.

12. Michael Miklaucic and Juan Carlos Pinzón, "Partnership: The Colombia-U.S. Experience," in Kerr and Miklaucic, 282.

13. Lina M. Gonzalez, Aaron C. Taliaferro, and Wade P. Hinkle, *The Colombian Ministry of National Defense's "Transformation and Future Initiative": Retrospective on a 9-Year Cooperative Effort Between the United States Department of Defense and the Colombian Ministry of National Defense* (Alexandria, VA: Institute for Defense Analyses, October 2017).

14. Organisation for Economic Co-operation and Development, *Colombia: Policy Priorities for Inclusive Development* (Paris: OECD, January 2015), 45–50.

15. Congressional Research Service, *Georgia: Background and U.S. Policy* (Washington, DC: CRS, April 2021), 17–20.

16. Ruslan Pukhov, *The Tanks of August* (Moscow: Center for Analysis of Strategies and Technologies, 2010).

17. NATO, "Defence Institution Building School: An Initiative of the Substantial NATO-Georgia Package," Fact sheet, 2016.

18. Embassy of Georgia to the United States of America, "Georgia Defense Readiness Program Kicks Off in Tbilisi," June 8, 2018.

19. One may be tempted to argue that the fact most Georgians identify themselves as Europeans has made it easier for them to absorb Western concepts in defense management, but that would be untrue. The issue of Georgian identity, and how it has evolved over centuries, is complicated. It also is probably irrelevant. Wanting to be part of the European Union and NATO doesn't equate with readily embracing the social agenda and values of Western Europeans. Indeed, the Georgians are a more religious and less individualistic bunch than the Americans or Western Europeans. But even if there were cultural compatibility, it wouldn't be the reason why the Georgians achieved some impressive milestones in defense reform. What did contribute to success was the fact that they managed to utilize the information and advice they received from their external partners and tailor it to their needs.

20. Fredrik Eriksson, *The Rapid Economic Liberalization and Ruthless Fight Against Corruption in Georgia: Interview with Dr. Tamara Kovziridze*, U4 Practitioner Experience Note 2017:1 (Bergen, Norway: Chr. Michelsen Institute, Anti-Corruption Resource Centre).

21. Institute for Development of Freedom of Information (IDFI), *Challenges of the Georgian Bureaucratic System in the Context of Public Administration Reform* (Tbilisi, Georgia: IDFI, 2017), 3.

22. James B. Linder, Eric J. Wesley, and Elliot S. Grant, "A New Breed of Advisory Team: Security Force Assistance Brigades to Collaborate with Special Operations Forces," Association of the United States Army, June 19, 2017.

23. Scott Gross and Lay Phonexayphova, "Joint, Interagency, and Tailored: Getting Security Force Assistance Right in Georgia," Modern War Institute at West Point, November 12, 2019.

24. Jason Gutierrez, "Philippines Backs Off Threat to Terminate Military Pact with U.S.," *New York Times*, June 2, 2020.

25. Ibid., 11.

26. Charles "Ken" Comer, "Philippine Defense Reform: Are We There Yet?" https://community.apan.org/wg/tradoc-g2/fmso/m/fmso-monographs/239227/ (accessed November 29, 2019), 28.

27. Ibid.

28. Gonzalez, Taliaferro, and Hinkle, *The Colombian Ministry of National Defense's "Transformation and Future Initiative."*

29. J. Patrick Work, "Fighting the Islamic State By, With, and Through: *How* Mattered as Much as *What*," *Joint Forces Quarterly* 2, no. 89 (April 2018): 56–62.

30. William M. Donnelly, "The Root Reforms and the National Guard," US Army Center of Military History, May 3, 2001, https://history.army.mil/documents/1901/Root-NG.htm.

31. Peter Munson, "The Limits of Security Cooperation," War on the Rocks, September 10, 2013, https://warontherocks.com/2013/09/the-limits-of-security-cooperation/.

32. Author's interview by phone, December 5, 2020. The source spoke on the condition of anonymity.

33. For one perspective on the likely relationship between democracy and military effectiveness, see Stephen Biddle and Stephen Long, "Democracy and Military Effectiveness: A Deeper Look," *Journal of Conflict Resolution* 48, no. 4 (August 2004): 525–546.

# Acronyms

| | |
|---|---|
| AFCENT | Air Forces Central |
| AFRICOM | Africa Command |
| AQAP | al-Qaeda in the Arabian Peninsula |
| AWACS | airborne warning and control system |
| C2 | command and control |
| C4ISR | command, control, communications, computers, intelligence surveillance, and reconnaissance |
| CAOC | Combined Air Operations Center |
| CDP | Capability Development Plan |
| CENTCOM | Central Command |
| CIA | Central Intelligence Agency |
| CTPF | Counterterrorism Partnership Fund |
| CTS | Counter Terrorism Service (Iraq) |
| DIB | defense institution building |
| DIILS | Defense Institute of International Legal Studies |
| DIRI | Defense Institution Reform Initiative |
| DOTMLPF-P | doctrine, organization, training, materiel, leadership and education, personnel, facilities, and policy |
| DSCA | Defense Security Cooperation Agency |
| EUCOM | European Command |
| FAO | foreign area officer |
| FMF | Foreign Military Financing |
| FMS | Foreign Military Sales |

| | |
|---|---|
| FY | fiscal year |
| FYSAR | five-year security assistance roadmap |
| GAMI | General Authority for Military Industries |
| GCC | geographic combatant command |
| GCC | Gulf Cooperation Council |
| GDRP | Georgia Defense Readiness Program |
| GHQ | general headquarters |
| GPS | Global Positioning System |
| HIMARS | high mobility artillery rocket systems |
| HRM | human resource management |
| ICB | institutional capacity building |
| IDF | Israel Defense Forces |
| IMET | International Military Education and Training |
| IRGC | Islamic Revolutionary Guard Corps |
| ISG | Institute for Security Governance |
| ISR | intelligence, surveillance, and reconnaissance |
| JAF | Jordanian Armed Forces |
| JBSP | Joint Border Security Program |
| JCIDS | Joint Capabilities Integration and Development System |
| JCP | joint capability planning |
| JDAM | Joint Direct Attack Munitions |
| JMC | Joint Military Commission |
| JOEP | Jordan Operational Engagement Program |
| JSPS | Joint Strategic Planning System |
| JTAC | joint terminal attack controller |
| KASOTC | King Abdullah II Special Operations Training Center |
| LAF | Lebanese Armed Forces |
| LAMP | Lebanese Army Modernization Program |
| LAV | light armored vehicle |
| LBRs | land border regiments |
| MAP-J | Military Assistance Program–Jordan |
| MBR | Mohammed bin Rashid |
| MBS | Mohammed bin Salman |
| MBZ | Mohammed bin Zayed |
| MoD | Ministry of Defense |
| MODA | Ministry of Defense Advisors |
| MOI | Ministry of Interior |
| MOI-MAG | Ministry of Interior–Military Assistance Group |
| NATO | North Atlantic Treaty Organization |
| NAVCENT | Naval Forces Central Command |
| NCO | noncommissioned officer |

| | |
|---|---|
| NDAA | National Defense Authorization Act |
| NDP | national defense policy |
| NDS | National Defense Strategy |
| NSC | National Security Council |
| OIR | Operation Inherent Resolve |
| OPM-SANG | Office of the Program Manager–Saudi Arabian National Guard |
| PG | Presidential Guard |
| PME | professional military education |
| QDR | Quadrennial Defense Review |
| QRF | quick reaction forces |
| R&D | research and development |
| RJAF | Royal Jordanian Air Force |
| ROTC | Reserve Officers Training Corps |
| RSADF | Royal Saudi Air Defense Force |
| RSAF | Royal Saudi Air Force |
| RSLF | Royal Saudi Land Forces |
| RSNF | Royal Saudi Naval Forces |
| RSSMF | Royal Saudi Strategic Missile Force |
| SAMI | Saudi Arabian Military Industries |
| SANG | Saudi Arabian National Guard |
| SDO/DATT | senior defense official/defense attaché |
| SDR | strategic defense review |
| SOCCENT | Special Operations Command Central |
| SOCOM | Special Operations Command |
| SOF | special operations forces |
| SO/LIC | special operations/low-intensity conflict |
| SSR | security sector reform |
| THAAD | Terminal High Altitude Area Defense |
| TRADOC | US Army Training and Doctrine Command |
| TSOC | theater special operations command |
| TTP | tactics, techniques, and procedures |
| UAE | United Arab Emirates |
| UAV | unmanned aerial vehicle |
| UN | United Nations |
| USAID | US Agency for International Development |
| USMTM | US Military Training Mission |

# Bibliography

Aanmoen, Oskar. "King Abdullah Opens New Military University College." *Royal Central*, February 3, 2021.

AbiNader, Jean R. "Facing High Public Employment, Morocco Continues to Build Support for Small and Medium Enterprises." Morocco on the Move, February 10, 2020. https://moroccoonthemove.com/2020/02/10/facing-high-public-employment-morocco-continues-to-build-support-for-small-and-medium-enterprises-jean-r-abinader/.

Abouzzohour, Yasmina, and Nejla Ben Mimoune. *Policy and Institutional Responses to COVID-19 in the Middle East and North Africa: Tunisia.* Washington, DC: Brookings, December 15, 2020.

Adams, Paul. "Gulf Crisis: Are We Heading for a New Tanker War?" *BBC*, June 21, 2019.

Addis, Casey L. *U.S. Security Assistance to Lebanon.* Washington, DC: Congressional Research Service, January 19, 2011.

Adler, Stephen J., Jeff Mason, and Steve Holland. "Exclusive: Trump Complains Saudis Not Paying Fair Share for U.S. Defense." Reuters, April 27, 2017.

Africa, Sandy. *The Transformation of the South African Security Sector: Lessons and Challenges.* Policy Paper No. 33. Geneva: Geneva Centre for the Democratic Control of Armed Forces (DCAF), March 2011.

Agence France-Presse. "Jordan Publicizes Defense Deal That Allows US Forces Free Entry into Kingdom." March 21, 2021.

———. "Pentagon Chief Says Some Coalition Partners in Fight Against Isis 'Do Nothing.'" January 22, 2016.

———. "Saudi Special Forces 'Involved in Yemen Ops.'" April 4, 2015.

*Air Force Magazine.* "Desert Falcons Travel Afar for Red Flag." February 4, 2011.

Alatawi, Naif H. "RSAF F-15 Reparable Items Capacity Planning & Execution." Thesis, Department of the Air Force, Air University, September 2017.

Alharahsheh, Ibrahim. "Jordanian Contributions to Afghanistan." *UNIPATH*, February 20, 2015.

Ali, Abbas. "Decision-Making Style, Individualism, and Attitudes Toward Risk of Arab Executives." *International Studies of Management and Organization* 23, no. 3 (1993): 53–73.

Almeida, Alex, and Michael Knights. *Gulf Coalition Operations in Yemen (Part 1): The Ground War.* PolicyWatch 2594. Washington, DC: Washington Institute for Near East Policy, March 25, 2016.

Angelo, Paul J., and Olga L. Illera Correal. *Colombian Military Culture.* Miami: Steven J. Green School of International & Public Affairs, Florida International University, 2020.

*Arab News.* "Saudi Air Force Completes 'Red Flag' Military Exercise in US." March 23, 2019.
———. "Saudi and US Air Forces Begin Joint Training Exercise." February 28, 2021.
———. "Saudi Women Invited to Join Ranks of the Armed Forces." October 3, 2019.
———. "UN Praises UAE for Arab Women Peacekeeper Training." February 8, 2019.
*Al Arabiya.* "Full Transcript of Prince Mohammed Bin Salman's Al Arabiya Interview." April 25, 2016.
Arango, Tim. "A Long-Awaited Apology for Shiites, but the Wounds Run Deep." *New York Times,* November 8, 2011.
Ardemagni, Eleonora. "The Saudi-Yemeni Militarized Borderland." *Sada* (Carnegie Endowment for International Peace), January 9, 2020.
Aronson, Geoffrey. *What Does Trump's Golan Proclamation Mean for UNDOF?* Washington, DC: Middle East Institute, June 3, 2019.
Arraf, Jane, and Eric Schmitt. "Iran's Proxies in Iraq Threaten U.S. with More Sophisticated Weapons." *New York Times,* June 4, 2021.
Ash, Nazanin, and Allison Grossman, *Modernizing US Security and Development Assistance in the Middle East.* Washington, DC: Center for Global Development, December 7, 2015.
Associated Press. "War in the Gulf: Military Briefing; Transcript of Briefing in Riyadh by the American Commander." February 25, 1991.
Atkinson, Rick, and David S. Broder. "U.S., Allies Launch Massive Air War Against Targets in Iraq and Kuwait." *Washington Post,* January 17, 1991.
Atlantic Council. "The Road to Camp David: The Future of the US-Gulf Partnership." Video, May 7, 2015. https://www.youtube.com/watch?v=lyUARa5w6iY&t=934s.
Awadallah, Alia, Hardin Lang, and Kristy Densmore. *Losing the War of Ideas: Countering Violent Extremism in the Age of Trump.* Washington, DC: Center for American Progress, August 17, 2017.
Axe, David. "Iran Is Close to Getting an Atomic Bomb—but It Could Still Choose to Stop." *Forbes,* February 9, 2021.
Ayubi, Nazih N. "Bureaucratization as Development: Administrative Development and Development Administration in the Arab World." *International Review of Administrative Sciences* 52, no. 2 (June 1986): 201–222.
———. *Over-stating the Arab State: Politics and Society in the Middle East.* London: I. B. Tauris, 1995.
Badawi, M. K. "Styles of Middle Eastern Managers." *California Management Review* 22, no. 2 (Spring 1980).
Baker, Peter, Eric Schmitt, and Helene Cooper. "ISIS Leader al-Baghdadi Is Dead, Trump Says." *New York Times,* October 27, 2019.
Bakri, Nada, and Graham Bowley. "Top Hezbollah Commander Killed in Syria." *New York Times,* February 13, 2008.
Barany, Zoltan. *Military Officers in the Gulf: Career Trajectories and Determinants.* Washington, DC: Center for Strategic and International Studies, November 5, 2019.
———. "Reforming Defense: Lessons for Arab Republics." *Strategic Studies Quarterly* 7, no. 4 (Winter 2013): 46–69.
Barbuscia, Davide. "Saudi Unemployment Spikes as Virus-Hit Economy Shrinks by 7% in Second-Quarter." Reuters, September 30, 2020.
Baron, Adam. "The Gulf Country That Will Shape the Future of Yemen." *Atlantic,* September 22, 2018.
Barrie, Douglas. "Iran's Drone Fleet." *Iran Primer* (United States Institute of Peace), August 20, 2020. https://iranprimer.usip.org/blog/2020/aug/20/irans-drone-fleet.
Al-Batati, Saeed, and Kareem Fahim. "Foreign Group Troops Join Yemen Fight." *New York Times,* August 3, 2015.
———. "Yemeni Fighters Trained in Persian Gulf Are Said to Join Saudi-Led Mission." *New York Times,* May 3, 2015.
Al-Batati, Saeed, Kareem Fahim, and Eric Schmitt. "Yemeni Troops, Backed by United Arab Emirates, Take City from Al Qaeda." *New York Times,* April 24, 2016.
Al-Batati, Saeed, and Eric Schmitt. "Thousands of Yemeni Forces Target Qaeda Stronghold." *New York Times,* August 6, 2017.
Bayoumy, Yara. "Lebanon Says 222 Militants Killed in Camp." Reuters, September 4, 2007.

*BBC News.* "Muslim Troops Help Win Afghan Minds." March 28, 2008.

———. "Libya Protests: Defiant Gaddafi Refuses to Quit." February 22, 2011.

Beauchamp, Zack. "The Syria War: A History." *Vox,* September 21, 2015.

Beckley, Michael. "The Myth of Entangling Alliances: Reassessing the Security Risks of U.S. Defense Pacts." *International Security* 39, no. 4 (Spring 2015): 12.

———. "The Power of Nations: Measuring What Matters." *International Security* 43, no. 2 (Fall 2018): 7–44.

Beehner, Lionel, and Gustav Meibauer. "The Futility of Buffer Zones in International Politics." *Orbis* 60, no. 2 (April 2016): 248–265.

Be'eri, Eliezer Be'eri. "The Waning of the Military in Coup Politics." *Middle Eastern Studies* 18, no. 3 (January 1982): 69.

Beirut Embassy. "Lebanon: Inaugural Joint Military Commission." Cable 08BEIRUT1497_a. WikiLeaks, October 20, 2008. https://wikileaks.org/plusd/cables/08BEIRUT1497_a.html.

Belser, Alan. "Jordanian NCOs Partner with U.S. Instructors." US Central Command, December 20, 2016.

Bensahel, Nora. "A Coalition of Coalitions: International Cooperation Against Terrorism." *Studies in Conflict and Terrorism* 29, no. 1 (2006): 35–49.

———. "The Coalition Paradox: The Politics of Military Cooperation." PhD diss., Stanford University, 1999.

———. *The Counterterror Coalitions: Cooperation with Europe, NATO, and the European Union.* Santa Monica, CA: RAND, 2003.

———. "Preparing for Coalition Operations." In *The U.S. Army and the New National Security Strategy,* edited by Lynn E. Davis and Jeremy Shapiro. Santa Monica, CA: RAND, 2003.

Berardino, Mike. "Mike Tyson Explains One of His Most Famous Quotes." *South Florida Sun Sentinel,* November 9, 2012.

Berger, Miriam. "Where U.S. Troops Are in the Middle East and Afghanistan, Visualized." *Washington Post,* January 4, 2020.

Bergman, Max, and Alexandra Schmitt. *A Plan to Reform U.S. Security Assistance.* Washington, DC: Center for American Progress, March 9, 2021.

Bertaut, Jules. *Napoleon: In His Own Words.* Chicago: A. C. McClurg & Co., 1916.

Biddle, Stephen, and Stephen Long. "Democracy and Military Effectiveness: A Deeper Look." *Journal of Conflict Resolution* 48, no. 4 (August 2004): 525–546.

Biddle, Stephen, and Robert Zirke. "Technology, Civil-Military Relations, and Warfare in the Developing World." *Journal of Strategic Studies* 19, no. 2 (June 1996): 171–212.

Bigelow, Christopher. "Security Enterprise Shares Logistics with Jordan." US Army, March 27, 2017.

Bipartisan Policy Center (BPC). *Digital Counterterrorism: Fighting Jihadists Online.* Washington, DC: BPC, March 2018.

Boucek, Christopher. *Saudi Arabia's "Soft" Counterterrorism Strategy: Prevention, Rehabilitation, and Aftercare.* Carnegie Papers No. 97. Washington, DC: Carnegie Endowment for International Peace, September 2008.

Bowman, Tom, and Monika Evstatieva. "The Afghan Army Collapsed in Days. Here Are the Reasons Why." NPR, August 20, 2021.

Boykin, William G. *The Origins of the United States Special Operations Command.* US Special Operations Command, April 24, 1980.

Boyne, Walter J. "Red Flag." *Air Force Magazine,* November 1, 2000.

Brender, Lance. "What Am I Doing in Saudi Arabia?" *Armor* 127, no. 2 (April–June 2016): 52–58.

Brinkley, Joel. "The Collapse of Lebanon's Army: U.S. Aid to Ignore Factionalism." *New York Times,* March 11, 1984.

Brodie, Bernard. "Strategy as a Science." *World Politics* 1, no. 4 (July 1949): 478.

Brooks, Risa A. "An Autocracy at War: Explaining Egypt's Military Effectiveness, 1967 and 1973." *Security Studies* 15, no. 3 (July–September 2006): 396–430.

———. "Civil-Military Relations in the Middle East." In *The Future Security Environment in the Middle East: Conflict, Stability, and Political Change,* edited by Nora Bensahel and Daniel L. Byman, 129–162. Santa Monica, CA: RAND, 2004.

———. "Making Military Might: Why Do States Fail and Succeed? A Review Essay." *International Security* 28, no. 2 (Fall 2003): 149–191.

———. *Shaping Strategy: The Civil-Military Politics of Strategic Assessment*. Princeton, NJ: Princeton University Press, 2008.

Brooks, Risa A., and Elizabeth Stanley. *Creating Military Power: The Sources of Military Effectiveness*. Stanford, CA: Stanford University Press, 2007.

Bruneau, Thomas C. *Ministries of Defense and Democratic Civil-Military Relations*. Occasional Paper. Monterey, CA: Center for Civil-Military Relations Naval Postgraduate School, August 2001.

Buitrago, Rachel. "PSAB Hosts Joint Air Defense Training with RSAF Forces." US Air Forces Central, May 22, 2021. https://www.afcent.af.mil/Units/378th-Air-Expeditionary-Wing /News/Article/2626794/psab-hosts-joint-air-defense-training-with-rsaf-forces/.

Bulos, Nabih, and David S. Cloud. "As Top Allies Scale Back in Yemen, Saudi Arabia Faces Prospect of an Unwinnable War." *Los Angeles Times*, August 11, 2019.

Bumgarder, Richard. "MOI-MAG Advise and Train in Saudi Arabia." US Army, November 6, 2019. https://www.army.mil/article/229552/moi_mag_advise_and_train_in_saudi_arabia.

*Business Insider.* "The World's Special Forces Train at This Base in Jordan." March 31, 2018. https://www.wearethemighty.com/tactical/the-worlds-special-forces-train-at-this-base-in -jordan/.

Byman, Daniel. "Can Al Qaeda in the Arabian Peninsula Survive the Death of Its Leader?" *Foreign Policy*, June 16, 2015.

———. "Friends Like These: Counterinsurgency at the War on Terrorism." *International Security* 31, no. 2 (Fall 2006): 79–115.

———. "The Homecomings: What Happens When Arab Foreign Fighters in Iraq and Syria Return?" *Studies in Conflict and Terrorism* 38, no. 8 (May 2015): 581–602.

———. *Prepared Testimony Before the House Committee on Foreign Affairs, Subcommittee on Terrorism, Nonproliferation, and Trade,* 114th Congress, May 24, 2016.

———. "US Counterterrorism Intelligence Cooperation with the Developing World and Its Limits." *Intelligence and National Security* 32, no. 2 (2017): 145–160.

Callimachi, Rukmini, Eric Schmitt, and Julia E. Barnes. "U.S. Strikes at Leader of Qaeda in Yemen." *New York Times*, January 31, 2020.

Cao, Sissi. "Saudi Arabia's Crown Prince Is Wildly Popular Among (His Own) Youth." *Observer*, May 10, 2018.

CAP Middle East Team. *Leveraging U.S. Power in the Middle East: A Blueprint for Strengthening Regional Partnerships*. Washington, DC: Center for American Progress (CAP), October 19, 2016.

Carter, Ash. *A Lasting Defeat: The Campaign to Destroy ISIS*. Cambridge, MA: Belfer Center for Science and International Affairs, Harvard Kennedy School, October 2017.

Carter, Jimmy. "President Carter's State of the Union Before a Joint Session of Congress." Washington, DC, January 23, 1980.

Casptack, Andreas. *Deradicalization Programs in Saudi Arabia: A Case Study*. Washington, DC: Middle East Institute, June 10, 2015.

Castillo, Mariano. "U.N. Rep Accuses Saudi-Led Coalition of Violating International Law." CNN, May 11, 2015.

Cawley, Janet, and George de Lama. "Reagan Says Saudi Talked of Contra Aid." *Chicago Tribune*, May 14, 1987.

*CBS News.* "Arab League Wants UN Peacekeepers in Syria." February 12, 2012.

Chairman of the Joint Chiefs of Staff Instruction. "Guidance for Developing and Implementing Joint Concepts." August 17, 2016. https://www.jcs.mil/Portals/36/Documents/Doctrine /concepts/cjcsi_3010_02e.pdf?ver=2018-08-01-134826-593.

Chandrasekaran, Rajiv. "In the UAE, the United States Has a Quiet, Potent Ally Nicknamed 'Little Sparta.'" *Washington Post*, November 9, 2014.

Chase, Michael S., Jeffrey Engstrom, Tai Ming Cheung, Kristen A. Gunness, Scott Warren Harold, Susan Puska, and Samuel K. Berkowitz. *China's Incomplete Military Transformation*. Santa Monica, CA: RAND, 2015.

Chivers, C. J. "Supplier Under Scrutiny on Arms for Afghans." *New York Times*, March 27, 2008.

Chivers, C. J., and Eric Schmitt. "Saudis Step Up Help for Rebels in Syria with Croatian Arms." *New York Times*, February 25, 2013.

Chulov, Martin. "How Saudi Elite Became Five-Star Prisoners at the Riyadh Ritz-Carlton." *Guardian*, November 6, 2017.

Chulov, Martin, Fazel Hawramy, and Spencer Ackerman. "Iraqi Army Capitulates to Isis Militants in Four Cities." *Guardian*, June 11, 2014.

Churchill, Winston. "Give Us the Tools." Broadcast, London, February 9, 1941, International Churchill Society. https://winstonchurchill.org/resources/speeches/1941-1945-war-leader/give-us-the-tools/.

CIP Security Assistance Monitor. "Security Assistance Database." Center for International Policy (CIP). Accessed December 17, 2020. https://securityassistance.org/security-sector-assistance/.

Cohen, Ronald. "Warfare and State Formation: Wars Make States and States Make Wars." In *Warfare, Culture, and Environment,* edited by R. Brian Ferguson. Orlando: Academic Press, 1984.

Collins, Shannon. "Desert Storm: A Look Back." US Department of Defense, January 11, 2019. https://www.defense.gov/News/Feature-Stories/story/Article/1728715/desert-storm-a-look-back/.

Colvin, Ross. "'Cut Off Head of Snake' Saudis Told U.S. on Iran." Reuters, November 28, 2010.

Comer, Charles "Ken." "Philippine Defense Reform: Are We There Yet?" https://community.apan.org/wg/tradoc-g2/fmso/m/fmso-monographs/239227/ (accessed November 29, 2019).

Committee on International Relations, Committee on Foreign Relations. *Legislation on Foreign Relations Through 2002*, Volume I-A of Volumes I-A and I-B. US House of Representatives and US Senate, July 2003.

Congressional Research Service (CRS). *Georgia: Background and U.S. Policy.* Washington, DC: CRS, April 2021.

———. *Kuwait: Governance, Security, and U.S. Policy.* Washington, DC: CRS, updated June 3, 2020.

———. *Morocco: Background and U.S. Relations.* Washington, DC: CRS, October 26, 2018.

———. *Saudi Arabia: Background and U.S. Relations.* Washington, DC: CRS, February 18, 2020.

———. *U.S. Special Operations Forces (SOF): Background and Issues for Congress.* Washington, DC: CRS, updated March 22, 2019.

Consulate General of the United Arab Emirates. "Women in the UAE." Accessed May 4, 2021. https://boston.uae-embassy.org/about-uae/women-uae.

Cook, Leon. "Enlisted Leaders from CENTCOM Region Countries Discuss Role of NCO in Today's Military." US Central Command, June 8, 2015.

Cooper, Helene. "Attacks Expose Flaws in Saudi Arabia's Expensive Military." *New York Times,* September 19, 2019.

———. "Will Trump's Plans to Counter Iran Bring a Return of the 'Tanker War'?" *New York Times,* June 28, 2019.

Cooper, Helene, and Eric Schmitt. "Airstrikes by U.S. and Allies Hit ISIS Targets in Syria." *New York Times*, September 22, 2014.

Cooper, Helene, Thomas Gibbons-Neff, and Eric Schmitt. "Army Special Forces Secretly Help Saudis Combat Threat from Yemen Rebels." *New York Times*, May 3, 2018.

Cordesman, Anthony. *The Iranian Sea-Air-Missile Threat to Gulf Shipping.* With Aaron Lin. Washington, DC: Center for Strategic and International Studies, February 2015.

Cordesman, Anthony, and Nawaf Obaid. *Saudi Military Forces and Development: Challenges and Reforms.* Washington, DC: Center for Strategic and International Studies, May 30, 2004.

———. "The Saudi Security Apparatus: Military and Security Services—Challenges and Developments." Paper presented at the DCAF Working Group on Security Sector Governance and Reform in the Middle East and North Africa (MENA) Workshop on Challenges of Security Sector Governance in the Middle East, Geneva, July 2004.

Cordesman, Anthony H., and Abraham R. Wagner. *The Lessons of Modern War, Volume IV: The Gulf War.* Boulder: Westview Press, 1996.

Corey, Craig R. "The Air Force's Misconception of Integrated Air and Missile Defense." *Air & Space Power Journal* 31, no. 4 (Winter 2017): 81–90.

Covey, Stephen R., A. Roger Merrill, and Rebecca R. Merrill. *First Things First.* New York: Simon and Schuster, 1996.

Cowell, Alan. "War in the Gulf: Jordan; Jordanian Ends Neutrality, Assailing Allied War Effort." *New York Times,* February 7, 1991.

Cronin, Stephanie. "Tribes, Coups and Princes: Building a Modern Army in Saudi Arabia." *Middle Eastern Studies* 49, no. 1 (January 2013): 2–28.

Crough, Thomas. "Jordan Implements New NCO Training Program." US Central Command, March 30, 2018.

Crowley, Michael. "Israel, U.A.E. and Bahrain Sign Accords, with an Eager Trump Playing Host." *New York Times,* November 11, 2020.

Daigle, Craig A. "The Russians Are Going: Sadat, Nixon, and the Soviet Presence in Egypt, 1970–71." *Middle East Review of International Affairs* 8, no. 1 (March 2004): 1.

Dalton, Melissa. "Toward a Smaller, Smarter Force Posture in the Middle East." *Defense One,* August 26, 2018.

David, Severino Vicente T., Aaron Taliaferro, and Wade P. Hinkle. *Implementing the Philippine Defense Reform Through the Defense System of Management.* Alexandria, VA: Institute for Defense Analyses, October 2017.

De Atkine, Norvell B. "Why Arabs Lose Wars." *Middle East Quarterly* 6, no. 4 (December 1999).

De Luce, Dan. "The Rift in the Relationship Between the U.S. and Turkey May Be Permanent." NBC News, July 15, 2019.

Defense Security Cooperation Agency. "Jordan—F-16 Air Combat Training Center." Transmittal no. 20-50, February 11, 2021.

———. "Mission, Vision, and Values." Accessed May 17, 2021. https://www.dsca.mil/mission-vision-and-values.

———. *Security Assistance Management Manual,* Chapter 16 under Title 10 of the US Code of Law. http://www.samm.dsca.mil/chapter/chapter-1.

DeLozier, Elana. "UAE Drawdown May Isolate Saudi Arabia in Yemen." PolicyWatch 3148. Washington, DC: Washington Institute for Near East Policy, July 2, 2019.

Department of the Navy, Naval Sea Systems Command. *Suez Canal Salvage Operations in 1974,* accessed on June 1, 2020. https://www.governmentattic.org/2docs/SUPSALV-Report_SuezCanal_1974.pdf.

Desch, Michael C. *Civilian Control of the Military: The Changing Security Environment.* Baltimore: Johns Hopkins University Press, 1999.

———. *Power and Military Effectiveness: The Fallacy of Democratic Triumphalism.* Baltimore: Johns Hopkins University Press, 2008.

DeYoung, Karen, and Dan Lamothe. "Qatar to Upgrade Air Base Used by U.S. to Fight Terrorism." *Washington Post,* July 24, 2018.

Dixon, Florence. "'We Are All Lebanese': Emotional Soldiers Break into Tears After Being Told to Confront Protesters." *New Arab,* October 23, 2019.

Donnelly, William M. "The Root Reforms and the National Guard." US Army Center of Military History, May 3, 2001. https://history.army.mil/documents/1901/Root-NG.htm.

Dreyfuss, Bob. "Washington's Weak Response to the Arab Awakening." *The Nation,* August 24, 2011.

Dudley, Dominic. "The 10 Strongest Military Forces in the Middle East." *Forbes,* February 26, 2018.

Duncan, Jonathan M. *The Dilemma for USSOCOM: Transitioning SOF-Peculiar to Service-Common.* Maxwell Air Force Base, AL: Air War College, Air University, February 15, 2012.

Ebo, Adedeji. "The Challenges and Lessons of Security Sector Reform in Post-conflict Sierra Leone." *Conflict, Security and Development* 6, no. 4 (2006): 481–501.

*Economist.* "Saudi Aramco: An Overburdened Champion." February 19, 2015.

———. "How America and Its Allies Are Keeping Tabs on Iran at Sea." January 2, 2020.

Eisenstadt, Michael, and Kenneth M. Pollack. "Armies of Snow and Armies of Sand: The Impact of Soviet Military Doctrine on Arab Militaries." *Middle East Journal* 55, no. 4 (2001): 549–578.

———. "Training Better Armies." *Parameters* 50, no. 3 (2020): 95–111.

El Massnaoui, Khalid, and Mhamed Biygautine. *Downsizing Morocco's Public Sector: Lessons from the Voluntary Retirement Program.* Case Studies in Governance and Public Management in the Middle East and North Africa, no. 2. Dubai: World Bank and Dubai School of Government, November 2011.

Elliott, Bryan, and Ernest Wang. "U.S. Army and Jordan Armed Forces Continue Partnership Mission Despite COVID-19 Challenges." US Central Command, May 26, 2020.

Embassy of Georgia to the United States of America. "Georgia Defense Readiness Program Kicks Off in Tbilisi." June 8, 2018.

Embassy of the United Arab Emirates (Washington, DC). "Foreign Aid." Accessed on July 2, 2020. https://www.uae-embassy.org/about-uae/foreign-policy/foreign-aid-0.

Emmons, Alex. "Secret Report Reveals Saudi Incompetence and Widespread Use of U.S. Weapons in Yemen." *The Intercept,* April 15, 2019.

Engelberg, Stephen. "U.S.-Saudi Deals in 90's Shifting Away from Cash Toward Credit." *New York Times,* August 23, 1993.

England, Andrew, and Ahmed Al Omran. "Saudi Arabia: Why Jobs Overhaul Could Define MBS's Rule." *Financial Times,* February 28, 2019.

Eriksson, Fredrik. *The Rapid Economic Liberalization and Ruthless Fight Against Corruption in Georgia: Interview with Dr. Tamara Kovziridze.* U4 Practitioner Experience Note 2017:1. Bergen, Norway: Chr. Michelsen Institute, Anti-Corruption Resource Centre.

Erlanger, Steven, and Eric Schmitt. "NATO Set to Take Full Command of Libyan Campaign." *New York Times,* March 25, 2011.

Estep, Chris. *Slow and Steady: Improving U.S.-Arab Cooperation to Counter Irregular Warfare.* Washington, DC: Center for a New American Security, April 25, 2019.

Exum, Andrew. "What Progressives Miss About Arms Sales." *Atlantic,* May 23, 2017.

Faddis, Charles. "Bin Ladin's Location Reveals Limits of Liaison Intelligence Relationships." *CTC Sentinel,* Special Yemen Issue (May 2011): 15–16.

Fahim, Kareem. "Houthi Rebels Kill 45 U.A.E. Soldiers in Yemen Fighting." *New York Times,* September 4, 2015.

Fahim, Kareem, and David D. Kirkpatrick. "Airstrikes Clear Way for Libyan Rebels' First Major Advance." *New York Times,* March 26, 2011.

Farazmand, Ali. "Bureaucracy and the Alternatives in the Middle East." In *Bureaucracy and the Alternatives in World Perspective,* edited by K. M. Henderson, O. P. Dwivedi, and Timothy M. Shaw. London: Palgrave MacMillan, 1999.

Fathallah, Hadi. "Challenges of Public Policymaking in Saudi Arabia." *Sada* (Carnegie Endowment for International Peace), May 22, 2019.

Feaver, Peter. "Civil-Military Relations." *Annual Review of Political Science* 2, no. 1 (1999): 211–241.

Feierstein, Gerald M. *The Times Have Changed, but the Need for a US-Led MFO Hasn't.* Washington, DC: Middle East Institute, April 16, 2020.

Fisher, Lucy. "British Officer Sent Home for Being 'Too Close to King.'" *The Times,* November 11, 2019.

Fisher, Max, Eric Schmitt, Audrey Carlsen, and Malachy Browne. "Did American Missile Defense Fail in Saudi Arabia?" *New York Times,* December 4, 2017.

Fitch, Asa. "U.S. Navy Ship Interdicts a Weapons Shipment in the Arabian Sea." *Wall Street Journal,* April 4, 2016.

Fitchetz, Joseph. "Paris Aid to Saudis Cited in Ending Mosque Siege." *International Herald Tribune,* January 28, 1980.

Foote, Michael. "Operationalizing Strategic Policy in Lebanon." *Special Warfare* 25, no. 2 (April–June 2012): 31–34.

Foreign Assistance Act of 1961. Section 622(c). Public Law no. 87-194. 75 Stat. 424 (1961).

*Frag Out! Magazine.* "Lebanese Air Force Completes First MD 530F Helicopters Training Class." March 17, 2021.

Freeh, Louis J. *Testimony Before the Joint Intelligence Committees,* 107th Congress, October 9, 2002.

Gable, Benjamin. "Senior NCOs from CENTCOM Nations Meet." US Army, August 9, 2010.

Gambrell, Jon. "US, UAE Troops Hold Major Exercise Amid Virus, Iran Tensions." Associated Press, March 23, 2020.

Gawrych, George. *The Albatross of Decisive Victory: War and Policy Between Egypt and Israel in the 1967 and 1973 Arab-Israeli Wars.* Westport, CT: Greenwood Press, 2000.

General Authority for Military Industries. Home page. Website. Accessed on October 13, 2010, gami.gov.sa/en.

Gerth, Jeff. "New Report of Saudi Money for Contras." *New York Times,* January 13, 1987.

———. "Saudi Stability Hit by Heavy Spending over Last Decade." *New York Times,* August 22, 1993.

———. "The White House Crisis: Evidence Points to Big Saudi Role in Iranian and Contra Arms Deals." *New York Times,* November 30, 1986.

Ghobari, Mohammed. "Yemen's War-Damaged Hodeidah Port Struggles to Bring in Vital Supplies." Reuters, November 24, 2016.

Ghobari, Mohammed, and Mohammed Mukhashaf. "Saudi-Led Planes Bomb Sanaa Airport to Stop Iranian Plane Landing." Reuters, April 28, 2015.

Glass, Andrew. "Reagan Brands Soviet Union 'Evil Empire,' March 8, 1983." *Politico*, March 8, 2018.

Glenn, Cameron, Mattisan Rowan, John Caves, and Garret Nada. *Timeline: The Rise, Spread, and Fall of the Islamic State*. Washington, DC: Wilson Center, October 28, 2019.

Godinho, Varun. "Two-Thirds of Saudi Arabia's Population Is Under the Age of 35." *Gulf Business*, August 10, 2020.

Goldberg, Jeffrey. "Ash Carter: Gulf Arabs Need to Get in the Fight." *Atlantic*, November 6, 2015.

———. "The Obama Doctrine." *Atlantic*, April 2016.

Goldman, Adam, and Declan Walsh. "Arab Raid Led to Freedom for American Hostage in Yemen." *New York Times*, March 6, 2019.

Gonzalez, Lina M., Aaron C. Taliaferro, and Wade P. Hinkle. *The Colombian Ministry of National Defense's "Transformation and Future Initiative": Retrospective on a 9-Year Cooperative Effort Between the United States Department of Defense and the Colombian Ministry of National Defense*. Alexandria, VA: Institute for Defense Analyses, October 2017.

Gordon, Michael R. "1991 Victory over Iraq Was Swift, but Hardly Flawless." *New York Times*, December 31, 2012.

Gould, Joe, Tara Copp, and Shawn Snow. "Pentagon Says Iraqi Train-and-Equip Mission Could End if Attacks on Kurds Continue." *Defense News*, October 16, 2017.

Government Accountability Office (GAO). *Security Assistance: Lapses in Human Rights Screening in North African Countries Indicate Need for Further Oversight*. Washington, DC: GAO, July 31, 2006.

Grant, Rebecca. "The Epic Little Battle of Khafji." *Air Force Magazine*, February 1, 1998.

Gross, Scott, and Lay Phonexayphova. "Joint, Interagency, and Tailored: Getting Security Force Assistance Right in Georgia." Modern War Institute at West Point, November 12, 2019.

Gutierrez, Jason. "Philippines Backs Off Threat to Terminate Military Pact with U.S." *New York Times*, June 2, 2020.

Haase, Thomas W. "A Challenging State of Affairs: Public Administration in the Republic of Lebanon." *International Journal of Public Administration* 41, no. 10 (2018): 792–806.

Haass, Richard N. "Desert Storm, the Last Classic War." *Wall Street Journal*, July 31, 2015.

Habib, Randa. "Jordan Playing Key Role in Anti-Terrorist Intelligence Gathering." *Jordan Times*, November 23–24, 2001.

Hajjar, Remi. "What Lessons Did We Learn (or Re-Learn) About Military Advising After 9/11?" *Military Review*, November–December 2014, 63–75.

Hakeem, Shaiyla. "Jordan, America Launch New Training Cycle." US Central Command, July 26, 2019.

Halloran, Richard. "2 Iranian Fighters Reported Downed by Saudi Air Force." *New York Times*, June 6, 1984.

Hamre, John J. *Reflections: Looking Back at the Need for Goldwater-Nichols*. Washington, DC: Center for Strategic and International Studies, January 27, 2016.

Al Harbi, Bandar O. Nahil. *Saudi Arabia National Guard (SANG)*. Carlisle Barracks, PA: US Army War College, March 27, 1991.

Harris, Shane. "The Mouse That Roars." *Foreign Policy*, September 12, 2014.

Hartung, William D. "Defense Contractors Are Tightening Their Grip on Our Government." *The Nation*, July 16, 2019.

———. "Nixon's Children: Bill Clinton and the Permanent Arms Bazaar." *World Policy Journal* 12, no. 2 (Summer 1995): 25–35.

Hartung, William D., and Seth Binder. *U.S. Security Assistance to Egypt: Examining the Return on Investment*. Washington, DC: Project on Middle East Democracy and Center for International Policy, May 2020.

Head, William P. "The Battle for Ra's Al-Khafji and the Effects of Air Power January 29–February 1, 1991." *Air Power History* 60, no. 1 (Spring 2013): 4–33.

Hearn, Jaccob. "1 TSC, Jordan Armed Forces Strengthen Partnership Through Logistics Training." US Army, September 25, 2017.

Al-Hegelan, Abdelrahman, and Monte Palmer. "Bureaucracy and Development in Saudi Arabia." *Middle East Journal* 39, no. 1 (Winter 1985): 48–68.

Heisterberg, Melissa. "U.S., Saudi Forces Conduct Joint Military Exercises on Saudi Islands." US Marines, May 29, 2020. https://www.marines.mil/News/News-Display/Article/2201371/us-saudi-forces-conduct-joint-military-exercises-on-saudi-islands/.

Helou, Agnes. "Lebanese Air Force Commander on Expanding the Light-Attack Fleet." *Defense News*, July 3, 2019.

———. "UAE Launches 'Edge' Conglomerate to Address Its 'Antiquated Military Industry.'" *Defense News,* November 6, 2019.

Hennessey, Kathleen, Lolita C. Baldor, and Adam Schreck. "Obama Pushes Saudis, Gulf Allies to Set Up Iraq Aid." Associated Press, April 20, 2016.

Hertog, Steffen. "Shaping the Saudi State: Human Agency's Shifting Role in Rentier-State Formation." *International Journal of Middle East Studies* 39, no. 4 (November 2007): 539–563.

Hoffman, Hugh F. T. "Lessons from Iraq." In Kerr and Miklaucic, *Effective, Legitimate, Secure,* 329–358.

Hollings, Alex. "The Birth of SOCOM: How America's Special Operations Command Was Born of Tragedy." SOFREP, March 7, 2019. https://sofrep.com/specialoperations/the-birth-of-socom-how-americas-special-operations-command-was-born-of-tragedy/.

Hosenball, Mark, and Matt Spetalnick. "Drone Strike Ends Long Hunt for U.S.-Born Awlaki." Reuters, September 30, 2011.

Hubbard, Ben. "Cables Released by WikiLeaks Reveal Saudis' Checkbook Diplomacy." *New York Times*, June 20, 2015.

———. "Inside Saudi Arabia's Re-education Prison for Jihadists." *New York Times*, April 9, 2016.

Hubbard, Ben, and Shuaib Almosawa. "Biden Ends Military Aid for Saudi War in Yemen. Ending the War Is Harder." *New York Times*, February 5, 2021.

Hubbard, Ben, Charlie Savage, Eric Schmitt, and Patrick Kingsley. "Abandoned by U.S. in Syria, Kurds Find New Ally in American Foe." *New York Times,* October 23, 2019.

Huber, Mark. "ISG Wins SECDEF Award for Excellence in Maintenance Training, Advice, and Assistance of Foreign Security Forces—Ministerial Category." Institute for Security Governance, November 3, 2020. https://instituteforsecuritygovernance.org/-/isg-wins-secdef.

Human Rights Watch. *Hiding Behind the Coalition.* New York, August 24, 2018.

———. *Stateless Again: Palestinian-Origin Jordanians Deprived of Their Nationality.* New York, February 1, 2010.

———. "Yemen Events of 2019." Accessed February 25, 2021. https://www.hrw.org/world-report/2020/country-chapters/yemen#.

Hunt, Peter. "Coalition Warfare: Considerations for the Air Component Commander." Thesis, Department of the Air Force, Air University Press, March 1998.

Huntington, Samuel P. *Political Order in Changing Societies.* New Haven, CT: Yale University Press, 1968.

———. *The Soldier and the State: The Theory and Politics of Civil-Military Relations.* Cambridge, MA: The Belknap Press of Harvard University Press, 1957.

Ibrahim, Youssef M. "Gulf War's Cost to Arabs Estimated at $620 Billion." *New York Times*, September 8, 1992.

Ignatius, David. "How to Rebuild Lebanon." *Foreign Affairs* 61, no. 5 (Summer 1983): 146.

IHS Markit. *Coalition's Failure to Secure Mocha Coastline Indicates Limits of Planned Offensive on Yemen's Hodeidah.* London: IHS Markit, April 14, 2017.

Indyk, Martin. "The Middle East Isn't Worth It Anymore." *Wall Street Journal*, January 17, 2020.

Insinna, Valerie. "In Newly Inked Deal, F-25 Price Falls to $78 Million a Copy." *Defense News*, October 29, 2019.

Inspector General of the Department of Defense. *Lead Inspector General for Operation Yukon Journey.* Quarterly Report to the United States Congress, October 1, 2019–December 31, 2019.

Institute for Development of Freedom of Information (IDFI). *Challenges of the Georgian Bureaucratic System in the Context of Public Administration Reform.* Tbilisi, Georgia: IDFI, 2017.

International Monetary Fund (IMF). "Arab Republic of Egypt." IMF Country Report No. 18/14. Washington, DC: IMF, January 2018.

International Peace Institute (IPI). *A New Approach? Deradicalization Programs and Counterterrorism.* New York: IPI, June 2010.

Jalal, Ibrahim. *The UAE May Have Withdrawn from Yemen, but Its Influence Remains Strong.* Washington, DC: Middle East Institute, February 25, 2020.

Al Jazeera. "Houthis Claim Attack on Military Target in Saudi Capital Riyadh." August 26, 2019.

*Jordan Times.* "Military's Afghanistan Mission Completed." January 5, 2015.

Joseph, Uri Bar. "The Egyptian Spy Who Saved Israel in the Yom Kippur War." *Daily Beast,* July 12, 2017.

Jreisat, Jamil E. "Managing National Development in the Arab States." *Arab Studies Quarterly* 14, no. 2/3 (Spring/Summer 1992): 1–17.

Kalin, Stephen, and Sylvia Westall. "Costly Saudi Defenses Prove No Match for Drones, Cruise Missiles." Reuters, September 17, 2019.

Kamrava, Mehran. "Military Professionalization and Civil-Military Relations in the Middle East." *Political Science Quarterly* 115, no. 1 (Spring 2000): 67–92.

Karlin, Mara E. *Building Militaries in Fragile States: Challenges for the United States.* Philadelphia: University of Pennsylvania Press, 2019.

Karlin, Mara, and Tamara Cofman Wittes. "America's Middle East Purgatory: The Case for Doing Less." *Foreign Affairs,* January/February 2019.

Katzman, Kenneth. *The United Arab Emirates (UAE): Issues for U.S. Policy.* CRS Report No. RS21852. Washington, DC: Congressional Research Service, March 3, 2020.

Kavanagh, Jennifer, Bryan Frederick, Alexandra Stark, Nathan Chandler, Meagan L. Smith, Matthew Povlock, Lynn E. Davis, and Edward Geist. *Characteristics of Successful U.S. Military Interventions.* Santa Monica, CA: RAND, 2019.

Kawar, Jumana. "Jordan: US Security Assistance and Border Defense Capacity Building." Middle East Institute, October 6, 2020.

Keaney, Thomas A., and Eliot A. Cohen. *Gulf War Air Power Survey.* Summary Report. Washington, DC: US Air Force, December 22, 1993.

Kelly, Fergus. "Lebanon Army Receives 8 Bradley Fighting Vehicles from the US." *Defense Post,* August 4, 2018.

Kendall, Elisabeth. *Contemporary Jihadi Militancy in Yemen.* Policy Paper 2018-7. Washington, DC: Middle East Institute, July 2018.

Kenner, David. "All ISIS Has Left Is Money. Lots of It." *Atlantic,* March 24, 2019.

Kerr, Alexandra, and Michael Miklaucic (eds.). *Effective, Legitimate, Secure: Insights for Defense Institution Building.* Washington, DC: National Defense University Press, 2017.

Kerr, Simeon. "Houthis Claim Capture of Thousands in Yemeni Offensive." *Financial Times,* September 29, 2019.

Kessler, Glenn. "Trump's Claim the Saudis Will Pay '100 Percent of the Cost.'" *Washington Post,* October 21, 2019.

Khaleel, Sangar, and Jane Arraf. "Rocket Attack in Iraq Kills a U.S. Military Contractor." *New York Times,* March 3, 2021.

Khatib, Lina. *Political Culture in the Arab World: Assumptions and Complexities.* Med Dialogue Series no. 34. Berlin: Konrad Adenauer Stiftung, January 2021.

Khouri, Rami. "Jordanian Unit Going to Aid Iraq 6 Hussein Will Join Volunteer Force Fighting Iranians." *Washington Post,* January 29, 1982.

Kirkpatrick, David D. "Secret Alliance: Israel Carries Out Airstrikes in Egypt, with Cairo's O.K." *New York Times,* February 3, 2018.

Klare, Michael T. "Fueling the Fire: How We Armed the Middle East." *Bulletin of Atomic Scientists* (January–February 1990): 18–26.

Knights, Michael. "Is the Yemen War Really Deadlocked? Think Again." Washington Institute for Near East Policy, September 2018. https://www.washingtoninstitute.org/policy-analysis /yemen-war-really-deadlocked-think-again.

———. "The U.A.E. Approach to Counterinsurgency in Yemen." War on the Rocks, May 23, 2016.

Koffler, Keith. "'Pay Us Back': Trump Says Troops Will Not Leave Airbase Unless Iraq Compensates US." *Washington Examiner,* January 5, 2020.

Krebs, Ronald R. "A School for the Nation? How Military Service Does Not Build Nations, and How It Might." *International Security* 28, no. 4 (Spring 2004): 85–124.

Al-Kubaisi, Ali. "A Model in the Administrative Development of Arab Gulf Countries." *The Arab Gulf 17*, no. 2 (1985): 29–48.

Kube, Courtney. "U.S. Military Has Begun Reestablishing Air Base Inside Saudi Arabia." NBC News, July 19, 2019.

Kuttab, Daoud. "Jordan Orders Army Conscription for 25–29-Year-Olds to Help Tackle Unemployment." *Arab News*, September 9, 2020.

LaForgia, Michael, and Walt Bogdanich. "Why Bombs Made in America Have Been Killing Civilians in Yemen." *New York Times*, May 16, 2020.

Lambeth, Benjamin S. *Air Power Against Terror: America's Conduct of Operation Enduring Freedom.* Santa Monica, CA: RAND, 2005.

Lamothe, Dan. "U.S. Troops in Iraq Move Closer to the Front Lines in Fight for Mosul." *Washington Post*, February 20, 2017.

Land, Hardin, William Wechsler, and Alia Awadallah. *The Future of U.S.-Jordanian Counterterrorism Cooperation.* Washington, DC: Center for American Progress, November 30, 2017.

Landler, Mark. "Obama Criticizes the 'Free Riders' Among America's Allies." *New York Times*, March 10, 2016.

Lang, Hardin, Peter Juul, and Trevor Sutton. *Confronting the Terror Finance Challenge in Today's Middle East.* Washington, DC: Center for American Progress, November 2015.

Lang, Hardin, William Wechsler, and Alia Awadallah. *The Future of U.S.-Jordanian Counterterrorism Cooperation.* Washington, DC: Center for American Progress, November 2017.

Layne, Christopher. "America's Middle East Grand Strategy After Iraq: The Moment for Offshore Balancing Has Arrived." *Review of International Studies* 35, no. 1 (January 2009): 5–25.

Lead Inspector General Report to United States Congress. *Operation Inherent Resolve, January 1, 2019–March 31, 2019.*

———. *Operation Inherent Resolve, April 1, 2019–June 30, 2019.* August 2, 2019.

Leaf, Barbara A., and Elana DeLozier. *The UAE and Yemen's Islah: A Coalition Coalesces.* Policywatch 3046. Washington, DC: Washington Institute for Near East Policy, December 6, 2018.

Legal Information Institute. "10 U.S. Code § 331. Friendly Foreign Countries: Authority to Provide Support for Conduct of Operations." Cornell Law School, 2016. https://www.law.cornell.edu/uscode/text/10/331.

Leone, Dario. "The Strange Case of the First Kills Scored by RSAF (or USAF) F-15 Pilots." *Aviation Geek Club*, June 4, 2018.

Lescaze, Lee. "Hill Battle Looms as Reagan Proposes Sale of AWACS to Saudis." *Washington Post*, August 25, 1981.

Levitt, Matthew. "Stemming the Flow of Terrorist Financing: Practical and Conceptual Challenges." *Fletcher Forum of World Affairs* (Winter–Spring 2003).

———. *Testimony Submitted to the House Foreign Affairs Subcommittee on the Middle East and North Africa,* 115th Congress, July 26, 2017.

Lewis, Jeffery. "Patriot Missiles Are Made in America and Fail Everywhere." *Foreign Policy*, March 28, 2018.

Lewis, Paul. "War on Oil Tankers Heats Up in the Persian Gulf." *New York Times*, May 18, 1986.

Lichtblau, Eric, and Eric Schmitt. "Cash Flow to Terrorists Evades U.S. Efforts." *New York Times*, December 5, 2010.

Linder, James B., Eric J. Wesley, and Elliot S. Grant. "A New Breed of Advisory Team: Security Force Assistance Brigades to Collaborate with Special Operations Forces." Association of the United States Army, June 19, 2017.

Liptak, Kevin. "King of Jordan Says ISIS Could Be Defeated 'Fairly Quickly.'" CNN, January 13, 2016.

Lister, Tim. "The Billions Saudi Arabia Spends on Air Defenses May Be Wasted in the Age of Drone Warfare." CNN, September 19, 2019.

Lubold, Gordon. "U.S. Works Up New Effort to Shift Military's Focus to Asia." *Wall Street Journal*, October 23, 2019.

Luck, Taylor. "New Aran Military Force to Reckon with as 'Little Sparta' Rises." *Christian Science Monitor*, February 28, 2019.

———. "U.S., Jordan Stepping Up Training of Syrian Opposition." *Washington Post*, April 2, 2013.

Lumpe, Lora. "Bill Clinton's America: Arms Merchant of the World." *Nonviolent Activist* (May–June 1995).

Macias, Amanda. "Saudi Arabia, US Take a Significant Step Toward Closing $15 Billion Deal for Lockheed Martin's THAAD Missile Defense System." CNBC, November 28, 2018.

Mackintosh, Eliza. "ISIS Leader Abu Bakr al-Baghdadi Is Dead. Here Are 6 Things You Need to Know." CNN, October 29, 2019.

Maclean, William, Noah Browning, and Yara Bayoumy. "Yemen Counter-terrorism Mission Shows UAE Military Ambition." Reuters, June 28, 2016.

Macmanus, Joseph E., and Elizabeth L. King. 2011. *Letters of Joseph E. Macmanus, and Elizabeth L. to Speaker of the House John A. Boehner.* US Activities in Libya, June 15, 2011.

Mahan, Erin R., and Jeffrey A. Larsen. *The Ascendency of the Secretary of Defense: Robert McNamara 1961–1963.* Cold War Foreign Policy Series, Special Study 4. Historical Office, Office of the Secretary of Defense, July 2013.

Maher, Ahmed. "UAE and US Forces Commence Iron Union 14 Military Exercise." *The National*, January 30, 2021.

Malsin, Jared, and Summer Said. "Saudi Arabia Promised Support to Libyan Warlord in Push to Seize Tripoli." *Wall Street Journal*, April 12, 2019.

Mansoor, Peter R., and Williamson Murray (eds.). *The Culture of Military Organizations.* Cambridge: Cambridge University Press, 2019.

Mapp, Jerome. *Ex-leader in Saudi Embraces Flexibility, Communication.* US Army, July 28, 2020.

Marquis, Susan L. *Unconventional Warfare: Rebuilding U.S. Special Operations Forces.* Washington, DC: Brookings Institution Press, 1997.

Marshall, Shana R. "The New Politics of Patronage: The Arms Trade and Clientelism in the Arab World." PhD diss., University of Maryland, 2012.

Massadeh, Abd El-Mahdi. "The Structure of Public Administration in Jordan: A Constitutional and Administrative Law Perspective." *Arab Law Quarterly* 14, no. 2 (1999): 91–111.

Matamoros, Cristina Abellan. "Saudi King Would Not Last 'Two Weeks' in Power Without US Support: Trump." *Euronews*, March 10, 2018.

Matisek, Jahara. "The Crisis of American Military Assistance: Strategic Dithering and Fabergé Egg Armies." *Defense & Security Analysis* 34, no. 3 (2008): 1–24.

Mazzei, Patricia, and Eric Schmitt. "Pentagon Restricts Training for Saudi Military Students." *New York Times*, December 12, 2019.

Mazzetti, Mark, and Matt Apuzzo. "U.S. Relies Heavily on Saudi Money to Support Syrian Rebels." *New York Times*, January 23, 2016.

McCain, John. "We Need a Strategy for the Middle East." *New York Times*, October 24, 2017.

McCarthy, Niall. "The Cost of Training U.S. Air Force Fighter Pilots." *Forbes*, April 9, 2019.

McDowall, Angus, Phil Stewart, and David Rohde. "Yemen's Guerrilla War Tests Military Ambitions of Big-Spending Saudis." Reuters, April 19, 2016.

McGlinchey, Stephen, and Robert W. Murray. "Jimmy Carter and the Sale of the AWACS to Iran in 1977." *Diplomacy & Statecraft* 28, no. 2 (2017): 254–276.

McGovern, Matthew. "SNCO Academy Brings First-Ever PME Course to Jordan." US Air Forces Central, July 1, 2019.

McInnis, Kathleen J. *Coalition Contributions to Countering the Islamic State.* Washington, DC: Congressional Research Service, August 24, 2016.

McKay, Hollie. "Billions Wasted? Iraqi Pilots Claim Pricey F-16 Program Is Falling Apart." *Fox News*, August 26, 2020.

McLeary, Paul. "Can Trump Find a Better Deal Than the U.S. Air Base in Qatar?" *Foreign Policy,* July 20, 2017.

McMahon, R. Blake, and Branislav L. Slantchev. "The Guardianship Dilemma: Regime Security Through and from the Armed Forces." *American Political Science Review* 109, no. 2 (May 2015): 297–313.

McNabb, Veronica. "NCO Exchange Between U.S. Army and Jordan Armed Forces." US Army Central, April 18, 2019.

McNeeley, Ty. "Jordanian, U.S. Partnership Revamps Noncommissioned Officer Training." US Army Central, November 5, 2017.

Mearsheimer, John J., and Stephen M. Walt. "The Case for Offshore Balancing: A Superior U.S. Grand Strategy." *Foreign Affairs,* July/August 2016.
Mehta, Aaron. "After Reshuffling, Israel Could Create 'Opportunities' for Regional Military Cooperation." *Defense News,* February 8, 2021.
———. "Global Defense Spending Sees Biggest Spike in a Decade." *Defense News,* April 27, 2019.
Memmott, Mark. "New Details on How U.S. 'Helped Saddam as He Gassed Iran.'" NPR, August 26, 2013.
Mezher, Chyrine. "Lebanon: Donated Helicopters Highlight Close, Continuing US Ties." *Breaking Defense,* March 18, 2021.
Michael, Maggie. "Details of Deals Between US-Backed Coalition, Yemen al-Qaida." Associated Press, August 6, 2018.
Michaels, Jim. "U.S. Military Needs Egypt for Access to Critical Area." *USA Today,* August 17, 2013.
Miller, Andrew. "Commentary: Five Myths About U.S. Aid to Egypt." Reuters, August 13, 2018.
Moore, Jack. "NATO Officially Initiates UAE into Afghan Mission." *The National,* July 12, 2018.
Moran, Michael. *Modern Military Force Structures.* New York: Council on Foreign Relations, October 26, 2006.
Morell, Michael. "The Giant Al Qaeda Defeat That No One's Talking About." *Politico Magazine,* May 2, 2016.
Mukashaf, Mohammad. "Pakistan Declines Saudi Call for Armed Support in Yemen Fight." Reuters, April 10, 2015.
Al-Mulhim, Abdulateef. "Saudi Youth, the Issue of Unemployment and Work Ethic." *Arab News,* March 9, 2013.
Mulroy, Michael Patrick, and Eric S. Oehlerich. *A Tale of Two Partners: Comparing Two Approaches for Partner Force Operations.* Washington, DC: Middle East Institute, January 29, 2020.
Munson, Peter. "The Limits of Security Cooperation." War on the Rocks, September 10, 2013.
Myers, Meghann. "'Up or Out' Is on Its Way Out, and It's Time for 'Perform or Out,' Army Secretary Says." *Army Times,* January 24, 2019.
Myers, Steven Lee. "U.S. Joins Effort to Equip and Pay Rebels in Syria." *New York Times,* April 1, 2012.
Myers, Steven Lee, and Rachel Donadio. "U.S. Seeks to Aid Libyan Rebels with Seized Assets." *New York Times,* May 5, 2011.
National Defense Authorization Act for Fiscal Year 2017. Public Law no. 114-328, 130 Stat. 2000 (2016). https://www.congress.gov/114/plaws/publ328/PLAW-114publ328.pdf.
National Defense Strategy Commission. *Providing for the Common Defense: An Assessment and Recommendations of the National Defense Strategy Commission.* Washington, DC: United States Institute of Peace, November 2018.
*National Security Decision Directive 166.* PDF. Federation of American Scientists. March 27, 1985. https://irp.fas.org/offdocs/nsdd/nsdd-166.pdf.
NATO. "Defence Institution Building School: An Initiative of the Substantial NATO-Georgia Package." Fact sheet, 2016.
———. "NATO Integrated Air and Missile Defence." Accessed on November 4, 2020. https://www.nato.int/cps/en/natohq/topics_8206.htm.
Naylor, Hugh. "Saudi-Led Coalition Plans Ground Attacks in Yemen After Taking Key City." *Washington Post,* July 29, 2015.
NBC News. "Splitting the Check: When Allies Helped Pay for Middle East War." September 14, 2014.
Neese-Bybee, Ashley-Louise, Paul Clarke, and Alexander H. Noyes. *Defense Institution Building in Africa: Toward a New Model for Low-Capacity, High-Threat African States.* Alexandria, VA: Institute for Defense Analyses, September 2018.
Neill, Martin, Aaron C. Taliaferro, Mark E. Tillman, Gary D. Morgan, and Wade P. Hinkle. *Defense Governance and Management: Improving the Defense Management Capabilities of Foreign Defense Institutions.* Alexandria, VA: Institute for Defense Analyses, March 2017.

Nelson, Rick "Ozzie," and Scott Goosens. *Counter-Piracy in the Arabian Sea: Challenges and Opportunities for GCC Action.* Washington, DC: Center for Strategic and International Studies, May 2011.

*New York Times.* "A Break in the Khobar Towers Case," August 28, 2015.

———. "Rice and Gates Seek Arabs' Help on Iraq." July 31, 2007.

Nissenbaum, Dion. "U.A.E. Moves to Extricate Itself from Saudi-Led War in Yemen." *Wall Street Journal,* July 2, 2019.

NPR. "Bush Announces $20 Billion Arms Deal for Saudis." January 14, 2008.

———. "Ike's Warning of Military Expansion, 50 Years Later." January 17, 2011.

Nunn, Frederick M. "Emil Korner and the Prussianization of the Chilean Army: Origins, Process, and Consequences, 1885–1920." *Hispanic American Historical Review* 50, no. 2 (May 1970): 300–322.

O'Flaherty, Kate. "The Iran Cyber Warfare Threat: Everything You Need to Know." *Forbes,* January 6, 2020.

O'Hanlon, Michael. "Access to Suez Is Convenient but Not Essential for U.S." *Washington Post,* August 22, 2013.

Al Omran, Ahmed, and Asa Fitch. "Saudi Arabia Forms Muslim Antiterror Coalition." *Wall Street Journal,* December 15, 2015.

Opall-Rome, Barbara. "Raytheon: Arab-Operated Patriots Intercepted Over 100 Tactical Ballistic Missiles Since 2015." *Defense News,* November 14, 2017.

Organisation for Economic Co-operation and Development (OECD). *Colombia: Policy Priorities for Inclusive Development.* Paris: OECD, January 2015.

Al-Otaiba, Yousef. "The Arab Coalition Is Making Progress Against Extremists in Yemen." *Washington Post,* September 12, 2018.

Ottaway, David B. "Egyptians Indicate Limited Readiness to Aid Iraq in War." *Washington Post,* May 21, 1982.

Parker, Claire, and Rick Noack. "Iran Has Invested in Allies and Proxies Across the Middle East. Here's Where They Stand After Soleimani's Death." *Washington Post,* January 3, 2020.

Partrick, Neil. "Saudi Defense and Security Reform." *Sada* (Carnegie Endowment for International Peace), May 31, 2018.

Pawlyk, Oriana. "US Had Light Footprint in Recent UAE-Led Exercise." Military.com, January 25, 2019.

Pawlyk, Oriana, and Phillip Swarts. "25 Years Later: What We Learned from Desert Storm." *Air Force Times,* January 21, 2016.

Pear, Robert. "Arming Afghan Guerillas: A Huge Effort Led by U.S." *New York Times,* April 18, 1988.

Perry, Mark. "US Generals: Saudi Intervention in Yemen a 'Bad Idea.'" Al Jazeera America, April 17, 2015.

Pew Research Center. *Saudi Arabia's Mohammed bin Salman Garners Little Trust from People in the Region and the U.S.* Washington, DC: Pew Research Center, January 29, 2020.

Philips, Samuel J. "Jordanian NCOs Learn to Be Warrior Leaders." *NCO Journal* 20, no. 6 (June 2011): 35–37.

Plumer, Brad. "The U.S. Gives Egypt $1.5 Billion a Year in Aid. Here's What It Does." *Washington Post,* July 9, 2013.

Pollack, Kenneth M. *Arabs at War: Military Effectiveness, 1948–1991.* Lincoln: University of Nebraska Press, 2002.

———. *Armies of Sand: The Past, Present, and Future of Arab Military Effectiveness.* Oxford: Oxford University Press, 2019.

———. *Security and Public Order.* Washington, DC: Atlantic Council and Brookings Institution, February 2016.

———. *Sizing Up Little Sparta: Understanding UAE Military Effectiveness.* Washington, DC: American Enterprise Institute, October 27, 2020.

Pollak, Nadav, and Michael Knights. *Gulf Coalition Operations in Yemen (Part 3): Maritime and Aerial Blockade.* PolicyWatch 2596. Washington, DC: Washington Institute for Near East Policy, March 25, 2016.

Porges, Marisa L. *The Saudi Deradicalization Experiment.* New York: Council on Foreign Relations, January 22, 2010.

Price, Bryan C. "Targeting Top Terrorists: How Leadership Decapitation Contributes to Coun-terterrorism." *International Security* 36, no. 4 (Spring 2012): 9–46.

Price, Daniel E. "Presidential Power as a Domestic Constraint on Foreign Policy: Case Stud-ies Examining Arms Sales to Saudi Arabia." *Presidential Studies Quarterly* 26, no. 4 (1996): 1099–1113.

Pukhov, Ruslan. *The Tanks of August.* Moscow: Center for Analysis of Strategies and Tech-nologies, 2010.

Quanrud, Pamela. "The Global Coalition to Defeat ISIS: A Success Story." *Foreign Service Journal* (January/February 2018).

Rahman, Redwanur, and Ameerah Qattan. "Vision 2030 and Sustainable Development: State Capacity to Revitalize the Healthcare System in Saudi Arabia." *Journal of Health Care* 58 (January–December 2021): 1–10.

Rank, Joseph, and Bill Saba. "Building Partnership Capacity 201: The New Jordan Armed Forces Noncommissioned Officer Corps." *Military Review* (September–October 2014): 24–35.

Rashad, Marwa, Sarah Dadouch, and Abdulrahman al-Ansi. "Barrage of Missiles on Saudi Arabia Ramps Up Yemen War." Reuters, March 26, 2018.

Rauen, Brian, Terri Erisman, and Edward Ballanco. "More Is Not Better: Fixing Security Cooperation." *War Room* (US Army War College), June 22, 2018.

Razoux, Pierre. *The Iran-Iraq War.* Cambridge, MA: Belknap Press/Harvard University Press, 2015.

Remnick, David. "Going the Distance." *New Yorker,* January 27, 2014.

Reuters. "Addiction and Intrigue: Inside the Saudi Palace Coup." July 19, 2017.

———. "Egypt's Suez Canal Reports Record High $5.585 Billion Annual Revenue." June 17, 2018.

———. "Factbox: U.S. Forces in Gulf Region and Iraq." January 8, 2020.

———. "Jordan: Royal Military Academy—the Basis of Jordan's Army." October 15, 1971.

———. "Saudi Arabia Boosts Troop Levels in South Yemen as Tensions Rise." September 3, 2019.

———. "Saudi King Orders National Guard to Take Part in Yemen Campaign." April 21, 2015.

———. "Saudi-Led Coalition Starts Military Operation Against Yemen's Houthis." July 1, 2020.

———. "UAE to Boost Troop Presence in Afghanistan for Training: Officials." June 8, 2018.

———. "UAE, U.S. Activate Defence Cooperation Pact: State News Agency." May 29, 2019.

———. "Yemen Houthis Say Attacked 'Important Target' in Riyadh with Missile, Drones." September 10, 2020.

———. "Yemen's Houthis Say They Fired Drones at Saudi Arabia's Abha Airport." Septem-ber 7, 2020.

Riedel, Bruce. "The $110 Billion Arms Deal to Saudi Arabia Is Fake News." *Markaz* (blog). Brookings Institution, June 5, 2017. https://www.brookings.edu/blog/markaz/2017/06/05 /the-110-billion-arms-deal-to-saudi-arabia-is-fake-news/.

———. *Lessons from America's First War with Iran.* Washington, DC: Brookings Institution, May 22, 2013.

Risen, James. "Iraqi Says He Made Up Tale of Biological Weapons Before War." *New York Times,* February 15, 2011.

Robbins, Michael, and Kathrin Thomas. "Tunisia at a Crossroads: Findings from the Fifth Wave of the Arab Barometer." Presentation. Arab Barometer, July 9, 2019.

Roberts, Steven V. "Prop for U.S. Policy: Secret Saudi Funds." *New York Times,* June 21, 1987.

Robertson, Nic, and Hakim Almasmari. "Saudi Special Forces Help Oppose Houthi Rebels in Yemen, Source Says." CNN, April 3, 2015.

Roblin, Sebastien. "The Army Decided to Replace Bradley Fighting Vehicles 17 Years and $22b Ago. They Still Don't Have a Prototype." NBC News, February 13, 2020.

———. "Why U.S. Patriot Missiles Failed to Stop Drones and Cruise Missiles Attacking Saudi Oil Sites." *NBC*, September 23, 2019.

Rosenfeld, Henry. "The Social Composition of the Military in the Process of State Formation in the Arabian Desert." *Journal of the Royal Anthropological Institute of Great Britain and Ireland* 95, no. 2 (July–December 1965): 174–194.

Rosenthal, Andrew. "The 1992 Campaign: Republicans; Jet Sale to Saudis Approved by Bush, Saving Jobs in U.S." *New York Times*, September 12, 1992.

Ross, Michael. "Secret Plan Told: Egypt Weighs Military Aid to Gulf States." *Los Angeles Times*, December 21, 1987.

Ross, Thomas W., Jr. "Defining the Discipline in Theory and Practice." In Kerr and Miklaucic, *Effective, Legitimate, Secure*, 21–46.

Rothschild, Emma. "Carter and Arms Sales." *New York Times*, May 10, 1978.

Saab, Bilal Y., *Beyond the Proxy Powder Keg: The Specter of War Between Saudi Arabia and Iran*. Policy Paper 2-2018. Washington, DC: Middle East Institute, 2018.

———. "Blindsiding the Gulf." *National Interest*, no. 168 (July/August 2020): 52–65.

———. "Broken Partnerships: Can Washington Get Security Cooperation Right?" *Washington Quarterly* 42, no. 3 (Fall 2019): 77–89.

———. "Can Mohamed bin Salman Reshape Saudi Arabia?" *Foreign Affairs*, January 5, 2017.

———. *The Gulf Rising: Defense Industrialization in Saudi Arabia and the UAE*. Washington, DC: Atlantic Council, May 2014.

———. "Houthi and the Blowback: Saudi Arabia Steps into Yemen." *Foreign Affairs*, March 29, 2015.

———. "The Incredible Shrinking Buffer: UN Peacekeepers Face Crisis in the Golan Heights." *Foreign Affairs*, October 28, 2013.

———. *Iran's Long Game in Bahrain*. Washington, DC: Atlantic Council, December 2017.

———. "The Lebanese Army Needs Cash." *Foreign Policy*, June 18, 2021.

———. "Trump's Curious Multilateralism." *Foreign Policy*, January 28, 2020.

———. "Trump's New Arms-Sales Policy Is Good but Sounds Awful." *Defense One*, April 27, 2018.

———. "The United States Has No Gulf Allies." *Foreign Affairs*, April 12, 2016.

———. "Washington Should Back, Not Punish, the Lebanese Military." *Foreign Policy*, November 5, 2019.

———. "What Does America Get for Its Military Aid?" *National Interest*, March/April 2018.

———. "What a New Iran Nuclear Deal Really Requires." *Foreign Policy*, January 27, 2020.

Saab, Bilal Y., and Michael Elleman. *Precision Fire: A Strategic Assessment of Iran's Conventional Missile Program*. Washington, DC: Atlantic Council, September 2016.

Saab, Bilal Y., and Michael P. Mulroy. "For Now, U.S. Troops Are Likely in Iraq to Stay." *Foreign Policy*, January 29, 2020.

Saab, Bilal Y., and Barry Pavel. *Artful Balance: Future US Defense Strategy and Force Posture in the Gulf*. Washington, DC: Atlantic Council, March 2015.

———. *Beyond Camp David: A Gradualist Strategy to Upgrade the US-Gulf Security Partnership*. Washington, DC: Atlantic Council, May 2015.

Saab, Bilal Y., and Joseph Votel. "We Need a Better China Policy in the Middle East." *Defense One*, July 28, 2020.

Samaan, Jean-Loup. "The Strategy Behind New Gulf War Colleges." *Sada* (Carnegie Endowment for International Peace), March 5, 2019.

Sanderson, Daniel. "Exclusive: Inside the 'Iron Union' as US and UAE Troops Train for Combat." *The National*, December 23, 2019.

Saudi Arabian Military Industries. Home page. Accessed on October 27, 2020. https://sami.com.sa.

Saudi Arabian National Guard (SANG), Home page [in Arabic]. Accessed on November 11, 2020. https://mngdp.sang.gov.sa.

*Saudi Gazette*. "Ministry of Defense Opens Doors for Women in Four Key Sectors." October 4, 2019.

———. "Studies Show Need for Intensive Work Ethics Training in Saudi Arabia." February 27, 2016.

Saul, Jonathan, Parisa Hafezi, and Michael Georgy. "Exclusive: Iran Steps Up Support for Houthis in Yemen's War." Reuters, March 21, 2017.

Schanz, Marc V. "Eager Lion." *Air Force Magazine* (September 2013): 56–64.

Scheck, Justin, Shane Harris, and Summer Said. "How a Saudi Prince Unseated His Cousin to Become the Kingdom's Heir Apparent." *Wall Street Journal*, July 19, 2017.

Schmidt, Susan. "U.S. Officials Press Saudis on Aiding Terror." *Washington Post*, August 6, 2003.

Schmitt, Eric. "Killing of Terrorist Leader in Yemen Is Latest Blow to Qaeda Affiliate." *New York Times,* February 10, 2020.

———. "Saudi Arabia Tries to Ease Concerns over Civilian Deaths in Yemen." *New York Times*, June 14, 2017.

Schmitt, Eric, Helene Cooper, and Julia E. Barnes. "Trump's Syria Troop Withdrawal Complicated Plans for al-Baghdadi Raid." *New York Times*, October 27, 2019.

Schmitt, Eric., Alissa J. Rubin, and Thomas Gibbons-Neff. "ISIS Is Regaining Strength in Iraq and Syria." *New York Times*, August 19, 2019.

Schneller, Robert J., Jr. *Anchor of Resolve: A History of U.S. Naval Forces Central Command/Fifth Fleet.* Washington, DC: Naval Historical Center, 2007.

Schwartz, Felicia. "U.S. Increases Surveillance, Military Advisers in Iraq." *Wall Street Journal*, July 23, 2014.

Sedra, Mark, ed. *The Future of Security Sector Reform.* Waterloo, ON: Centre for International Governance Innovation, 2010.

Senior NATO Logisticians' Conference Secretariat. *NATO Logistics Handbook.* Brussels: NATO Headquarters, October 1997.

Setzekorn, Eric. "Eisenhower's Mutual Security Program and Congress: Defense and Economic Assistance for Cold War Asia." *Federal History*, no. 9 (2017): 7–25.

Shapiro, Andrew. "Ensuring Israel's Qualitative Military Edge." Remarks by the Assistant Secretary for the Bureau of Political-Military Affairs to the Washington Institute for Near East Policy, Washington, DC, November 4, 2011.

Sharp, Jeremy M. "Jordan: Background and U.S. Relations." Congressional Research Service, June 18, 2020.

Sheehan, Edward R. F. "Why Sadat Packed Off the Russians." *New York Times*, August 6, 1972.

Sheeley, Zach. "Fortifying the Backbone." Colorado National Guard, August 29, 2018. https://co.ng.mil/News/Archives/Article/1632500/fortifying-the-backbone/.

Shehata, Samer. *Shop Floor Culture and Politics in Egypt.* Albany, NY: SUNY Press, 2009.

Shield, Ralph. "The Saudi Air War in Yemen: A Case of Coercive Success Through Battlefield Denial." *Journal of Strategic Studies* 41, no. 3 (2018): 461–489.

Silverfarb, Daniel. "Great Britain, Iraq, and Saudi Arabia: The Revolt of the Ikhwan, 1927–1930." *The International History Review* 4, no. 2 (May 1982): 222–248.

Smith, Cary. "378 AEW, RSAF Partner Together in Training Exercise." US Air Forces Central, September 12, 2020. https://www.afcent.af.mil/News/Article/2345817/378-aew-rsaf-partner-together-in-training-exercise/.

———. "USAF, RSAF Conduct Exercise Desert Eagle in CENTCOM AOR." US Air Forces Central, September 14, 2020. https://www.afcent.af.mil/Units/378th-Air-Expeditionary-Wing/News/Article/2346303/usaf-rsaf-conduct-exercise-desert-eagle-in-centcom-aor/.

Smith, James D. *Saudi Arabian National Guard Modernization Through U.S. Army Project Management.* Carlisle Barracks, PA: US Army War College, August 25, 1975.

Snow, Shawn. "Pentagon Eyes Big Expansion of Foreign Military Training Program." *Military Times*, December 3, 2019.

Sonmez, Felicia, Paige Winfield Cunningham, and Tony Room. "Pompeo Dismissed Iraqi Leader's Call for All Foreign Troops to Leave." *Washington Post,* January 5, 2020.

South, Todd. "Senators Want to Know if US Military Advisers in Yemen Are Helping or Hurting the Conflict." *Army Times,* April 18, 2018.

Spetalnick, Matt. "Trump Recommits to U.S. Allies but Says They Must Pay 'Fair Share.'" Reuters, February 28, 2017.

Stephens, Michael. "Mixed Success for Saudi Military Operation in Yemen." *BBC News*, May 12, 2015.

Stevens, Michael. "FAST Marines Train with Lebanese Armed Forces." US Central Command, May 6, 2010.

Stewart, Phil, and Yara Bayoumy. "In Yemen Conflict, a Window into Deepening U.S.-Gulf Ties." Reuters, April 27, 2017.

Stockholm International Peace Research Institute (SIPRI). *Global Military Expenditure Sees Largest Annual Increase in a Decade—Says SIPRI—Reaching $1917 Billion in 2019.* Stockholm, Sweden: SIPRI, April 27, 2020.

Sukman, Daniel. *The Institutional Level of War.* Washington, DC: Strategy Bridge, May 5, 2016.

Sutherland, J. J. "U.S. Air Raid Kills Terror Figure Zarqawi." NPR, June 8, 2006.

Svolik, Milan W. *The Politics of Authoritarian Rule.* New York: Cambridge University Press, 2012.

Szoldra, Paul. "Pentagon Says US Military 'Advisers' Are Fighting Inside Mosul." *Business Insider,* January 6, 2017.

Taliaferro, Aaron. *A Framework for Security Cooperation Planning.* Alexandria, VA: Institute for Defense Analyses, August 2018.

———. *IDA's Standard Model: Defining the Defense Management Domain.* Alexandria, VA: Institute for Defense Analyses, August 2019.

Talmadge, Caitlin. *The Dictator's Army: Battlefield Effectiveness in Authoritarian Regimes.* Ithaca, NY: Cornell University Press, 2015.

Tankel, Stephen. *With Us and Against Us: How America's Partners Help and Hinder the War on Terror.* New York: Columbia University Press, 2018.

Tarpgaard, Peter T. "McNamara and the Rise of Analysis in Defense Planning: A Retrospective." *Naval War College Review* 48, no. 4 (Autumn 1995): 67–87.

Taylor, Adam. "For Saudi Arabia, an Oil Field Attack Was a Disaster. For Russia, It's a Weapons Sales Pitch." *Washington Post,* September 20, 2019.

———. "Saudi Arabia's 'Islamic Military Alliance' Against Terrorism Makes No Sense." *Washington Post,* December 17, 2015.

Tell, Tariq. *Early Spring in Jordan: The Revolt of the Military Veterans.* Beirut: Carnegie Middle East Center, November 4, 2015.

Tellis, Ashley J., Janice Bially, Christopher Layne, and Melissa McPherson. *Measuring National Power in the Postindustrial Age.* Santa Monica, CA: RAND, 2000.

10 U.S.C. 16–Security Cooperation, §301–386. US Government Publishing Office, December 30, 2016. https://www.govinfo.gov/app/details/USCODE-2016-title10/USCODE-2016 -title10-subtitleA-partI-chap16.

Tenet, George. *At the Center of the Storm: My Years at the CIA.* New York: HarperCollins, 2007.

Tharoor, Ishaan. "U.A.E.'s First Female Fighter Pilot Dropped Bombs on the Islamic State." *Washington Post,* September 25, 2014.

Thomas, Clayton. *Arms Sales in the Middle East: Trends and Analytical Perspectives for U.S. Policy.* Washington, DC: Congressional Research Service, October 11, 2017.

Thornbury, Chris. "Falcon Shield Strengthens Coalition's Air Defense." 380th Air Expeditionary Wing Public Affairs, US Air Forces Central, October 8, 2019.

Tilly, Charles, ed. *The Formation of National States in Western Europe.* Princeton, NJ: Princeton University Press, 1975.

*The Times.* "Saudi Bombs Kill 60 After Yemeni Peace Plan Fails." October 31, 2016.

Titus, James. *The Battle of Khafji: An Overview and Preliminary Analysis.* Maxwell Air Force Base, AL: Air University, September 1996.

Toosi, Nahal. "Trump Plan Would Steer Foreign Aid to 'Friends and Allies.'" *Politico,* September 6, 2019.

Toronto, Nathan W. *How Militaries Learn: Human Capital, Military Education, and Battlefield Effectiveness.* London: Lexington Books, 2018.

Toumi, Habib. "Saudi Shura Opposes Military Conscription." *Gulf News,* February 12, 2018.

Trevithick, Joseph. "Houthi Rebels Trounce Saudi Force amid Concerns over the Kingdom's Military Competence." *War Zone,* September 30, 2019.

———. "Russia Is Extending One of the Runways at Its Syrian Airbase." *War Zone,* February 5, 2021.

Tucker-Jones, Anthony. *Iran-Iraq War: The Lion of Babylon 1980–1988.* South Yorkshire, UK: Pen and Sword Military, 2018.

Turak, Natasha. "How Saudi Arabia Failed to Protect Itself from Drone and Missile Attacks Despite Billions Spent on Defense Systems." *CNBC,* September 19, 2019.

*UNIPATH.* "Fostering Special Forces: Col. Sufyan Subhi Al Sulaihat Exemplifies Jordan's Commitment to Partnerships and Peacekeeping." October 25, 2019.

United Arab Emirates Abu Dhabi. "2004 Report to Congress on Allied Contributions to the Common Defense: UAE Submission." Cable 03ABUDHABI5390_a. WikiLeaks, December 23, 2003. https://wikileaks.org/plusd/cables/03ABUDHABI5390_a.html.

United Nations. "Security Council Demands End to Yemen Violence, Adopting Resolution 2216 (2015), with Russian Federation Abstaining." Meeting coverage. April 14, 2015. https://www.un.org/press/en/2015/sc11859.doc.htm.

———. "A Year After the Stockholm Agreement: Where Are We Now?" Office of the Special Envoy of the Secretary-General for Yemen, accessed July 21, 2021. https://osesgy.unmissions.org/year-after-stockholm-agreement-where-are-we-now.

United Nations Development Programme (UNDP). *Arab Human Development Report 2002: Creating Opportunities for Future Generations* (New York: UNDP, February 13, 2003)

———. *Arab Human Development Report 2004: Towards Freedom in the Arab World.* New York: UNDP, April 15, 2005.

United Nations Security Council. *The Rule of Law and Transitional Justice in Conflict and Post-conflict Societies.* Report of the Secretary-General. New York: UN, August 23, 2004.

United States Institute of Peace and United States Army Peacekeeping and Stability Institute. *Guiding Principles for Stabilization and Reconstruction.* Washington, DC: Endowment of the United States Institute of Peace, 2009.

US Army. *Advising at the Senior Level: Lessons and Best Practices.* Handbook 19-06. Fort Leavenworth, KS: Center for Army Lessons Learned, January 2019.

US Army Training and Doctrine Command. Home page. Accessed on November 10, 2020. http://www.tradoc.army.mil.

US Central Command. "115th Field Artillery Brigade and 4-133rd Field Artillery Regiment Participate in Bilateral Exercises with UAE." April 3, 2020.

———. *Operation Desert Shield/Desert Storm,* Executive Summary. July 11, 1991.

———. "UAE, U.S. Forces Conduct Aviation Live Fire Exercise in Arabian Gulf." August 17, 2020.

US Department of Defense. *Conduct of the Persian Gulf War: Final Report to Congress.* April 1992.

———. *Department of Defense Operations at U.S. Embassies.* DOD Directive 5105.75. December 21, 2007.

———. *Joint Operations.* Joint Publication 3-0. August 11, 2011.

———. *Defense Institution Building (DIB).* DOD Directive 5205.82. January 27, 2016.

———. *Quadrennial Defense Review Report.* February 6, 2006.

US Department of State. "Leahy Law Fact Sheet." Bureau of Democracy, Human Rights, and Labor, January 22, 2019. https://www.state.gov/key-topics-bureau-of-democracy-human-rights-and-labor/human-rights/leahy-law-fact-sheet.

———. "U.S. Relations with Saudi Arabia." Bureau of Near Eastern Affairs, December 15, 2020. https://www.state.gov/u-s-relations-with-saudi-arabia/.

———. "U.S. Security Cooperation with Jordan, Fact Sheet." Bureau of Political-Military Affairs, April 8, 2020. https://www.state.gov/u-s-security-cooperation-with-jordan/.

———. "U.S. Security Cooperation with Jordan, Fact Sheet," Bureau of Political-Military Affairs, January 20, 2021. https://www.state.gov/u-s-security-cooperation-with-jordan/.

———. "U.S. Security Cooperation with Lebanon, Fact Sheet." Bureau of Political-Military Affairs, May 1, 2020. https://www.state.gov/u-s-security-cooperation-with-lebanon/.

———. "U.S. Security Cooperation with Oman, Fact Sheet." Bureau of Political-Military Affairs, June 15, 2021. https://www.state.gov/u-s-security-cooperation-with-oman/.

US Department of the Treasury. "Terrorist Financing Targeting Center Hosts Exercise on Disrupting Illicit Finance." Press release. March 27, 2019.

US Energy Information Administration (EIA). "World Oil Transit Chokepoints." July 25, 2017.

US Joint Forces Command. *Handbook for Military Support to Rule of Law and Security Sector Reform.* February 19, 2016.

US Marine Corps. *Logistics.* Marine Corps Doctrinal Publication 4. Washington, DC: US Government Printing Office, 1997.

US Naval Forces Central Command Public Affairs Office. "Saudi, UK, U.S. Forces Complete Exercise Nautical Defender 21." US Naval Forces Central Command, Combined Maritime Forces–US 5th Fleet, February 4, 2021.

————. "Saudi, U.S. Forces Conduct Joint Aviation Integration Exercise in Arabian Gulf." US Navy, December 21, 2020.

US Overseas Loans and Grants. *Greenbook 2015*. Washington, DC: USAID, 2015.

"USS *Little Rock* CLG 4 at the Re-Opening of the Suez Canal 05-06 June 1975." USS Little Rock Association, May 30, 2017. https://www.usslittlerock.org/historic-events/suez_canal.html.

Van Der Heide, Liesbeth, and Jip Geenen. "Children of the Caliphate: Young IS Returnees and the Reintegration Challenge." *Terrorism and Counter-Terrorism Studies* 8, no. 10 (August 2017): 1–19.

Vinograd, Cassandra. "Burned Alive: ISIS Video Purports to Show Murder of Jordanian Pilot." NBC News, February 3, 2015.

Vision 2030: Kingdom of Saudi Arabia. https://www.vision2030.gov.sa/en.

Votel, Joseph L. *Testimony Before the United States Senate Committee on Armed Services*. 116th Congress, February 5, 2019.

Wadhams, Nick, and Jennifer Jacobs. "President Trump Reportedly Wants Allies to Pay Full Cost of Hosting U.S. Troops Abroad 'Plus 50%.'" *Time*, March 8, 2019.

Wafa, Dina. "Capacity-Building for the Transformation of Public Service: A Case of Managerial-Level Public Servants in Egypt." *Teaching Public Administration* 33, no. 2 (2015): 115–129.

Wald, Charles F. "New Thinking at USEUCOM: The Phase Zero Campaign." *Joint Forces Quarterly* 4, no. 43 (2006): 72–73.

Walker, Bryan, and Sarah A. Soule. "Changing Company Culture Requires a Movement, Not a Mandate." *Harvard Business Review*, June 20, 2017.

*Wall Street Journal*. "How Mecca Uprising Helped Give Birth to al Qaeda: New Book Documents U.S. Participation in 1979 Mosque Siege." September 18, 2007.

Walt, Stephen M. "Don't Knock Offshore Balancing Until You've Tried It." *Foreign Policy*, December 8, 2016.

Waltz, Michael G. *Warrior Diplomat: A Green Beret's Battles from Washington to Afghanistan*. Lincoln, NE: Potomac Books, 2014.

Warrick, Joby. "Hillary's War: How Conviction Replaced Skepticism in Libya Intervention." *Washington Post*, October 30, 2011.

————. "More Than 1,400 Killed in Syrian Chemical Weapons Attack, U.S. Says," *Washington Post*, August 30, 2013.

*Washington Post*. "Realigning Foreign Assistance for a New Era of Great Power Competition." September 19, 2019.

————. "Should U.S. Troops Put Their Lives on the Line for Saudi Arabia?" September 21, 2019.

————. "What the U.S. Can Learn from the Fight Against the Islamic State." March 25, 2019.

Wasser, Becca, Stacie L. Pettyjohn, Jeffrey Martini, Alexandra T. Evans, Karl P. Mueller, Nathaniel Edenfield, Gabrielle Tarini, Ryan Haberman, and Jalen Zeman. *The Air War Against the Islamic State: The Role of Airpower in Operation Inherent Resolve*. Santa Monica, CA: RAND, 2021.

Weisgerber, Marcus, and Caroline Houck. "Obama's Final Arms-Export Tally More Than Doubles Bush's." *Defense One*, November 8, 2016.

Weeks, Jessica L. P. *Dictators at War and Peace*. Ithaca, NY: Cornell University Press, 2014.

Werner, Ben. "Pentagon Officials Call Out Iranian-Backed Weapons Smugglers." *USNI News*, February 19, 2020.

Westermeyer, Paul W. *U.S. Marines in Battle: Al Khafji, January 28–February 1, 1991*. Washington, DC: US Marine Corps History Division, 2008.

The White House. *U.S. Policy Toward the Persian Gulf*. National Security Directive 26, October 2, 1989.

————. *Conventional Arms Transfer Policy*. Presidential Directive/NSC-13, May 13, 1977.

Whitlock, Craig. "The Afghanistan Papers: A Secret History of the War." *Washington Post*, December 9, 2019.

WikiLeaks Cable. "Lebanon: Scene Setter for CENTCOM Commander General David Petraeus." November 28, 2008.

Williams, Dan. "Israel Will Not Oppose U.S. Sale of F-35 to UAE." Reuters, October 23, 2020.

Williams, Ian, and Shaan Shaikh. "Lessons from Yemen's Missile War." *Defense One*, June 11, 2020.

———. *The Missile War in Yemen*. Washington, DC: Center for Strategic and International Studies, June 2020.

Williams, Michael, and Samuel C. Lindsey. "A Social Psychological Critique of the Saudi Terrorism Risk Reduction Initiative." *Psychology, Crime & Law* 20, no. 2 (2014): 138.

Wilson, Benjamin. "F-16 Fighting Falcon News: U.A.E. Crosses Atlantic for Red Flag." F-16.net, February 3, 2011.

Wilson, Tod J. "Morocco: A Friend and a Moderating Arab Voice." *The DISAM Journal of International Security Assistance Management* 11, no. 1 (Fall 1988): 10.

Wintour, Patrick. "Yemen: UAE Confirms Withdrawal from Port City of Hodeidah." *Guardian*, July 9, 2019.

Wittes, Tamara Cofman. *Freedom's Unsteady March: America's Role in Building Arab Democracy*. Washington, DC: Brookings Institution Press, 2008.

Work, J. Patrick. "Fighting the Islamic State By, With, and Through: *How* Mattered as Much as *What*." *Joint Forces Quarterly* 2, no. 89 (April 2018): 56–62.

World Bank. *Unemployment, Youth Total (% of Total Labor Force Ages 15–24) (Modeled ILO Estimate)—Saudi Arabia*. Washington, DC: World Bank, June 21, 2020.

Worth, Robert F. "Saudis Strike Yemeni Rebels Along Border." *New York Times*, November 5, 2009.

Worth, Robert F., and Eric Lipton. "U.S. Resupplies Lebanon Military to Stabilize Ally." *New York Times*, October 25, 2008.

Wright, Claudia. "Reagan Arms Policy, the Arabs and Israel: Protectorate or Protection Racket?" *Third World Quarterly* 6, no. 3 (July 1984): 638–656.

Wright, Robin. "The Demise of Hezbollah's Untraceable Ghost." *New Yorker,* May 13, 2016.

———. "Saudis Propose Islamic Force in Iraq." *Washington Post*, July 29, 2004.

Young, Thomas-Durell. "Experimentation Can Help Build Better Security Partners." War on the Rocks, August 30, 2019. https://warontherocks.com/2019/08/experimentation-can-help-build-better-security-partners/.

Zambelis, Chris. "Is There a Nexus Between Torture and Radicalization?" *Terrorism Monitor* 6, no. 13 (June 26, 2008).

Zelin, Aaron Y. *Tunisia Turns a Corner Against the Jihadist Movement*. Washington, DC: Washington Institute for Near East Policy, January 27, 2020.

Zemrani, Aziza. "Teaching Public Administration: The Case of Morocco." *Journal of Public Affairs Education* 20, no. 4 (Fall 2014): 515–528.

Zengerle, Patricia. "Biden Administration Proceeding with $23 Billion Weapons Sale to UAE." Reuters, April 14, 2021.

Zraick, Karen. "What to Know About the Death of Iranian General Suleimani." *New York Times*, January 3, 2020.

# Index

Abdullah bin Abdulaziz Al Saud (king of Saudi Arabia), 26
Abdullah Ibn Abdul Aziz (prince of Saudi Arabia), 54
Abdullah II (king of Jordan): aviation school inauguration, 102; defense reform, 16, 98; military career, 30, 32, 93
Abraham Accords, 9
academies, military: in Jordan, 101–103; in Lebanon, 122; in Saudi Arabia, 60–63; in United Arab Emirates, 144–147. *See also* educational systems; names of specific universities
access, basing, and overflight rights, 7, 15, 52, 162, 187, 207
accounting. *See* acquisition policies; names of specific funding programs
acquisition policies, 16, 38–39, 43, 185–186. *See also under* names of specific countries
administrative capacity: Arab countries and, 14, 172–177; country variation in, 173–174; cultural and political aspects, 176–177; DIB and, 18, 40–44, 172–177; MAPs challenges, 176–177; public administration, 172–173, 174–177

advising constructs. *See* defense institution building (DIB): advising constructs
AFCENT (Air Forces Central), 55
Afghanistan, Soviet invasion, 25
Afghanistan War (2001-2021): Arab troops in, 29, 88, 137–138; impact on US attitudes, 2, 37–38, 157–158; MODA and, 46
airborne warning and control system (AWACS), 25, 47n4
air defenses: arms transfers, 9, 25–27, 134, 135, 147; JTEs, 55, 73, 119, 135, 136; operational capability, 71–73, 75, 88, 148–150; weaknesses, 2, 78, 116
Aoun, Joseph, 128
AQAP (al-Qaeda in the Arabian Peninsula). *See* al-Qaeda
*Arab Human Development Report,* 172
Arabian Sea. *See* maritime security
Arab-Israeli War (1973), 13
Arab Spring (2011), 7, 8, 9, 157–158
Arafat, Yasser, 90, 115
Aramco (Saudi Arabia), 18, 174
Arms Export Control Act (1976), 31–32
arms transfers: Abraham Accords and, 9; economic motivations, 26, 168; history of, 8–9, 23, 24–27; usage

# About the Book

AFTER DECADES OF US MILITARY ASSISTANCE IN THE MIDDLE East—providing expensive weapons systems and conducting military exercises—why are the military capabilities of US allies in the region still lacking? Why does it matter? And what can be done to remedy the status quo?

Bilal Saab addresses these vexing questions through a set of in-depth case studies. Identifying the pitfalls of diverse assistance programs, Saab convincingly demonstrates the importance of institution building in efforts to achieve effective security cooperation in a region that remains of great strategic significance.

**Bilal Y. Saab** is a former senior adviser in the Office of the Secretary of Defense with oversight responsibilities for security cooperation in the broader Middle East. At present, he is senior fellow and director of the Defense and Security Program at the Middle East Institute in Washington, DC, and an adjunct assistant professor in the Security Studies Program of Georgetown University's School of Foreign Service.